Hame

Julie-Ann Rowell

Published by Nine Pens Press

2024

www.ninepens.co.uk

ISBN: 978-1-917150-03-3

023

Cover artwork by Lesley Murdoch

Contents

Hame: Orcadian for home.

Dounby, Orkney

Our village sits at a crossroads. A woman is seen
with a box of firelighters where the pharmacy
greets the butchers, which shuts at three.
Times are important in Dounby: the surgery,
the pub, the post office, the care home;
a hub reliant on its opening hours
to be appreciated. We know the Co-op well
with its two petrol pumps. Inside the aisles
so narrow you get through by dancing.
When dad was ill, we used it for wine
gin, olives and chocolate to bear us up.
Mum dropped and died filling her car there
after dad had gone. We pop in every other day.
The village is easily overlooked, on its way to
somewhere else, Skara Brae, coast and spire.
But now its virus lockdown, we're all stuck –
the Co-op serves on, measures out
the queue, disinfects, restocks, reloads,
advertises its times, gives advice, its staff
as friendly as they go, working relentlessly.
It's on a crossroads, our village, a dot on a map,
but centre of our lives and deaths for all that.

Building the Croft House

Peat-cutting, stone-getting, stone-dressing, stone-setting
that summer when they built the croft on the rise
above the Dounby road. Stones piled up topped by lintel,
the hearth stone set, then roof-beams, door frame, doorstep.

Liveable, end-facing the valley wind that liked to test its measure,
smoke a signal from the chimney. Oil lamps filling in windows
puncturing night, the vale peppered with shining eyes.
Warm bed sanctuaries inside, sleep as deep as an Orca's throat.

The croft is roofless now, doorless, the window glass long purloined.
Indoors tussocks rise thick over floors, impossible for feet to ply.
House Martins nest in gaps but stones still interconnect
holding tight to the past. Nothing loose wasted: gone to repair gates, fences.

We carry stones in a two-handled basket up to the ruin.
We dig out the binding tussocks and lay slate. An expert in wood
carves beams while we drink Scapa Special Ale from a stoneware bottle
engraved with Norn. We embed the final stone before the snow encrusts.

Lambing Snow

They say April; the road edges
primed by daffodils. I've planted
seedlings in the garden room
of sheltering stone wall. Lambing
snow, wet and sloppy, streams over
dips and risings. 'Don't
take your coat off until May!'
is the best advice I've never taken.

Cold, the kind which carves wrinkles
drives around the house. We are the north
and beauty comes in disguise.
To my surprise, the seedlings of chard,
turnip, broccoli survive, pokes
of green I cover with plastic wrap.
We shall eat well. Lambs snow-born,
long gone; forgotten.

Crystal Jellyfish

strewn at Skaill
shining Caithness glass
their pink innards on show.

So many I have to watch my step,
tiptoe between or slip on translucence.
I can't imagine them glowing,

or being among them, my pink
on the outside. Onshore wind
drives them in after they've multiplied.
I am taken

by the regularity of their death spread.
So close still to their world.
So dead to it.

The Polar Bears Club

Buffed up by the wind,
only our faces exposed, we see
one another through red-raw eyes.

The women arrive, stumbling down
the pebble bank to the beach
in their swimsuits and bathing caps.

The sea is flint. They break
its silvertone surface and seal-swim,
calling to each other as they surge,

orange swim buoys
like human bladderwrack. I shudder
at the tenderness of skin

against sunless water. We both feel colder
than they do, these water-women,
euphoric in their float and backstroke.

I can't surface in my quilt wrap,
hood and hat, gloves for far north
Winter blade. Layer upon layer.

The polar bears are rushing out now,
as they dashed in, whooping, laughing
in the blue air under a whale grey sky.

They don their dry robes, chatting away,
energy to spare. We're huddling
in our winter plumage, our lack of dare.

Late Summer

Effe says summer is over because the puffins have gone
and the nights are sinking in. The barley is nearly ready
for harvesting. The hay is baled. The kye will soon be inside.
I gaze into their lime-green fields and think of murder. Effe's right,
each evening the sun drinks in the house less and less.
A countdown to nothingness, the landscape wiped out.

Yet swallows continue to whizz over meadows, our heads,
at speeds unaccountable. The sunsets are brilliant crimson
and in the south it's already dark, lights on, curtains drawn.
We lounge in the sitooterie for every second's caress.
We neither read nor talk, nothing to express. Bosquoy Loch
a shimmer, an invitation, summer is still talking, hear it.

Barley

From the window, the barley is a swathe of copper.
I want to run my hand over it.
It's windy out. The garage door's complaining.

Mum would say: 'Don't open any windows!'
We always knew if one was open: the bungalow
became a vortex when the wind got in.

The barley is a burnished wave. In the sun
the sitooterie is a heat trough we can hardly bear.
We won't close the blinds but daren't open the windows.

Mum was a stickler for household rules.
She hated going into town. Put up with Dounby Co-op.
One door opens and another slams.

I want to paint the barley, but the colour is beyond me.
It shines in its maturity, a last outburst of growth
cascading over a softly sloping ridge.

Mum wouldn't notice it. She'd only go out
to hang laundry on the industrial strength washing line.
The wind swishes through the barley defiantly.

Peedie

She liked peedie things: the wren, the goldcrest:
a nestled dormouse. But the brown hare in the garden
she'd happily take a gun to. The beast in the field
was a lump of flesh, nothing more. Grotesque,
its great head an offence, its pink
mashing gums, spools of saliva – its bulk
only of interest when bloody on the butcher's slab.

She kept tongue in the fridge for sandwiches,
made oxtail soup, a bister broth filling
the house with fleshy emanations, no hiding
from what it was. But crumbs from the bread board
were scattered on the patio for birds
which could fit in her palm. She was peedie like them;
a small woman with a fortress inside.

Groatie Buckies

I found one once, the size of my baby fingernail,
a pink-white, ridged back cowrie, someone's
home of porcelain – a mollusc's died, moved on.

The shore wouldn't mind if I owned it, removed it,
tiny as it was, a moment of delicacy in among
kelp and rough-hewn pebbles.

How such delicacy could survive the thrashing
of sea, the bludgeoning of coast, the tide
only ever retreating with minor courtesy.

If I found another would I keep it? I'm not sure,
the ocean must have millions more and when
deposited they would only be ground to grains.

Only later did I discover the collecting frenzy,
the museum of finds: photos on Facebook of five hundred,
a thousand, hoards galore, and I felt for the sand.

Quoyloo

I always cringe at the waste yard sited
at the crossroads. Cemetery for tractors, balers,
ploughs, car carcasses, mowers, field cultivators,
shredders, rusting in abandonment, skeletons
of industry among weeds getting their own back.
This junk has no energy. It looks disgraced, unworthy
as if it once disappointed at the point of delivery
even in its bright plumage of reds, greens, yellows.
It's so solitary in its decaying togetherness.
I can never pass by without regret, so I usually
take the Skaill road as if avoiding the site of an accident.

Entrapped

A stoat trap's been installed at the end of our road
under the Give Way sign. Two more in the copse
up the lane. Long narrow boxes, a wire window
at one end, entry at the other. Redesigned because
the previous sort killed two cats.

Thousands of stoats caught so far, a world record
for a cull of animals per square mile of land and human
population. We're saving the Orkney vole,
which exists only here, and ground-nesting birds –
they need all the help they can get. So, if I see a stoat's
bounding gait across a field I must report the sighting.

I love the stoat, its soft white neck, sharp eyes,
the viciousness. I love the Orkney vole
(several nest in our garden), the hedgehog, brown hare,
rabbit. The red-throated divers and Arctic terns.
I love the Orkney vole, hedgehog, brown hare,
short-eared owl, rabbit, corncrake, and puffin too.
I love the snow goose. I love the sea eagle. I love the stoat.

Boom

The sky cracked,
a split of sound ripped the ground
from under us.

The pony in the field opposite
raced around, ears flattened,
kye bellowed; pain raked my head.

I nearly threw myself down
but managed with a shriek and a *Jesus*
to hold on.

I've always hated
explosions, even fireworks
send me running.

Effe stopped her car at the gate,
'It's that bloody fighter jet again.'
I felt the booming ripple resonating

in my chest – can you die from sound?
'They've started practising over here.'
Imagine the islands passing at that speed,

to them we're a gulp, a hiccough,
a whip of light, houses, byres, reduced to nothing
people not even dots.

'We'll get used to it,' Effe said,
'like explosives at the quarry.'
But you couldn't hear that in Dounby –

this *boom* could shatter anywhere
slamming our small selves on the map,
back into a world we regret.

Wind

decides whether I can go out,
if rain or hail can stay.

This day it's a hooley, pampas
grass stretched flat, greylag

trying to fly, their usual V
formation disconcerted.

I stand at the sitooterie's sliding door
built to aircraft standards

air whistling as if in panic.
A sparrow makes it to the guttering

crouches in. I can't see how it manages,
each gust is like a birthing pang

pulling across the body of the land
its grassy hummocks and moorland hills.

No one could stride out in this
nothing to cling to, not even the self.

Severe Clear

September, and greylag geese are arriving in their dozens,
that must mean summer's over. The sky's an unrealistic blue
as on that day. Sun that can't hold back makes
glass shimmer before it breaks. We're quiet. In the next
field the farmer harvests dark gold. Cities don't exist,

all that steel and cement. All that crowding together
we loved so much. Our lawn is citrine. Rain foreign.
'It had to be, didn't it?' you say. 'Not a cloud in sight.'
'You'd still remember,' I tell you. 'Whatever.' Me too,
waiting hours for your call, phone lines scrambled across the world.

Sky have pity! A contrail carves the blue. You look the plane
up on your App: 'It's going to Montreal.' Comforting.
Letting go of arguments, reasons. We can stop thinking in that way.
When its evening at last, it's past. Over. But aftermath.
'Okay, we'll watch *Dix Pour Cent*,' tonight,' I say, 'from the beginning.'

Drought in Orkney

No rain. For Months. The burns dry, skeletal beds –
white and studded with pebble. Our acre
is scorched, scarred with patches of yellow,
any green is pale. The same is true of the field beyond
where hares run. Crops are drying in the sun
too early for harvest, though the farmers
are baling and they must top up the livestock troughs,
they won't fill themselves. I drove past a bull
drool spilling from its lips almost to the ground.
No one can keep up with this. Lochs are low
their boundaries exposed, they never normally
have baked sandy rims. There's plenty of cloud, and the haar
is dank with dampness but we need a drenching.

Today, at Stromness, I saw two huge tankers of water
roll off the ferry from Scrabster, never known before.
The clunk of their wheels over the lip to shore,
heading off in different directions, which part
of the isles needs it more? I put out trays of water
for the birds, they often drink rainwater from the guttering
but the guttering's dry. We're asked by
the Council to conserve water. The question
of taking flowers to our parents' grave,
filling the bottle to top up the vase. Our habits
are changing. We obsess. It's summer but no one
is lying on towels, except visitors. The rest of us
are watching the sky, holding our breath.

Driftwood

Few trees here, driftwood's set aside to be claimed.
'This must be valuable,' I say as we come across
a table leg, separated from its meaning

once turned and honed. 'How did it get here?'
The dog mouths it. No one beachcombs
in the dark anymore to get the best stuff.

Still, building essentials are harder to come by –
our friend's garage unrepaired for ten months,
she must get in her car in a force ten gale,

snow, hail, wind like a barber's blade.
'Time's turning in on itself,' you remark,
wrangling with the dog over the table leg.

Expect delays. We hear it constantly. How can
there be a shortage of cement? The horizon
is too far away, the vanishing point. I dream

of woods sprinkled with light. Trees nuzzling.
A quantity of something. Island life: you take
what you find. A table leg is useful surely

but we're too smitten with shops, Internet.
Someone will give the heap of driftwood purpose.
I gift it the gnawed table leg.

Mallimack

I'm looking for faces in these bodies'
unbending flight   gullies and rock trench drop
soul-filled   must be uncomfortable
carrying your bird self   and a human

vying for a view   waves like shelves
only sailors apparently deserve homes
in fish-stink   cacking solidarity   pairs of birds
snuggling on blunt ledges

chicks bloating with newly-freed souls
A boat went down last week   one man lost –
is he now inveigling his way into   this life
no, this, the one on that precipice

where sea thrift thrives   gales are weights
air is heavy   is it only seamen
slipping into embryo   waiting for the first plunge
feathers streamline   nothing out of place?

I swear I saw *you* in one long sweep over
the sea's threat   soaring for once   not giving
a shit   free in flight   rising above a sea wake
one two three DROP   letting your hurt self go

Ferry

The Hamnavoe sits alongside Stromness quay.
I can hear its engine's thrum even from inside the car,
rain slashing the windows, I've put the wipers on.
She's lit up against the swamp of night. Windows burning.
Water is jumping in the harbour, so what will it be like out there,
in the Firth, when land is gone, so gone it's lost from memory?

A cheery *bong* and the captain speaks over the intercom.
I can hear him clearly even through the car window.
It's the welcome and safety drill that no one listens to,
all is well, imbued with the everyday, we know the way, assurance
only crew can give. I'd trust them with my life
have done before. The ship starts a slow reverse and turn.

Then, she seems to be moving quickly into night
(which begins at four o'clock). White bulk tunnelling nothinginess,
a lone red flashing light marking the way.
She vanishes, just the clatter of rain. How can
this bring such loneliness? I imagine passengers finding
their place, the womb of cabin, the ship beginning to tilt, rise, fall.

Arriving at Papa Westray

It's something only the stranger will understand
this stepping from jittery craft to shore
the land a shrunken thing.

The boatman ignores my shocking balance
on the stone-peppered beach, dwindling dunes –
the wind has been hard at work

for incalculable time. I wear a hat
made for city winters, and no gloves
in the splintering wind bucking cold.

I wonder how I ever got this far
to this creeping path, these patches of field,
grey sheep for mutton made. Too much horizon.

But there's the pattern of houses,
chimneys full of puff, their hearths loaded with peat
and unknowingly I'm someone's hero.

The Blue House

nestles in the crib of the hill.
It catches the eye. Houses aren't usually
painted such colours here. Makes one wonder why.
Why this blue? It's not sky-like
or even sea-like, though it's sea and sky
all around. Sky never bigger nor sea broader.
It's a middle blue, but not tame.
Maybe it's blow-ins who want to make
a show, *Hey, we're up here! Hello!*
or Orcadians bored with pebbledash and grey.
But we're not Shetland or Norway.
Perhaps it's the start of a craze,
seduced by pink, yellow, red,
no longer consumed by neutral, we'll be
trumpeting not blending. Every time
we drive past I say, 'Look, it's the blue house,'
and when we see the sign at the end of a lane
saying *Shalom* I always say *Shalom* back,
more than a greeting, a benediction.
It means we've reached the end of the Lyde road
over the heather moors and we're hame.

Acknowledgements:

Dounby, Orkney
First published as *'Dounby'* in in *City, Town and Village*
chapbook, Figment Books, 2020

Building the Croft House
Published online as part of the George Mackay Fellowship
project, Working with Words, 2021

Peedie
Orbis, Spring edition, 2021

Notes:

p.8: *Building the Croft House* is the title of a poem by George Mackay Brown, and the first line is also from the poem.

p.12: *Kye* is Orcadian for cattle.

p.14: *Peedie* is Orcadian for something very small.

p.21: *Severe Clear* – an aviation term used by pilots to describe a bright blue sky with unlimited visibility.

p.24: *Mallimack* is Orcadian for Fulmar.

p.26: *Papa Westray* (Papay in Orcadian) is one of the smaller islands. It hosts the oldest stone houses in northern Europe at the Knap of Howar.

Praise for 'Hame'

Julie-Ann Rowell's touching and acutely observed Orkney poems show how local, everyday details dwell at the very 'centre of our lives and deaths'. In beautifully phrased poems that sing with an integral music, these poems are suffused in local specifics and language - Groatie Buckies (cowries), wild and hardy swimming women, swarms of jellyfish, puffins, hares in the field, and coasting mallimacks (fulmars)- leaving you feeling like you've just visited Orkney yourself. In a prayer-like poem about the conservation struggle between the stoat and the Orkney vole, Julie-Ann begs vital questions of how humans live with nature, while the man-made and natural sounds are ever present in the sonic boom of passing fighter jets or the hooley of the northern wind. These poems show Julie-Ann's gift to be able to capture tiny details and open them up to much wider significances, such as a driftwood table leg that is washed up and 'separated from its meaning'. Resonant and replete new poems from a poet keenly attuned to her environs.

Andy Brown

Julie-ann Rowell sings her beloved Orkney in sharply observed, deftly crafted lyrics. Spare and grounded in harsh realities and industrial wreckage as much as the island's wild beauty, these poems are unromantic in the best sense, marrying vivid sensory perceptions with the shock of tough lives lived at the margins. Both hard and tender, like the 'small woman with the fortress inside' who won't hesitate to shoot an animal when required but lovingly scatters crumbs for the birds, these poems are alert to the changing weathers, ugliness and loveliness of life as it is actually lived, with all its irreconcilable contrasts and discrepancies.

Matthew Barton

Praise for 'Hame'

Julie-ann Rowell's new collections, book-length or pamphlets, are always a cause for celebration. I don't often say that these days. Rowell's voice is unique, and Hame is the poet at her best: lyrical, image-rich words, intimate, lacing together outer and inner, fleeting joys or darker moments.

Rowell is a poet unafraid of writing about cruelty and death; and yet the poems are not heavy. She sees deeply into the nature of being in the outer world; observing keenly, commenting minimally but personally. Whether she's writing about seasons, town or city concerns, greylag geese or the trapping of stoats, she brings a penetrating passion to what she perceives.

Roselle Angwin

Milton Keynes UK
Ingram Content Group UK Ltd.
UKHW010745100724
445379UK00006BA/157

AUSTRALIAN
STEAM LOCOMOTIVES
1896–1958

WRITTEN & ILLUSTRATED BY

JIM TURNER

Kangaroo Press

*Phillip with a painting of locomotive No 210
of B205 class, which entered service with
NSWGR in February 1882*

THIS BOOK IS DEDICATED TO MY CHILDREN JESSICA AND PHILLIP
WHO BOTH LOVE STEAM TRAINS

Designed by Kerry Klinner
Cover designed by Darian Causby

© Jim Turner 1997

First published in 1997 by Kangaroo Press Pty Ltd
3 Whitehall Road Kenthurst NSW 2156 Australia
PO Box 6125 Dural Delivery Centre NSW 2158 Australia
Printed in Hong Kong by South China Printing Co. (1988) Ltd

ISBN 0 86417 778 X

CONTENTS

FOREWORD

The steam locomotive has been an object of examination and interest for many generations. Despite the fact that twenty-five years and more have elapsed since regular steam operation has been seen on Australia's main lines, the fascination of steam remains strong and active, as is evident from new books such as this continuing to be published.

The steam days were characterised by the very diverse and individualistic designs of rolling stock of the various rail systems. Relative to today's railway scene, there was little or no design standardisation evident. This great variety in the type and design of locomotives was a major feature of their appeal, as well as being a source of endless discussion between railwaymen and enthusiasts alike.

In this book, James Turner has set out to provide an illustrated compendium of the locomotives operating for the government in Australia in the second half of the steam era. The hand-painted watercolour illustrations give a vivid indication of variety and the pictorial index, with the additional small drawings done to scale, allows a comparison of size and power. This approach will be of interest to those enthusiasts who have not experienced the excitement of seeing these locomotives in service.

The artistic illustrations together with the associated description of the principal features of each locomotive class, will be a source of both information and pleasure to today's enthusiasts and will encourage many to take up a more detailed study of those features that capture their imagination.

And so the wheel of interest in steam goes on into the future.

John Glastonbury

PREFACE

I have always had a love of steam locomotives, and while the modern diesel locomotives may have superior performance and reliability, for me they lack the distinctive sound and individual personality of the steam locomotives of days gone by.

A steam locomotive is like a living thing—each one is different. With the steam and smoke, the sounds and smells, every trip along the same line is unique.

This book began by accident in a garbage bin. For a number of years I worked at a high school where my job included emptying about a hundred garbage bins twice a day. During a clean out by the art department I found dozens of old outline diagrams for NSWGR steam locomotives in a bin, so I gathered them up and took them home. After speaking with Neil Cram a series of paintings evolved over a period of time, and in order to make the detail of the paintings as accurate as possible, I spent quite a lot of time in research and looking at old photos. I found that in many cases it was difficult to find the information I was after, so I have tried to include some basic details about each locomotive and their time in service, their size and weight and the colours they were painted.

Covering the period from 1896 to 1958, this book deals specifically with steam locomotives which were in the service of individual state government railway departments around Australia, even though some of these locomotives were made from spare parts and said to be virtually useless when in service.

Each locomotive has been depicted twice, with the small illustrations all to the same scale in the pictorial index, so that the reader can compare their size. While I have endeavoured to make both the text and each illustration as accurate as possible, the illustrations are intended only as an introduction to the locomotives and not as a technically correct drawing of each. Also included are details of the locomotives that have been preserved, and where they may been seen.

I hope that this book will be of interest to all readers, from those with only a passing interest in steam locomotives right through to that band of dedicated enthusiasts who spend their weekends restoring or riding on trains hauled by those few locomotives that survived the scrapper's torch.

ACKNOWLEDGMENTS

The author wishes to acknowledge the support and assistance of the following people who made it possible to complete this book.

In N.S.W.: Neil Cram for his encouragement early in the project and continuing help, Peter Neve for his help with text and illustrations, Victor Poljanski of State Rail Authority Archives, Transport House, Sydney for diagrams and technical details. The staff at ARHS Sydney archives who wish to remain anonymous (S.S., D.H. & G.B.) for their help with many hours of photocopying and finding references.

In Queensland: Del Cuddihy from the Queensland Railway Historical Centre for diagrams and technical details, John Armstrong for his help with text and illustrations, also Bob Mawson, John Lees and Tony Poulos from Courtaulds Coatings.

In Victoria: Colin Kemp of PTC Photo archives, Ian R Barkla from the ARHS Victorian Division, Frank Kelly and Norman Cave for help with text and illustrations, and Norman W. De Pomeroy for help with the text.

In Tasmania: Michael Dix for help with text and illustrations and Rene Mouchet from the Australian Archives, Rosney Park, Tasmania and Dr Jim Stokes from Australian Archives in Canberra.

In South Australia: Steve McNicoll for his help with text and illustrations.

For Western Australia: Adrian Gunzburg for his help with text and illustrations for WAGR locomotives.

Built by James Martin & Co of Gawler, South Australia, No 62 entered service on 8 July 1896 with No 63 arriving a few weeks later on 1 August 1896. On 8 September No 63 hauled the first train from Coolgardie to Kalgoorlie. Both locomotives were used on the main passenger service and were the same as the South Australian Z class, except for their bogie tenders. These were four feet longer than the six-wheel Z class tenders and carried 150 more gallons of water, but not as much coal. The locomotives were the only two of this class bought by Western Australian Government Railways.

The more powerful R class was introduced in February 1897, replacing the P class on main line passenger services. The P remained in Government service until 1912, when No 62 was withdrawn

P CLASS (WA)
WHEEL ARRANGEMENT: 4-4-0
PASSENGER LOCOMOTIVE
2 IN CLASS
FINAL NOS: 62, 63

from service on 24 April. No 63 met the same fate a few months later. They were both sold to the Midland Railway Company, but were found unsuitable for main line use as they were underpowered when compared with both the B and G classes then in service with the Midland Railway. No 62 was hired out to the Public Works Department for £20 per week for just over a year and returned to Midland in June 1914. It was then used for spare parts to keep No 63 in service. Midland was unable to find a buyer for No 63, which was then renumbered 12 and worked as a shunter until the 1920s. Both locomotives were scrapped in 1929.

Builder: James Martin & Co, Gawler, S.A. 2

Preserved: Nil

Above: Built by James Martin & Co of Gawler, South Australia in 1896, No 63 entered service on 1 August 1896 with Western Australian Government Railways. Within months it was replaced by more powerful locomotives and was withdrawn from service on 23 July 1912. Sold to Midland Railways, it was scrapped in 1929. Listed weight in working order of locomotive and tender was 51 tons 1 cwt with a combined length of 46 ft, from buffer to buffer. For more details see A History of W.A.G.R. Steam Locomotives, A. Gunzburg, ARHS(WA) 1984, p. 48.

H1 was the first of this class, built in Germany by Lokomotivfabrik Krauss & Co in 1896, to be bought by Tasmanian Government Railways. H1 was used for construction work and regular services, until it was withdrawn and stored at Zeehan where it rusted away. The second H2 was bought in 1898 and in 1906 it was sold to the Victorian Public Works Department, who later sold it to the Corrimal Colliery in New South Wales. Withdrawn from service in 1933, it was still rusting beside the line in 1956. A third locomotive, H3, was bought in 1899 and was sold in turn to the Victorian Public Works Department about 1906. It was sold again in 1910, to the Rubicon Timber Co of Victoria, where it remained in service until 1935 before being scrapped in the early 1950s.

H CLASS (TAS)
WHEEL ARRANGEMENT: 0-4-0WT
SMALL WELL-TANK GOODS
LOCOMOTIVE
4 IN CLASS
FINAL NOS: H1-H4

powerful locomotives.

Builder: Lokomotivfabrik Krauss & Co, Germany 4
Preserved: Nil

These three locomotives were all bought second-hand; however, H4 was bought new from the locomotive builders in Germany in 1899 and remained in service until 1927. Following this it was then sold to the Catamaran Colliery in Tasmania in 1927, and was withdrawn and scrapped in 1938. These small locomotives were mostly used to haul ore traffic, shunting and operating the railway lines near smelters, but with the rapid increase in traffic they were soon replaced by the larger and more

Above: Built by Lokomotivfabrik Krauss & Co in Germany in 1889, H1 was bought second-hand and entered service with Tasmanian Government Railways in 1896. It was used on construction work and then in service. Stored at Zeehan after being withdrawn from service, it rusted away in the railyard. Listed weight in working order of this locomotive was 7 tons 8 cwt and it was about 13 ft 7 in from buffer to buffer. For more details see Railways of the Zeehan District, *L.B. Manny, ARHS Bulletin No. 313, November 1963, p. 165–6.*

The expansion of the Eastern Railway in 1896 resulted in an extreme shortage of locomotives, and plans and orders were placed with builders in Britain. Meanwhile the colony's Consulting Engineer in London obtained two tank locomotives built by R & W Hawthorn Leslie & Co Ltd in 1895. They were part of a cancelled South African order and were sold to Western Australian Government Railways in May 1896. Nos 138 and 139 both entered service on 19 August 1896. Four more locomotives of the same type had been ordered weeks before, on 24 April. All were built in 1896, with the first to enter service being No. 140 on 5 December 1896, followed by No. 141 on 20 January 1897, and Nos 142 and 143 on 13 March 1897.

Q CLASS (WA)
WHEEL ARRANGEMENT: 4-6-2T
TANK LOCOMOTIVE
6 IN CLASS
FINAL NOS: 138-143

The only difference between Nos 138–139, and the later Nos 140 to 143, was in the shape of the cab side window and the different-shaped side tanks due to the extension of the running board along to the buffer beam. They were all used as shunters in the Fremantle and Midland areas. By 1909 only Nos 138 and 139 were still in use as shunters, working the industrial sidings and wharfs of the Rocky Bay branch line, and North Fremantle to Fremantle. Nos 140 to 143 had all been converted to form the Qa class. Both Nos 138 and 139 were withdrawn from service on 31 January 1924 and scrapped.

Builder: R & W Hawthorn Leslie & Co 6
Preserved: Nil

Above: Built by R & W Hawthorn Leslie & Co in 1895, this locomotive was intended for delivery to South Africa as No. 2 General Smit. After the order was cancelled, it entered service with Western Australian Government Railways on 19 August 1896 as No. 139. It was withdrawn from service on 31 January 1924 after about twenty-eight years in service. Listed weight in working order of this locomotive was 41 tons and it had a length of 34 ft 1 in from buffer to buffer. For more details see A History of W.A.G.R. Steam Locomotives, A. Gunzburg, ARHS(WA) 1984, p. 49–51.

The first locomotives of this class were built by Beyer Peacock & Co and arrived in 1885, with the first entering service with South Australian Government Railways on 9 September 1885. The final locomotive, No. 179, was the first built by the Islington Workshops and entered service on 29 September 1898. The Y class was assigned to hauling ore trains from Cockburn to Port Pirie, and long distance services such as Oodnadatta to Port Augusta.

In 1901 Nos 70 and 76 collided head on near Walloway station. The northbound mixed goods train was hit by a southbound cattle train, which was unable to stop after descending the Walloway hills.

Before 1910, racks were fitted to the tops of their tenders to enable them to carry more coal. Only

Y CLASS (SA)
WHEEL ARRANGEMENT: 2-6-0
NARROW GAUGE GOODS
LOCOMOTIVE
129 IN CLASS
FINAL NOS: 22, 38, 43, 49, 57–106, 108–142, 147–79
NOS DUPLICATED: 153–158

a few other modifications were made in the 1920s, with electric lighting, stovepipe chimneys and extended smokeboxes. A survey taken in 1948 found that only seventeen Y class were still in service. By the early 1960s No. 97 was the only one of its class in service. With the nickname of 'the rat' it remained in use as a shunter at the Peterborough roundhouse until January 1970. It was condemned on 14 May 1970, after eighty years in service.

Builders: Beyer Peacock & Co, England 48; J. Martin & Co, Gawler, S.A. 76; S.A.R. Islington Workshops 2

Preserved: No 71, at ARHS Museum, Bassendean, W.A.; No 82, at children's playground, Grove St, Peterborough; No 97, at Port Dock Railway Museum, Adelaide; No 157, at Timber Museum, Manjimup, W.A.

Above: Built by James Martin & Co at Gawler, South Australia, No 165 entered service with South Australian Government Railways on 7 September 1896. It was rebuilt with a larger boiler and classified Yx class on 27 February 1907. Condemned on 21 March 1928, it was cut up on 30 June 1930. Listed weight in working order of locomotive and tender was 47 tons 15 cwt with a combined length of 39 ft 3⅛ in from buffer to buffer. For more details see Narrow Gauge Memories The Locomotives, S. McNicol, Railmac Publications, 1993, p. 142–54.

The first of two locomotives in this class was built by Kitson &
Co in 1888, and entered service with the Great Southern
Railway on 1 August. It was named *Princess*. The second loco-
motive, also built by Kitson, was named *Duchess*; it was built in 1892 and
entered service with the Great Southern Railway on 1 May 1892. Built
as small shunting engines, they were able to be used on light wharf and
jetty lines.

On 1 December 1896, both locomotives entered service with Western Australian Government
Railways and were numbered 162 and 163. They were used continuously for the next twenty years until
they were again sold, this time to the Commonwealth Government. They were used south of

S CLASS (WA)
WHEEL ARRANGEMENT: 0-6-0T
SMALL WELL TANK LOCOMOTIVE
2 IN CLASS
FINAL NOS: 162, 163

Fremantle for a time in the construction of the Henderson Naval Base,
and when work there ceased in 1923, they were both sent to Canberra
carrying bricks needed in the construction of Parliament House and other
buildings. In 1927 they were both sold again, this time to the New South
Wales Associated Blue Metal Quarries. Renumbered again, they became
Nos 1 and 2 and were used to carry stone to the crusher from the quarry
face. In 1932 No 2 (163) was scrapped at Bass Point Quarry near Shellharbour. No 1 (162) lasted until
1938, when it too was scrapped and its place taken by lorries.

Builder: Kitson & Co, England 2
Preserved: Nil

Above: Built by Kitson & Co in England in 1888, No 162 entered service with Western Australian Government Railways on 1 December 1896. It was withdrawn from service on 18 November 1915, after about nineteen years in service.
Listed weight in working order of this locomotive was 17 tons and it was 20 ft from buffer to buffer. For more details see A History of W.A.G.R. Steam Locomotives, A. Gunzburg, ARHS(WA) 1984, p. 59–60.

T CLASS (WA)
WHEEL ARRANGEMENT: 4-4-0
GOODS LOCOMOTIVE
10 IN CLASS
FINAL NOS: 164-173

Built by Beyer Peacock & Co in England in 1887, the first of six locomotives sold to the W.A. Land Company for use on their Great Southern Railway entered service on 10 November 1888. A further four locomotives were built by Kitson & Co to make a total of ten, the last of which, No 172, entered service on 6 August 1890. Used on mail, goods and passenger trains on the main line, they also often worked between the port of Albany and Perth, a distance of over 350 kilometres. On 1 December 1896, all ten locomotives entered service with Western Australian Government Railways as Nos 164 to 173. After a few years of main line work, more powerful locomotives entered service and the T class was relegated to shunting work. For many years No 167 was used to haul the Commissioner's inspection train.

Between 1924 and 1926, Nos 164, 165, 166, 168, 172 and 173 were all withdrawn and scrapped. The remainder were all stored for a number of years. In early 1940 two more, Nos 167 and 169, were also withdrawn from service. No 171 which had been fitted with a bogie tender from R150, was withdrawn from service on 19 October 1948 after more than fifty-nine years in service. The last to go was No 170, which had been fitted with a bogie tender from R228. It was withdrawn on 14 February 1952 after sixty-two years in service

Builders: Beyer Peacock & Co, England 6; Kitson & Co, England 4
Preserved: Nil

Above: Built by Kitson & Co in 1888, this locomotive was delivered to the W.A. Land Company and worked on the Great Southern Railway carrying the name plate Mount Barker. *It entered service with Western Australian Government Railways on 1 December 1896 as No 167, and was withdrawn from service on 31 March 1940. Listed weight in working order of locomotive and tender was 49 tons 16 cwt with a combined length of 43 ft 3 in from buffer to buffer. For more details see* A History of W.A.G.R. Steam Locomotives, *A. Gunzburg, ARHS(WA) 1984. p. 61–2.*

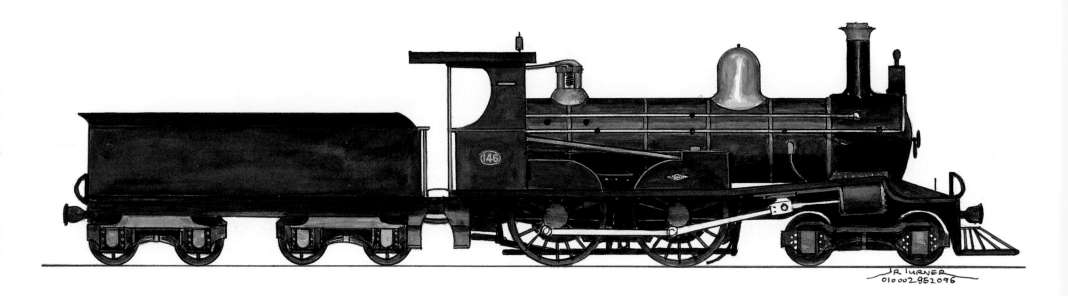

Built by Dubs & Co in England in 1896 for use as express passenger locomotives, these were the largest engines used up to that time on Western Australian Government Railways. When the initial order of twelve arrived, No 144 entered service on 25 February 1897 with obvious success, and on 13 July 1897 a second batch of twelve locomotives was ordered from Dubs. The second batch was all built in 1898 and all entered service in mid 1899. Painted Royal blue with polished brass domes, chimney caps and boiler bands, the R class was used for about five years on express passenger and mail trains on the eastern Goldfields and northern lines.

On 21 March 1907 two R class locomotives, Nos 174 and 228, were involved in transporting divers

R CLASS (WA)
WHEEL ARRANGEMENT: 4-4-0
EXPRESS PASSENGER LOCOMOTIVE
24 IN CLASS
FINAL NOS: 144-55, 174-79, 227-32

and rescue equipment from Perth to Southern Cross. Ec 246 completed the delivery of the equipment to Coolgardie, to rescue a trapped miner.

Between 1909 and 1913 twelve R class locomotives were converted to the 4-4-2 Ra class. However, by mid 1914 seven of these had been changed back to R class. Between 1922 and 1926, a total of thirteen R and five Ra class were scrapped. Of those that remained, three were converted for a second time to Ra class. After withdrawals in 1947, only No 150 remained and it was written off on 19 October 1948, after about fifty-one years in service.

Builder: Dubs & Co, England 24

Preserved: No 174, at Centrepoint Shopping Centre, Midland, Perth.

Above: Built by Dubs & Co in 1896, No 146 entered service with Western Australian Government Railways on 28 February 1897 and was withdrawn after about twenty-seven years service on 31 January 1924. The listed weight in working order of locomotive and tender was 55 tons 16 cwt with a combined length of 48 ft 6 in from buffer to buffer. For more details see A History of W.A.G.R. Steam Locomotives, A. Gunzburg, ARHS(WA) 1984, p. 63–5.

These locomotives were bought by Tasmanian Government Railways from Sharp, Stewart & Co in Scotland, and entered service in 1896 and 1898. A boiler explosion at Zeehan on 16 May 1899 completely destroyed G–1 and killed its crew. The boiler is said to have landed 230 metres away, and apart from the smokebox, everything else above the frame was destroyed. A replacement locomotive arrived in 1900 from Sharp, Stewart & Co and also carried the number G–1. These locomotives were used on the Williamsford line which included solid rock cuttings and 1:40 grades

G CLASS (TAS)
WHEEL ARRANGEMENT: 0–4–2T
SMALL NARROW GAUGE TANK
LOCOMOTIVE
3 IN CLASS
FINAL NOS: G–1, G–2

Preserved: Nil

with sharp curves. It passed through some of the most isolated, rugged country on the west coast of Tasmania.

With the closure of most of the west coast narrow gauge lines, both locomotives were withdrawn from service and sold to the Isis Central sugar mill in Queensland, where they were converted to tender engines and continued in service until the early 1960s.

Builder: Sharp, Stewart & Co, Scotland 3

Above: Built by Sharp, Stewart & Co in Scotland, G–1 entered service with Tasmanian Government Railways in 1896 and was used on isolated narrow gauge lines in the Zeehan area on the west coast of Tasmania. Listed weight in working order of this locomotive was 19 tons 15 cwt with a length of 20 ft from buffer to buffer. For more details see The Tasmanian 'G' Class 2 ft Gauge Locomotive, Light Railways, Summer, 1973–74, p. 11–15.

R TURNER
003 026 900 096

EE CLASS (VIC)
WHEEL ARRANGEMENT: 0–6–2T
SHUNTING TANK LOCOMOTIVE
29 IN CLASS
FINAL NOS: 350–353, 355–357, 359, 361, 367, 369-381, 390

Built by the Phoenix Foundry Company of Ballarat in the late 1880s as a 2–4–2T E class locomotive, No 496 was converted at Newport Workshops in June 1898 to an 0–6–2T and was renumbered as EE No 371. It became one of seven tank engines used for shunting work in the Melbourne goods yard, until the electrification of the suburban system had been completed.

As more of the E class locomotives were converted to EE class, they had their 17-inch cylinders replaced with 18-inch ones which increased their power. During 1923–24, No 371 had its cylinders changed from 17 to 18-inch. Some EE class were moved from Melbourne and were used for shunting at Seymour and Benalla.

A number of changes were made over the years, with automatic couplers fitted and the old pip-squeak whistle replaced with a cast-iron three-tone type. During their time in service the EE class had several bad accidents; in one instance the driver involved was sacked. On 11 February 1908 he drove his locomotive EE 478 through a dead end at Ringwood, and it ended up on its side on the embankment alongside Wantirina Rd. In another accident on 15 May 1908, EE 468 ended up in one of the turntable pits at the North Melbourne Locomotive Yard. Between the early 1920s and early 1930s all the EE class were reclassified as E class.

By the mid 1950s twenty of the class had been scrapped, and in February 1962 Nos 377, 369 and 379 were the last to go, after more than seventy years in service.

Builder: David Munro 11; Phoenix Foundry Company Ballarat 18; Converted from E class at Newport Workshops 24

Preserved: No 369, at ARHS Railway Museum, Champion Rd, North Williamstown; No 371, at Castlemaine & Maldon Railway Preservation Society.

Above: Built in the late 1880's at Phoenix Foundry Company of Ballarat as an E class, No 496 was converted to EE class during 1898 and renumbered 371. Withdrawn from service, it was stored and is one of two of its class to have been preserved. Listed weight in working order of this locomotive was 55 tons and it was 33 ft 8 in from buffer to buffer. For more details see The EE Class 0–6–2 Shunting Tank Engines, M.H.W. Clark, ARHS Bulletin No 518, December 1980, p. 258–63.

The initial order of thirty-six O class locomotives was supplied by Neilson & Co, England, between 1896–1897, with an additional ten locomotives from Dubs & Co built in 1898. The first locomotive to enter service was No 74 on 19 September 1896. The last was built by Dubs & Co and entered service on 11 October 1898. The O class had been designed to operate on both 45 lb and 60 lb rails, and was similar to the K class but lighter. They had a number of obvious differences, such as a bogie tender as well as side tanks which carried 500 gallons of water. This increased their range over the K class.

On entering service they were used on the eastern goldfields hauling heavy goods traffic, and

O CLASS (WA)
WHEEL ARRANGEMENT: 2–8–0
HEAVY GOODS TENDER-TANK
LOCOMOTIVE
46 IN CLASS
FINAL NOS: 74-100, 208-226

were found to be very economical to operate. They were also used for hauling goods on the Collie line. By 1901 they were being replaced on the eastern Goldfields by the Ec class, and in 1903 the K class replaced them on the Collie line. Most were then stored until 1907, when parts taken from ten locomotives were used in the construction of N class locomotives for the Perth suburban passenger services. Over the following years a number of O class were converted to Oa or Os, and then back to O class again. The final seven locomotives were all withdrawn from service on 25 July 1971 after over sixty years in service.

Builders: Neilson & Co, England 36; Dubs & Co, England 10

Preserved: No 218, at ARHS Railway Museum, Bassendean.

Above: Built by Dubs & Co in 1898, No 218 entered service with Western Australian Government Railways on 11 October 1898, and was withdrawn from service on 25 July 1961. This locomotive is preserved at the ARHS Railway Museum at Bassendean in Perth, WA. Listed weight in working order of this locomotive and tender was 62 tons 17 cwt with a combined length of 47 ft 4 in from buffer to buffer. For more details see A History of W.A.G.R. Steam Locomotives, A. Gunzburg, ARHS(WA) 1984, p. 52–5.

Built by Dubs & Co in England, these locomotives were assembled in Rockhampton and went into service in October 1898. They had been bought specifically for use on the steep 1:16½ gradient that lay on the track between Moonmera and Moongan, which linked Mount Morgan with Rockhampton via Kabra. To negotiate the dangerous steep section, the locomotives used Roman Abt's patent type, which used a pair of staggered racks centrally mounted between the rails. These were engaged by pinion wheels on the locomotives.

Because of the difficult conditions under which they operated, the locomotives were often in

4D11½ ABT CLASS (QLD)
WHEEL ARRANGEMENT: 0-4-2T
SMALL TANK RACK LOCOMOTIVE
2 IN CLASS
FINAL NOS: 339 40

was written off in December 1922.

Builder: Dubs & Co, England 2

Preserved: Nil

need of repair, and with little space under the boiler they were difficult to work on. Queensland Government Railways also had no previous experience with this type of locomotive. They were quite powerful for their size, but the problems with servicing meant they were used as little as possible when larger rack engines entered service in October 1898. No 340 spent its last years as a boiler washout plant at Mount Morgan, and

Above: Built by Dubs & Co in England, No 339 entered service with Queensland Government Railways in October 1898. Designed for use on steep gradients, it was bought for use on the Kabra to Mount Morgan line. No 339 was little used after newer engines arrived in October 1900 and was written off in September 1916. Listed weight in working order of this locomotive was 26 tons 17 cwt with 15 cwt of coal and was 23 ft 5½ in long. For more details see Locomotives in the Tropics Volume 1, J. Armstrong, ARHS(QLD) p. 66.

This class was originally introduced as the 79 class tender engine, with No 79, delivered from Beyer Peacock & Co in England, entering service in May 1877. By the mid 1890s, a shortage of suburban engines resulted in the experimental conversion of the class leader C79 to a side tank engine and it was reclassed as CC79, with the tender version becoming the C80 class. The success of this experiment resulted in twenty being converted between 1896 and 1902. Initially they were used on the outer suburban services around Sydney, but with the introduction of the new S(636) class in 1903, they were moved to the Newcastle area, and then further out to minor branch lines.

CC(79) CLASS (Z)13 (NSW)
WHEEL ARRANGEMENT: 4-4-2T
SUBURBAN PASSENGER
SIDE TANK LOCO
20 IN CLASS
FINAL NOS: 1301-1316, 83, 84, 87, 149

In later years they were used at Ballina, Picton, Yass, Coffs Harbour and Casino. In 1962, No 1301 was assigned for use on vintage trains, but spent most of its time working as a shunter at various depots around the state. It was the last of its class to be withdrawn in September 1973, after ninety-six years in service and travelling 1 623 021 miles.

Builders: Beyer Peacock & Co 17; Dubs & Co 2; Atlas Engineering Co, Sydney 1

Preserved: Nos 1301, 1307 and 1308, at Rail Transport Museum, Thirlmere.

Above: Delivered to N.S.W. Government Railways from Beyer Peacock & Co as a tender locomotive, it was numbered 37N and entered service in February 1879. It was then renumbered 415 in 1889, rebuilt as a tank type in July 1899, and then in 1924 it was renumbered 1311. Withdrawn from service in December 1963, it was scrapped on 1 May 1964, having travelled 1 458 854 miles during eighty-four years in service. The locomotive weighed 54 tons 7 cwt and was 35 ft 8¼ in from buffer to buffer. For more details see A Compendium of NSW Steam Locomotives, compiled by A. Grunbach, ARHS(NSW) 1989, p. 136–7.

G CLASS (SA)
WHEEL ARRANGEMENT: 2-4-0T
SMALL TANK ENGINE
8 IN CLASS
FINAL NOS: 156, 161-2

Whilst there were eight locomotives in this class, we refer here to only three of them. They all entered service with South Australian Government Railways on 16 December 1899, when it acquired the Glenelg Railway Company. All three locomotives had been built by Beyer Peacock & Co in 1879 and delivered to the Holdfast Bay Railway Company, whose private line began at the South Australian Government-owned North Terrace station, and linked it to the one-time port of Glenelg, about seven miles away. Initially numbered 1, 2 and 3, they were renumbered in November 1881 to become numbers 2, 7 and 8 when Holdfast Bay merged with the Glenelg Railway Company. Smaller in size than the Gd class which entered service in 1880, they would probably have pulled trains made up of several carriages or wagons, or a mixture of both.

On entering service with South Australian Government Railways they were renumbered again as 156, 161 and 162. Most G class locomotives continued to work the Glenelg lines, until replaced in 1908 by the P and K tank engines. They then continued to work passenger services until they were transferred to Port Adelaide, where they finished their service as shunters. No 161 was condemned in December 1904, with Nos 156 and 162 being condemned on 5 June 1923, after about forty-four years in service.

Builder: Beyer Peacock & Co 3
Preserved: Nil

Above: Built in 1879 by Beyer Peacock & Co in England, it was imported by the Holdfast Bay Railway as No 2, sold to the Glenelg Railway Company in November 1881 and renumbered 7, then re-sold on 16 December 1899 to South Australian Government Railways with the number 161. It was withdrawn from service on 12 December 1904 and condemned. Listed weight in working order of this locomotive was 21 tons 5 cwt and it was 23 ft 2 in from buffer to buffer.
For more details see The G–Class Locomotives of South Australia, G. H. Eardley, ARHS Bulletin No 272, June 1960, p. 81–4.

GE CLASS (SA)
WHEEL ARRANGEMENT: 4–4–0T
SMALL SIDE-TANK LOCOMOTIVE
2 IN CLASS
FINAL NOS: 165–166

Delivered to the Glenelg Railway Company from Beyer Peacock & Co in England in 1897, they were numbered 11 and 12. It was thought the locomotives were lost when the SS *Mortiban* on which they were being carried caught fire and sank while entering port at Albany in Western Australia. After the locomotives had been salvaged and delivered to Adelaide in a somewhat rusty condition, a problem arose with cleaning them. SS *Mortiban* had also carried a large quantity of Sunlight soap in the same cargo hold, which had melted in the fire and filled all pipes and cavities on both locomotives.

Painted black with polished brass fittings and copper chimney cap, they were purchased by the South Australian Government Railways on 16 December 1899, and given the numbers 165 and 166.

The numbers were fixed to the front of the chimney with the class letters Ge on the back. They continued to operate the South Terrace-Glenelg and North Terrace–Glenelg services of up to five carriages at a time, and remained in service in this area until 1908, when newer locomotives replaced them. They were then assigned to Port Adelaide as shunters, with trips between the Mile End marshalling yard and Glanville. Both continued to work as shunters until withdrawn from service, with No 166 condemned on 8 April 1929 and No 165 on 4 June 1935, after about thirty-eight years of service.

Builder: Beyer Peacock & Co England 2
Preserved: Nil

Above: Delivered to the Adelaide and Glenelg United Railway Company in 1897 as No 12, it was renumbered 166 when it entered service with South Australian Government Railways on 16 December 1899. After working on passenger and goods services, it spent its final years as a shunter and was withdrawn in April 1929 after about thirty-two years in service. The listed weight in working order of this locomotive was 28 tons 18 cwt with a length of 25 ft 7 in.
For more details see The GE Class Locomotives of South Australia, *G. Eardley, ARHS Bulletin No 381, July 1969, p. 158–60.*

GD CLASS (SA)
WHEEL ARRANGEMENT: 0-4-4T
SMALL WELL TANK LOCOMOTIVE
2 IN CLASS
FINAL NOS: 163 AND 164

Delivered to the Holdfast Bay Railway Co in Adelaide and numbered 4 and 5, these locomotives arrived from Beyer Peacock & Co aboard the *Ironbark*, which sailed from England in June 1880. They entered service painted green with a black smoke box and polished dome, but in November 1881 Holdfast merged with the Adelaide, Glenelg and Suburban Railway Co, and the locomotives were renumbered 9 and 10.

In 1899 the company was taken over by the South Australian Government Railways, and the locomotives were again renumbered 163 and 164 before entering service on 16 December 1899. Having been painted black in 1895, the locomotives had polished brass numbers fitted mid way up the front of the funnel, with the class letters on the back. The number was also displayed on the rear

bunker of the locomotive.

These locomotives continued to operate on Holdfast Bay line trains until sometime after 1908 when the track was re-laid and P-class locomotives introduced. After having their chimneys shortened by nine inches to comply with regulations, they were also fitted with new brakes and then relegated to the Port Line and its extensions, working passenger and goods services until replaced by F class engines. They were then restricted to shunting duties around the Port Adelaide goods sidings, until they were withdrawn from service in February 1922 and condemned on 6 February 1925.

Builder: Beyer Peacock & Co. 2
Preserved: Nil

Above: After arriving in Adelaide from England in 1880, No 164 entered service with South Australian Government Railways on 16 December 1899. It was withdrawn from service in February 1922 and condemned on 6 February 1925, after about forty-five years of service. The listed weight in working order was 32 tons 4 cwt and it was 29 ft 3 in from buffer to buffer. For more detail see The Gd Class Locomotives of South Australia, G.H. Eardley, ARHS Bulletin No 351, January 1967, p. 14–17.

By the late 1890s the need for a new locomotive for passenger services was becoming more urgent, as new lines were completed in the Gladstone and Rockhampton areas. After the rejection of two proposed designs, a third was accepted. The first PB15 was delivered by Walkers Ltd in January 1899, and entered service as No 356. The final locomotive, No 609, was delivered in 1912. Locomotive No 12 was built for the Aramac Shire Tramway in 1924, and was eventually bought by Queensland Government Railways in February 1958.

Soon after entering service, the PB15 was assigned to hauling mail trains such as the Gladstone Boat Mail, Sydney Mail and Rockhampton Mail. With the expansion of the rail system into

PB15 CLASS (QLD)
WHEEL ARRANGEMENT: 4-6-0
PASSENGER LOCOMOTIVE
203 IN CLASS
FINAL NOS: 12, 347-609

south-western Queensland, more PB15s were ordered. Though larger engines were considered, the light track meant that they could not be used. Few modifications were required during their time in service, and while some were withdrawn from service during the 1930s and 1940s, most were not withdrawn until the 1960s, with the final few withdrawn in August 1970, after seventy years in service.

Builders: Walkers Limited 92; Evans, Anderson, Phelan & Co 70; Kitson & Co 20; Toowoomba Foundry 20; Ipswich Workshops 1

Preserved: No 444, at QR in storage; No 448, at Pioneer Steam Railway, Swanbank; No 454, at Bellarine Peninsular Railway, Queenscliff, Victoria.

Above: Built by Walkers Limited in 1899, No 356 entered service in December of that year. It was withdrawn from service in February 1969 after almost seventy years in service. Listed weight in working order of locomotive and tender was 56 tons 3 cwt with a combined length of 47 ft 6⅛ in from buffer to buffer. For more details see Locomotives in the Tropics *Volume 1, J. Armstrong, ARHS(QLD) p. 67–8.*

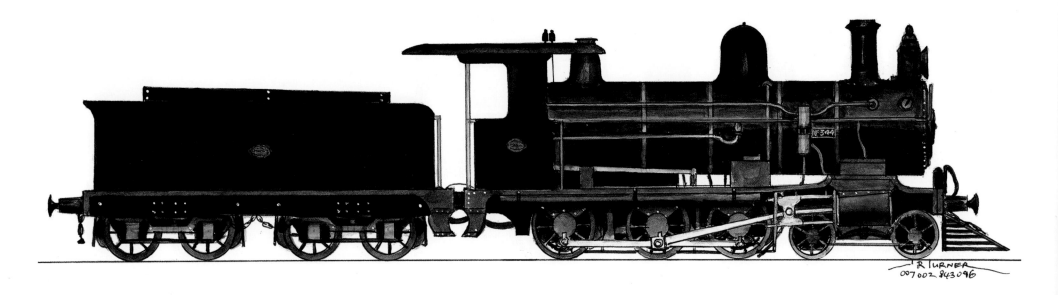

B15 CLASS (QLD)
WHEEL ARRANGEMENT: 4-6-0
GOODS LOCOMOTIVE
98 IN CLASS
FINAL NOS: 3, 23, 42, 54, 95, 205–219, 235–244, 270–280, 289–338, 341–346, 539

Tenders were called through the Agent-General's office in London for fifteen heavy traffic engines, and a quote from Nasmyth Wilson & Co of Manchester was accepted in 1889. The first of the new locomotives arrived in Rockhampton and Townsville later that year. The second batch of locomotives was built locally by Evans, Anderson and Phelan, and had boilers made of steel, which allowed for a higher working pressure. Many instances of broken rails were caused by these locomotives, which were reported to have severe grooving of tyres, especially when they had been used on livestock trains. A number of changes were made to cab layout, which were continued into later locomotives built for Queensland Government Railways. The final locomotive in this class was delivered in 1909 by Walkers Limited.

The problem of the broken rails continued, and in 1900 it was suggested that fitting larger diameter wheels might solve it. After some dispute, three sets of 45 inch diameter wheels were obtained from South Australian Railways, and fitted to No 336, along with some other changes, at Ipswich in November 1900. After testing on both goods and passenger trains and some further adjustments, the changes were a success, with No 336 being known as a B15 Converted. Over the next thirty years almost all in the class were modified.

Builders: Nasmyth Wilson & Co, England 15; Evans, Anderson & Phelan 21; Yorkshire Engine Co 10; Walkers Limited 52

Preserved: No 290, at QR, (stored at present); No 299, at Maryborough Station, Maryborough.

Above: Built by Walkers Limited in 1899, No 344 entered service in February 1900. It was converted in November 1903 and withdrawn from service in May 1953 after about fifty-four years in service. The listed weight in working order of locomotive and tender was 51 tons 7 cwt with a combined length of 45 ft 7 in from buffer to buffer. For more details see Locomotives in the Tropics *Volume 1, J. Armstrong, ARHS(QLD) p. 67–8.*

With the demand for railway lines continuing to grow, the combination of rising construction costs and difficult terrain resulted in the building of a series of narrow gauge lines in the late 1890s. The Baldwin Locomotive Works, Philadelphia, U.S.A. won the tender for the supply of two 2–6–2 tank engines able to work in either direction on a 1 in 30 grade with 2-chain curves. The first into service was No 1A on 26 September 1898, and the last, No 17A, on 4 April 1916, after seven months in storage. No 1A was used in the construction of the Wangaratta–Whitfield line, which opened on 14 March 1899. With more lines due to open, it was decided that Newport Workshops should build two more locomotives, using the spare parts and plans which had been sent by Baldwin with Nos 1A and 2A. No 3A entered service on 6 April 1900 and No 4A on 13 June 1900. They were identical copies of the first two locomotives, except that the water capacity had been increased to 780 gallons.

As the new lines were opened, Newport Workshops continued to build new locomotives to work them. Narrow gauge depots were established at Wangaratta, Colac, Moe and Upper Ferntree Gully. The repairs were done at Newport Workshops initially, using a pair of bogies fitted after the narrow gauge ones had been removed to allow transport on a broad gauge line. In 1926 a special transport wagon, 129 Q, was built at Newport Workshops. It had narrow gauge track fitted on it so that any narrow gauge wagon or engine could be rolled on and transported without removing the bogies.

Some were withdrawn from service in the late 1920s and mid 1930s, and 1950s. In March 1977 only Nos 6A, 7A, 12A and 14A were still in service, as part of the Puffing Billy railway at Belgrave.
Builders: Baldwin Locomotive Company 2; Newport Workshops, Melbourne 15
Preserved: Nos 3A, 6A, 7A, 8A, 12A and 14A, at the Puffing Billy Preservation Society,Belgrave.

Above: *The first NA class locomotive built by Newport Workshops, No 3A entered service on 6 April 1900. It was struck off the register on 29 November 1955, and placed in a park at the Lord Mayor's Camp at Portsea on 15 November 1960. Bought by the Puffing Billy Preservation Society, it arrived at Menzies Creek on 27 April 1977, It was then hauled to Belgrave by No 12A on 7 May 1977, where it was dismantled and all re-useable parts were stored for eventual restoration. Listed weight in working order of this locomotive was 34 tons 18 cwt and it was 30 ft 8¼ in long. For more details see* Victorian Railways, *M.H.W. Clark and J.L. Buckland, ARHS Bulletin No 473, March 1977, p. 49–61.*

The first pair of these locomotives was built by Dubs & Co in England, and entered service in October 1900. They were found to be better than the earlier, smaller rack locomotives, and as traffic increased, two more were ordered. By this time Dubs had been merged into the North British Locomotive Co, and North British built the next four locomotives, with two delivered in 1906 and the final pair in June 1915.

Using the Abt rack system, all six were based at Mount Morgan and spent their working life on the 4½ mile long section of rack track nearby. The only time they ventured further was when they went to Rockhampton for an overhaul. While No 202 was written off in June 1926 after ten years in

6D13½ ABT CLASS (QLD)
WHEEL ARRANGEMENT: 0–6–0T
TANK RACK LOCOMOTIVE
6 IN CLASS
FINAL NOS: 202–3, 383–4, 402–3

service, the other five continued until November 1952. The completion of a deviation meant that the rack section of track, which had been used for more than fifty years, was eliminated, and all five rack locomotives were written off. The new line meant that a single C17 locomotive could haul 275 tons up or 650 tons down the Razorback escarpment. This was a great improvement on the 125 tons up or 100 tons down on the old line that had been achieved with the assistance of Abt locomotives.

Builders: Dubs & Co, England 2; North British Locomotive Co 4
Preserved: Nil

Above: Built by Dubs & Co, No 383 entered service in October 1900. It was built especially for use on the section of rack track north of Mount Morgan. It was withdrawn from service in November 1952 and cut up after about fifty-two years in service. The listed weight in working order of this locomotive was 35 tons 3 cwt and it was 25 ft 2 in from buffer to buffer. For more details see Locomotives in the Tropics Vol. 1, J. Armstrong, ARHS(QLD) p. 77.

ME CLASS (VIC)
WHEEL ARRANGEMENT: 4-4-2T
SUBURBAN TANK LOCOMOTIVE
22 IN CLASS
FINAL NOS 40, 210–240, 312–320
(EVEN NUMBERS ONLY)

On 10 May 1879, a 4–4–0 tank engine was imported from England. Built by Beyer Peacock & Co, No 40 was used as the pattern for twenty-one identical locomotives, built at Phoenix Foundry in Ballarat between 1884 and 1886. In 1900, No 318 was the first to be classified ME when it was converted to a 4–4–2T wheel arrangement on 15 November. It also had a new boiler fitted at this time, but 18 inch cylinders were not fitted until 26 March 1904. Twelve of the class had boilers replaced as M class between 1895 and 1898, and whilst some had new cylinders fitted when converted to ME class, others had them fitted at a later date. Improved springs and a new front bogie with a bigger wheelbase, along with fitting the rear wheels allowed a much larger bunker to be added. They continued in service on the suburban lines, until the increase in traffic required larger trains which were hauled by the new E class tank locomotives.

Though they still performed well on the easier graded tracks, they were eventually to be seen only on the Burnley–Darling line. In 1913 the first of the class to be scrapped was No 240, on 27 December 1913. By 1922 only three remained in service—Nos 214, 228 and 318—all of which were scrapped on 20 May 1922, after thirty-six years in service.

Builder: Beyer Peacock & Co. 1; Phoenix Foundry Co 21
Preserved: Nil

Above: Built by Phoenix Foundry Co at Ballarat, No 226 entered service with Victorian Railways on 17 August 1885. It was converted to ME class on 28 June 1901, and had its boiler changed at the same time. On 21 October 1901 No 226 hauled its first train to Heidelberg via Collingwood. It had new 18 inch cylinders fitted on 29 June 1905, and also a shorter chimney—the only one of its class to do so. It was scrapped on 13 July 1918, after about thirty-three years in service. Listed weight in working order of this locomotive was 54 tons and it was 34 ft 9⅛ in from buffer to buffer. For more details see The Tank Locomotives of the Victorian Government Railways, *M.H. Clark & A. Madden, ARHS Bulletin No 384, October 1969, p. 221–40.*

The first true suburban tank locomotive to be used on Queensland Government Railways, No 363 was built by Walkers Limited at Maryborough, and entered service in May 1901. Nineteen more were built over the following year, and the final locomotive, No 382, entered service in July 1902. Problems were encountered during construction with difficulty in obtaining some materials specified in the tender.

Once in service, the combination of a single trailing truck and double front bogie caused a number of derailments, as well as problems with overheating bearings. The position of the flangeless driving wheels also caused problems. It took three years to resolve these problems, during which time the government came under attack when the cost of upgrading track and bridges was made known to the public. A number of solutions were proposed: one, in early 1904, was to scrap the whole class

6D16 CLASS (QLD)
WHEEL ARRANGEMENT: 4-6-2T
SUBURBAN TANK LOCOMOTIVE
20 IN CLASS
FINAL NOS: 363-382

rather than repair and upgrade the track they were continually damaging. Another was to convert them to tender engines.

At the time the 6D16s entered service only eight kilometres of track was ready for them. When used on existing light rails, it was not unusual for them to spread the track and derail on curves. In February 1904 the Premier became involved and by July, No 371 had been modified, with the front bogie and rear trailing wheels replaced with a four-wheel swinging bolster bogie fitted front and rear. This solved the derailment problem, and all in the class were converted to 4-6-4T between 1904 and 1905.

Builder: Walkers Limited, Maryborough 20

Preserved: Nil

Above: Built by Walkers Limited in 1901, No 364 entered service with Queensland Government Railways in June l901. It was converted to 4-6-4 wheel arrangement in 1904-1905, and then remained in service until June 1942, when it was written off after about forty-one years in service. The listed weight in working order of this locomotive was 58 tons 3 cwt and it was 36 ft 4 in from buffer to buffer. For more details see Locomotives in the Tropics *Volume 1, J. Armstrong, ARHS(Qld) p. 78–81.*

Built by the Baldwin Locomotive Works of Philadelphia, the Ec class was ordered in December 1900 as a stopgap measure to handle increasing traffic, until new locomotives arrived from Britain. With tracks upgraded to 60 lb rails, the Ecs were ideal, being able to handle heavy loads without the assistance of a second locomotive. The first of them arrived in Fremantle in July 1901. No 250 was the first to enter service on 7 August, with all twenty in service by 10 October when No 245 was completed.

While drivers were trained to operate these compound engines they soon used their own system. After a few years of service the frames began to crack behind the cylinders, and piston rods and crossheads were bent by improper use. Overall, the Ec class was a success. A number of changes

EC CLASS (WA)
WHEEL ARRANGEMENT: 4-6-2
HEAVY PASSENGER GOODS
LOCOMOTIVE
20 IN CLASS
FINAL NOS: 236–255

were made during their time in service, including the large soft coal chimney fitted between 1900 and 1902, and new front end frames and safety valves in 1906. In the early 1920s nine Ec locomotives were converted to the Eca class, to enable them to operate on the 45 lb rails of the Northam-Wongan Hills-Mullewa line.

However time was running out for the Ec class, and all were withdrawn from service between 1923 and 1925. No 240 was the last to go, on 24 August 1925, after about twenty-four years in service. Following rebuilding they were re-numbered and became the L class and survived another 30 years in service.

Builder: Baldwin Locomotive Works, U.S.A. 20

Preserved: Nil

Above: Built by the Baldwin Locomotive Works, No 249 entered service on 14 September 1901 and was withdrawn from service on 19 January 1925, after about twenty-four years of service. Listed weight in working order of this locomotive and tender was 73 tons with a combined length of 56 ft 8 in from buffer to buffer. For more details see A History of W.A.G.R. Steam Locomotives, A. Gunzburg, ARHS(WA) 1984, p. 69–71.

The need for a new heavy goods locomotive resulted in Victorian Railways importing a 2–8–0 locomotive built by the Baldwin Locomotive Works, Philadelphia, in 1889. In May 1900 it was used in tests on the 'Great Southern Railway', hauling coal trains between Melbourne and Nyora. It quickly showed itself to be superior to the R class then in service, being able to haul far heavier loads with ease. An order was then placed with the Phoenix Foundry Company of Ballarat to build fifteen identical locomotives. These were numbered 501–529 (odd numbers only) with the first, No 501, entering service in November 1901. No 529 was the last, in December 1902.

The cabs were large, with comfortable seats for the crew. Used on many lines they were most

V CLASS (VIC)
WHEEL ARRANGEMENT: 2-8-0
HEAVY GOODS LOCOMOTIVE
16 IN CLASS
NOS ON ENTERING SERVICE:
499–529 (ODD NUMBERS ONLY)
FINAL NOS: 200–215

Builder: Baldwin Locomotive Works 1; Phoenix Foundry 15

Preserved: Nil

often seen on the South Gippsland line as well as lines from Bendigo and Maryborough. During 1912–13, new boilers were needed, and as each of the class had them fitted the cylinders were changed from compound to simple. This change was due to high maintenance costs said to result from misuse by drivers on heavy grades. In the early 1920s they were condemned and scrapped as their boilers needed renewal, with No 413 the first to go in June 1924. No 200 (499) was the last to go in January 1930, after almost thirty years in service.

Above: Built by Phoenix Foundry in Ballarat in 1901, No 201 (501) entered service with Victorian Railways in November 1901. The boiler and cylinders were changed in August 1913, and the locomotive was withdrawn from service in January 1923 and scrapped in December 1924. Listed weight in working order of this locomotive and tender was 91 tons 3 cwt with a combined length of 60 ft 3 in from buffer to buffer. For more details see
The Victorian Railways V-Class Vauclain Compound Locomotives, M.H. Clark and J.L. Buckland, ARHS Bulletin No. 305, March 1963, p. 17–41

Built by Lokomotivfabrik Hagans in Erfurt, Germany, the Hagan's Patent, as it was known was the only one of its type in Australia. It arrived at Zeehan on the west coast of Tasmania in 1900. After a test run on the North-East Dundas tramway it was placed in service hauling ore trains and mixed goods services along the narrow gauge lines in the Zeehan area.

In 1901 an ore smelter was opened at Silver Bell, a few miles south-east of Zeehan, and a new line was built so that the ore could be shipped directly to the smelter. The first trainloads arrived on 6 March 1901. While some lines were used for ore traffic only, by 1910 the narrow gauge network around Zeehan had reached a total of twenty-four miles in length. Traffic increased again when the line from Zeehan to Williamsford became a popular tourist

J CLASS (TAS)
WHEEL ARRANGEMENT: 2-6-4-0T
NARROW GAUGE GOODS TANK LOCOMOTIVE
1 IN CLASS
FINAL NO: HAGAN'S PATENT

destination in the 1920s. Montezuma Falls became well known, as the line crossed a large timber trestle bridge at the foot of the falls.

By the late 1920s a rapid decline in mining activity, combined with the depression of the 1930s saw the last train run on the Zeehan–Williamsford line on 5 July 1932. Only the Zeehan–Comstock line was still in use, but even that section to the west of Zeehan also closed for good on 8 October 1933.

It was the last remaining section of 2 ft track to be used by the Tasmanian Government Railways. Along with a number of other locomotives, the Hagan's Patent was stored in the rail yard at Zeehan. In 1963 what remained of it after being stripped was still rusting away in the rail yard.

Builder: Lokomotivfabrik Hagans, Erfurt, Germany 1

Preserved: Nil

Above: Built by Lokomotivfabrik Hagans, in Erfurt, Germany, the J class or Hagan's Patent entered service with Tasmanian Government Railways in 1900. The only one of its kind to be used in Australia, it was withdrawn from service in the early 1930s with the closure of the narrow gauge lines at Zeehan. Listed weight in working order of this locomotive was 41 tons 10 cwt and it was 34 ft 7 in from buffer to buffer. For more details see Railways of the Zeehan District, L.B. Manny, ARHS Bulletin No 313, September 1963, p. 166–7.

C CLASS (WA)
WHEEL ARRANGEMENT: 4-6-0
MIXED TRAFFIC LOCOMOTIVE
12 IN CLASS
FINAL NOS: 264-275

The combination of a locomotive shortage, and delays of up to two years for delivery of new locomotives from England, resulted in an order for twelve locomotives being placed with the Baldwin Locomotive Works on 2 September 1901. They arrived at Fremantle in June 1902, with No 264 the first into service on 1 July 1902. No 268 was the last, on 15 August 1902. Used on mixed passenger and mail services on the Eastern, Eastern Goldfields and Great Southern railways, they were nicknamed 'Baby Yanks' and provided a better service than the locomotives they replaced on those lines.

In 1905 they were also working on the northern and South Western railways but required costly repairs to their boilers. To overcome this problem a new boiler was designed by the Midland Junction Workshops. It included a number of modifications, and was heavier than the previous boiler. A trailing bogie was fitted under the firebox to carry the extra weight. Two locomotives, Nos 270 and 272, were converted on 10 September 1908, and in 1909 it was reported that these locomotives were giving excellent results. All of the class were converted, with No 269 the last on 23 March 1918. No dates are given for conversion of Nos 264, 267 or 275.

Builder: Baldwin Locomotive Works 12

Preserved: Nil

Above: Built by the Baldwin Locomotive Works in 1901, No 267 entered service with Western Australian Government Railways on 7 August 1902. The date of its conversion to 4-6-2 is not known. It was withdrawn from service on 29 September 1950 after about forty-eight years in service. Listed weight in working order of this locomotive and tender was 67 tons 10 cwt with a combined length of 55 ft 3 in from buffer to buffer. For more details see A History of W.A.G.R. Steam Locomotives, A. Gunzburg, ARHS(WA) 1984, p. 72–5.

F CLASS (WA)
WHEEL ARRANGEMENT: 4-8-0
HEAVY GOODS LOCOMOTIVE
57 IN CLASS
FINAL NOS: 276–290, 356–367, 394–423

The order for fifteen F class locomotives was placed with Dubs & Co in 1900, with the first to enter service being No 276 on 16 August 1902. No 288 was the last of this group, on 15 November 1902. While trials proved them to be satisfactory, they needed boiler repairs soon after entering service, due to poor workmanship. These problems having been solved between 1905 and 1907 by re-riveting the boiler tube plates, the F class then performed well in service, and was used mostly on the Eastern Railway.

With traffic increasing, a second order for twelve locomotives was placed with North British Locomotive Co on 28 June 1911. Dubs & Co had been taken over by North British after the first order had been filled, and on 5 August 1912 a final order for thirty more of the F class was placed with North British. The last to enter service was No 423 on 21 March 1914. In late 1912, the last two locomotives of the 1912 order entered service. Nos 366 and 367 had been superheated, and a series of tests in 1913 showed savings of 35 percent in coal and 38 percent in water consumption. By the mid 1920s work began on converting the whole class to Fs or superheated, with the last being No 415 on 22 September 1950.

New locomotives were introduced in the 1950s, and the F class was relegated to shunting and local goods services around Perth, Bunbury, Collie and Narrogin. A large number was withdrawn in July 1969. No 407 was the last to go on 14 August 1972, after fifty-nine years in service.

Builders: Dubs & Co, Glasgow 15; North British Locomotive Co 42
Preserved: No 452, at Mining Museum, Collie; No 460, at ARHS Railway Museum, Bassendean.

Above: Built by Dubs & Co, No 290 entered service with Western Australian Government Railways on 18 October 1902. It was converted to Fs class on 29 November 1924 and was withdrawn from service on 1 March 1962. Listed weight in working order of this locomotive and tender was 85 tons 19 cwt with a combined length of 55 ft from buffer to buffer. For more details see A History of W.A.G.R. Steam Locomotives, A. Gunzburg, ARHS(WA) 1984, p.76–81.

The first group of A class locomotives had been built by Beyer Peacock in 1884, and the second was built from a Kitson design by the Phoenix Foundry Co, between 1889 and 1891. The third group, known as the AA class, was an improved version of the second group and was also built by the Phoenix Foundry Company, Ballarat. The first ten AA class Nos 530 to 548 (even numbers only) entered service in 1900 and 1901 with a six-wheel tender. The second group of ten, No 550 to 570 (even numbers only, with 560 omitted) all entered service in 1903, and had an eight-wheel bogie tender and minor changes to the boiler. No 550 was first in service on 30 April 1903, and No 570 the last, on 3 November 1903.

The bogie tender carried 4400 gallons of water and 5 tons of coal, which made the combined weight with the locomotive ten tons heavier than the locomotive with a six-wheeled tender. On delivery, all AA class locomotives arrived painted light and dark green with white lining, with polished

AA CLASS (VIC)
WHEEL ARRANGEMENT: 4–4–0
EXPRESS PASSENGER LOCOMOTIVE
20 IN CLASS
NOS ON ENTERING SERVICE: 530–558,
562–570 (EVEN NUMBERS ONLY)
FINAL NOS: 74–77, 82, 84, 86

class and number plates made of brass with vermilion backgrounds. Nos 546 and 552 worked Lord Tennyson's Special on December 1903. From 1904 the class was repainted Canadian red and chocolate, with the name plates painted over. They were used on all main line express and passenger trains until about 1911, when the new A2 class gradually replaced them on the main line. Nos 538 and 548 were used on the Royal tour of the Duke and Duchess of York in May 1901.

In 1919 the first of the class were scrapped. Another eleven followed in the mid 1920s. In January 1932 the last four of the class were all withdrawn over four days between 25 and 28 January 1932. The last to go was No 542, which had a six-wheel tender. It had travelled 574 330 miles during thirty-one years in service.

Builder: Phoenix Foundry Co. Ballarat 20
Preserved: Nil

Above: Built by the Phoenix Foundry Co of Ballarat, No 552 entered service on 3 June 1903. It was scrapped on 3 March 1926 after about twenty-three years in service, in which it travelled 470 705 miles. Listed weight in working order of this locomotive and tender was 91 tons 2 cwt with a combined length of 53 ft 8 in from buffer to buffer. For more details see The AA-Class 4–4–0 Express Locomotives, M.H. Clark and J.L. Buckland, ARHS Bulletin No 406, August 1971, p. 169–73.

Thirteen locomotives of this class were built by Beyer Peacock & Co. The first, No 14N, entered service in September 1865 as a 2–4–0 tender locomotive with N.S.W. Government Railways. Initially known as the 23 class, the first nine locomotives had 5 ft 9½ in driving wheels, while the remaining four had 5 ft 6 in wheels. The final locomotive of this class entered service in December 1870 as No 35. In 1889 they were classified as the G23 class 2–4–0.

In early 1903, work began on re-boilering the G23 class locomotives, which had been in storage at Eveleigh for about ten years. At the same time the single leading truck was replaced by a four-wheel bogie, making them almost identical to the C80 (Z12) class. After modification they were

CG CLASS (Z)14 (NSW)
WHEEL ARRANGEMENT: 4–4–0
PASSENGER LOCOMOTIVE
13 IN CLASS
FINAL NOS: 1401–1413

designated the Cg23 class 4–4–0, with a Belpaire boiler, Bissell pattern bogie and a steel-sided cab with circular window.

Used on outback lines, the Cg class was gradually replaced between 1928 and 1932 by the more modern (C)30T class engines. As traffic increased, they were reintroduced as fast passenger 'rail motors' until the mid 1930s, when most were withdrawn from service. However three remained in use until the mid 1940s, with No 1412 the last to be withdrawn in February 1948, having travelled 1 106 491 miles during seventy-eight years of service. It was scrapped in March 1952.

Builder: Beyer Peacock & Co, England 13

Preserved: Nil

Above: Built by Beyer Peacock & Co, No 25 was one of the first nine locomotives with 5 ft 9½ in driving wheels. In 1924 it was renumbered 1408 as a Z14 class 4–4–0. It was withdrawn from service in April 1935 and scrapped on 23 November 1939, having travelled 1 025 863 miles during its sixty-seven years of service. The combined weight of the rebuilt locomotive and tender was 62 tons 8 cwt with a combined length of 48 ft 3¼ in from buffer to buffer. For more details see A Compendium of NSW Steam Locomotives, compiled by A. Grunbach, ARHS(NSW), 1989, p. 140–1.

Built by Walkers Limited at Maryborough, these locomotives entered service during 1901–1902. After many problems during the first three years of service, they were all converted to the 4–6–4T wheel arrangement in 1904 and 1905. Though the initial problems of rail damage and derailments had now been overcome, new problems emerged with the smokebox, and then in 1908 with the Belpaire fireboxes; these were eventually solved by fitting new round-top boilers. This was done gradually between 1912 and 1918. During this time various tests were carried out using coke as a fuel, which eventually resulted in larger bunkers being fitted to all locomotives in the class during 1917.

The locomotives could haul between 160 and 175 tons tare weight on suburban passenger

6D16 CLASS (QLD)
WHEEL ARRANGEMENT: 4-6-4T
SUBURBAN TANK LOCOMOTIVE
20 IN CLASS
FINAL NOS: 363-382

trains. Also used on local livestock trains, they spent much of their time on lines in the Brisbane–Ipswich–Sandgate area. A couple also worked from south Brisbane as far as Kingston and Lota. Often used on all-station trains, they were capable of speeds up to 45 mph.

Two of the class were converted to tender engines, No 375 in July 1935 and No 376 in July 1939. These were known as the B16D class. During 1942 and 1943 twelve of the class were written off, with the remaining six and the two tender engines withdrawn from service during 1950 and 1951.

Builder: Walkers Limited, Maryborough 20

Preserved: Nil

Above: Built by Walkers Limited, Maryborough in 1901, No. 374 entered service in January 1902 as a 4–6–2T, and was converted to 4–6–4T during 1904–1905. It was withdrawn from service in January 1943. The listed weight in working order was 58 tons 2 cwt with a length of 36 ft 4 in from buffer to buffer. For more details see Locomotives in the Tropics Vol. 1, J. Armstrong, ARHS(QLD) p.78–81.

The first of a total of 145 locomotives of this class to be built by Beyer Peacock & Co in England, No 636 entered service with N.S.W. Government Railways on 10 December 1903. The final locomotive of the class entered service on 14 February 1917, as No 1073. With Sydney growing rapidly to the north and south, a locomotive which could handle both the steep grades and heavy traffic was needed. The S(636) was designed specifically to fill the gap, a job it did extremely well. But with electrification they were pushed to Sydney's outer suburbs, and to Newcastle and Wollongong. They were also used at Merriwa, Leeton, Casino and on the Wollongong–Moss Vale line.

S(636) CLASS (C)30 (NSW)
WHEEL ARRANGEMENT: 4-6-4T
SUBURBAN SIDE-TANK
LOCOMOTIVE
145 IN CLASS
FINAL NOS: 3001-3145

With the introduction of diesel-electric locomotives, mulitple-unit railcars and extensions to suburban electrification, the majority of the class were withdrawn from service in the late 1960s. No 3085 was withdrawn in February 1973, having travelled 1 536 652 miles during sixty-one years of service.

Builders: Beyer Peacock & Co, England 95. Eveleigh Workshops, Sydney 50.
Preserved: No 3013, at Lachlan Valley Railway, Cowra; No 3046, at Dorrigo Steam Railway & Museum; No 3112, privately owned, on loan to 3801 Ltd; No 3085, at Rail Transport Museum, Thirlmere; No 3137, at Rail Transport Museum, Thirlmere.

Above: Delivered to N.S.W. Government Railways on 10 December 1903, this locomotive was numbered 636. Later, in the renumbering and reclassification of August 1924, it was renumbered 3001. It was converted to a tender engine in June 1933, and superheated in March 1948, with its final number being 3001T. Withdrawn from service on 17 November 1967 after sixty-four years of service, it is now maintained in working order at the N.S.W. Rail Transport Museum at Thirlmere, south of Sydney. Listed weight in working order of this locomotive was 72 tons 3 cwt 1 qtr with a length of 40 ft 9¾ in from buffer to buffer. For more details see A Compendium of N.S.W. Steam Locomotives, *compiled by A. Grunbach, ARHS(NSW), 1989, p. 142–5.*

These locomotives were built at the Ipswich Railway Works in 1904, using wheel-sets from B15 goods locomotives and spare 13½ inch cylinders. The first locomotive, No 396, entered service in July 1904, with the last, No 401, entering service in April 1905. It was planned that only four would be built, but an extra two wheel-sets and cylinders were available, so six were built. When in service they worked in the Brisbane area, with some periods away. No 400 was used in tests on the rack line at Mount Morgan in 1907, while Nos 396 and 399 were used at Toowoomba. One is also reported to have worked in the Warwick area.

6D13½ CLASS (QLD)
WHEEL ARRANGEMENT: 0-6-0T
SMALL SHUNTING TANK LOCOMOTIVE
6 IN CLASS
FINAL NOS: 396–401

Builder: Ipswich Railway Works 6
Preserved: Nil; all converted to tender engines.

During its time in service a number of improvements were made, including the fitting of better brakes and pumps when they were re-boilered in 1928. During 1930 the cab roof was raised by nine inches for improved headroom. It was decided to convert all this class to tender engines, beginning with No 397 in 1932. The side tanks and bunker were removed and a tender from a B13 was added. They then became known as the B13½ Class,

Above: Built by Ipswich Railway Works, No 401 entered service with Queensland Government Railways in April 1905. In October 1937 it was stripped of its tanks and bunker and rebuilt as a tender engine, to become a Class B13½. The listed weight in working order of this locomotive was 30 tons 12 cwt and it was about 26 ft 6 in from buffer to buffer. For more details see Locomotives in the Tropics *Volume 1, J. Armstrong, ARHS(QLD), p. 88.*

The DD class entered service in 1902, and a total of 263 were eventually built. Newport Workshops built No 560, which was the first to enter service in October 1902. No 1052 was the last in December 1920, having been assembled at Ballarat using parts supplied by Thompsons of Castlemaine. The early DD locomotives had a low running board, wheel splashers and narrow cabs, while later models had the raised running board and wide cab which were typical of all later Victorian Railway locomotives. Of the 263 in the class, a total of 220 were built as saturated with 18 inch cylinders, and during their time in service they were modified to form a total of four classes. The D1 was the original saturated locomotive, D2 was fitted with a superheater, the D3 was fitted with a larger boiler and superheater while the D4 or DDE class was built new, as a 4–6–2 tank engine based on the DD class.

DD CLASS (VIC)
WHEEL ARRANGEMENT: 4-6-0
PASSENGER LOCOMOTIVE
263 IN CLASS
FINAL NO: 531-1052

On entering service it was planned that the DD would be used on main line services, but with their small boilers and the introduction of the A2 class, they were soon relegated to working branch lines throughout most of the state on both goods and passenger services. Many DD locomotives were converted to D2 or D3 classes during their time in service. With the change of a boiler, the locomotive often changed its number and these changes would make a book on their own. Many were withdrawn from service in the 1940s with some still in service in the early 1960s.

Builders: Newport Workshops 140; Ballarat 8; Bendigo 8; Phoenix Foundry 7; Thompsons 40; Beyer Peacock 20; Baldwin Locomotive Co 20; Walkers Ltd 20

Preserved: No 604 (DD 795), at ARHS Railway Museum, Champion Rd, North Williamstown.

Above: Built by Newport Workshops, No 654 entered service with Victorian Railways in March 1906. During its time in service it was never superheated. On 24 May 1921 No 654 collided head-on with D3 No 634 at Carrapooee, and was scrapped in October 1934. Listed weight in working order of this locomotive and tender was 94 tons with a combined length of 57 ft 3½ in from buffer to buffer. For more details see The Evolution of the DD Class Locomotive, M.H. Clark, ARHS Bulletin No 167, September 1951, p. 113–5.

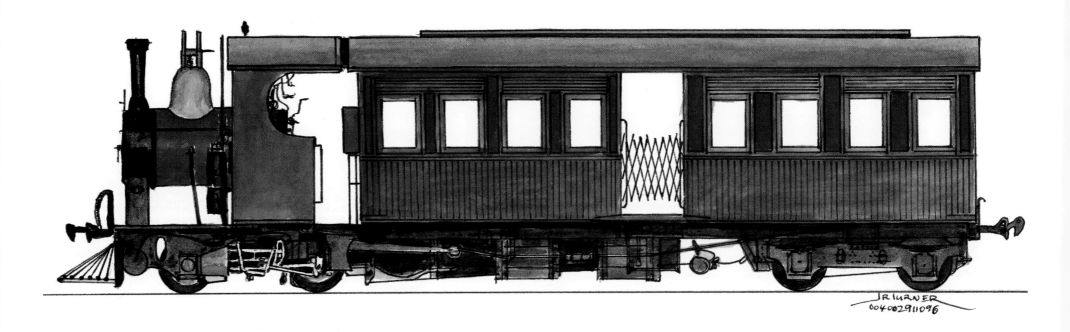

The need to provide a service on lines with low passenger numbers resulted in two combined engine and carriage units arriving from England in 1906. Built for use on narrow gauge lines, the well tank engine was built by Kitson & Co, while the coach was built by the Metropolitan Amalgamated Railway Carriage and Wagon Company of Birmingham, England.

The coach was able to carry twenty-two passengers, nine in First Class and thirteen in Second Class. Soon after entering service, the water capacity of No 1 was more than doubled and it was then able to carry only eighteen passengers. Used on the line between Quorn and Hawker, No 1 provided a weekly service, and had a small four-wheel van attached to the coach to carry mail and parcels.

STEAM MOTOR COACH (SA)
WHEEL ARRANGEMENT: 2-2-0WT
WELL TANK LOCOMOTIVE
WITH COACH
2 IN CLASS
NOS: 1, 2

After use on the Naracoorte to Kingston line, No 2 was sent to Mount Gambier where it provided a service to and from Beachport, and was able to carry a maximum of thirty-three adult passengers. Both coaches were popular with picnic and sports groups.

The Commonwealth Government took control of the Port Augusta to Oodnadatta line in 1911, and No 1, or the 'Coffee Pot' as it had been nicknamed was sold to them in 1924.

By the mid 1920s No 2 was rarely used. It was sold in September 1935 and converted for use as a shunter at Beachport.

Builder: Kitson & Co 2

Preserved: No 1, at Pichi Richi Railway Preservation Society, Quorn.

Above: Built by Kitson & Co in England, No 1 entered service with South Australian Government Railways in August 1906. It was transferred to the Commonwealth on 1 January 1911 and sold to them on 4 June 1924. It was then stored at Quorn from 1932–1955. After restoration it was displayed in Alice Springs, and then re-entered service at Quorn on 21 May 1984, carrying tourists. Listed weight in working order of this locomotive is 21 tons 18 cwt with a length of 39 ft 11½ in. For more details see Steam Locomotives and Railcars of the South Australian Railways, R.E. Fluck, R. Sampson & K.J. Bird, Mile End Railway Museum 1986, p. 145–6

E CLASS (TAS)
WHEEL ARRANGEMENT: 4-6-0
GOODS LOCOMOTIVE
2 IN CLASS
FINAL NOS: E1, E2

By the early 1900s the need for more powerful locomotives resulted in orders being placed with Beyer Peacock & Co in England, for two prototypes each of several new classes of locomotives. One of these was the E class, which was built in 1907 and was intended for use as the standard heavy goods locomotive on Tasmanian Government Railways. A lack of funds resulted in no further order being placed, and the two E class were based at Launceston hauling goods services on the Main and north-eastern lines. In the mid 1950s one was based at Launceston while the other was further east at Herrick.

With diesels and new steam locomotives in service, the E class was used only for shunting work between Launceston and Rocherlea to the north. In June 1958, E1 was withdrawn from service and remained stored at Launceston, being listed as stored awaiting scrapping in April 1965. E2 had been used for shunting work at Launceston until May 1961, but it had lost the boiler and cab by 1963, and was listed as partially dismantled at Launceston in April 1965.

Builder: Beyer Peacock & Co 2
Preserved: E1, at Apex Park, adjacent to river bridge, Deloraine.

Above: Built by Beyer Peacock & Co in 1907, E1 entered service with Tasmanian Government Railways that year. It was withdrawn from service in 1958 after about fifty-one years in service. Listed weight in working order of this locomotive and tender was 72 tons 3 cwt 3 qtr with a combined length of about 52 ft. For more details see The Decline of Steam Power on the Tasmanian Government Railways 1945–1965, H.J.W. Stokes, ARHS Bulletin No. 347, September 1966, p. 193–202.

A2 CLASS (VIC)
WHEEL ARRANGEMENT: 4-6-0
EXPRESS PASSENGER LOCOMOTIVE
185 IN CLASS
FINAL NOS: 816–999

During 1900 plans for a large 4–6–0 express passenger locomotive were under consideration at the Newport Workshops. However it was to be another seven years and many design changes before No 572, the first of the A2 class, was delivered by Newport Workshops on 2 December 1907. Following a series of tests, No 572 was put to work hauling the Sydney Express, which until that time had been hauled by two locomotives. After a number of modifications, five more A2 locomotives were ordered and delivered in 1908, with more being built every year. By 1915 there was a total of 125, all using the Stephenson's valve gear. The first A2 using the Walschaerts valve gear was No 983. Built at Newport, it entered service on 23 October 1915 and had a superheated boiler. Over the following seven years another sixty were built with Walschaerts valve gear.

From 1917 onward the early A2 locomotives were superheated when they were given new boilers. They continued to be used on all express passenger services, as well as express freight and goods services on lines throughout most of the state. In November 1935 they were fitted with smoke deflector plates. These improved the view of the crew on locomotives which had been fitted with a modified front end to improve performance. In 1946 over fifty of the Walschaerts series were converted to burn oil, and though it was expensive the reliability and superior performance of the A2 outweighed the cost involved.

By the late 1940s withdrawals began, and by September 1957 approximately thirty-one of the A2 class were still in service; some in storage and others being used as heavy shunters. On 16 April 1962 Nos 995 and 996 hauled the last broad gauge *Spirit of Progress* from Seymour to Melbourne.

Builder: Newport Workshops 175; Ballarat Workshops 5; Bendigo Workshops 5

Preserved: No 884 and 995, at ARHS Railway Museum, North Williamstown; No 964, at Edwards Lake Park City of Preston Reservoir; No 986, at Steamrail Victoria Ltd, Champion Rd, Newport; No 996, at Wharf Museum, Echuca.

Above: Built by the Newport Workshops, No 572 was the first of its class and entered service on 2 December 1907. It was superheated in March 1946, and was scrapped in September 1954. Listed weight in working order of this locomotive and tender was 114 tons 5 cwt with a combined length of 62 ft 6¾ in from buffer to buffer. For more details see The Jubilee of the A2-Class Locomotive, *M.H. Clark and J. Buckland, ARHS Bulletin No 243, January 1958, p. 1– 13.*

T CLASS (SA)
WHEEL ARRANGEMENT: 4-8-0
NARROW GAUGE LOCOMOTIVE
78 IN CLASS
FINAL NOS: 22, 23, 44–48, 50, 51, 180–186, 197–258

Designed by the South Australian Railways at Islington, No 180 was the first of the class to enter service on 16 February 1903. This locomotive was so successful that tenders were called for additional locomotives. They were able to haul 50 percent bigger loads than the Y class they replaced. With rail traffic having doubled between 1892 and 1900, the Y class was unable to cope. The final locomotive, No 258, entered service on 7 September 1917.

During 1923 a superheater was trialed on No 255. The tests were so successful that all T class locomotives were then superheated. By 1933 some of the class had had their copper cap chimneys and brass fittings removed. A number of modifications were carried out over the years. Fitting the Cyclone front end and spark arrester resulted in a second extension of the smoke box, which allowed the use of poorer quality Leigh Creek coal. Later about a dozen were converted to burn oil, with these locomotives being used on the Quorn to Hawker line.

Apart from a few withdrawn from service in 1959, most of the class were in use until the late 1960s, with the last few withdrawn in June 1970. A T class hauled the last regular steam service operated by South Australian Government Railways.

Builders: S.A.R. Islington Workshops 4; James Martin & Co, Gawler 34; Walkers Ltd, Maryborough, Qld 40

Preserved: No 186, at Pichi Richi Railway, Quorn; No 199, at Steamtown, Peterborough; No 224, at National Trust Museum, Millicent; No 251, at Bellarine Peninsula Railway, Queenscliff; No 253, at Port Dock Railway Museum, Adelaide.

Above: Shown here as it looked in the 1960s, No 44 was built at the South Australian railway workshops at Islington and entered service on 20 March 1907. During its time in service, No 44 worked in the South East Division of the state from the mid 1930s until September 1953. Later it was converted to burn oil, and worked in the Peterborough area, where double-headed T class trains which weighed up to 660 tons and were 1000 ft long were common until the mid 1950s. No 44 was withdrawn in January 1970 and condemned on 18 April 1970, after about sixty-three years of service. Listed weight in working order of this locomotive and tender was 78 tons 8 cwt with a combined length of 54 ft from buffer to buffer. For more details see Narrow Gauge Memories: The Locomotives, S. McNicol, Railmac Publications, 1993, p. 155–62.

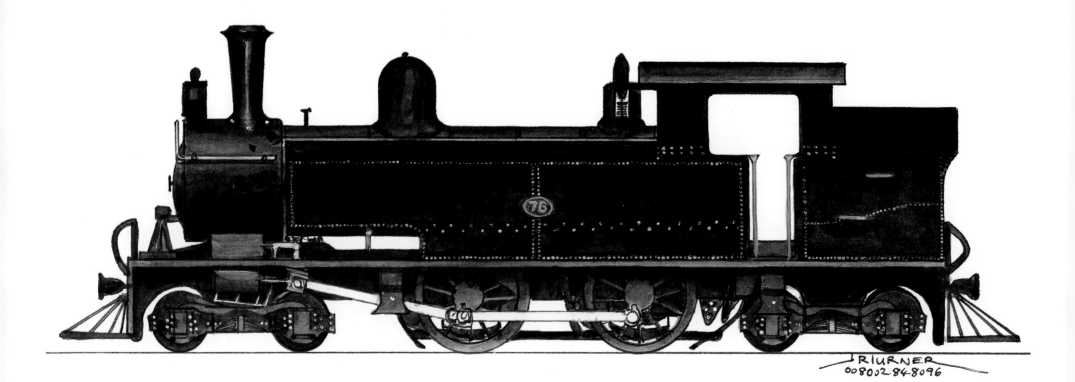

N CLASS (WA)
WHEEL ARRANGEMENT: 4-4-4T
SUBURBAN PASSENGER
TANK LOCOMOTIVE
42 IN CLASS
FINAL NOS: 1, 19, 20, 25–27, 69–73, 75–79,
85–87, 95, 96, 132, 196–207, 256–263

Built by Neilson & Co in England in 1896, the first of a batch of five locomotives, No 73 entered service on 10 September 1896. The last of the five, No 71, was in service just over a week later on 19 September. By July 1897 these locomotives had each averaged 28 000 miles without experiencing any problems. Over the following years more were delivered, making a total of forty-two in all, with No 75 the last to enter service on 27 June 1908.

Later that year it was reported that the locomotive shortage that had existed on suburban passenger services had been overcome. By 1912 the new D class tank engines entered service, working heavy passenger and goods trains, while the N class continued to handle most of the suburban passenger services. Over the years a variety of changes were made with larger bunkers, high inverted cone chimneys, new safety valves, cow catchers and new smokebox doors. In the mid 1940s the Ns were gradually replaced by the new Dd and Dm classes on the suburban lines. By 1960 only Nos 200 and 201 remained in service, and both were written off on 28 September of that year after about sixty-two years in service.

Builders: Neilson & Co, England 5; Nasmyth, Wilson & Co 15; Robert Stephenson & Co 12; W.A.G.R. 10

Preserved: No 201, at ARHS Railway Museum, Bassendean.

Above: Built by Neilson & Co in England in 1896, No 76 entered service with Western Australian Government Railways on 2 May 1908. It was withdrawn from service on 18 February 1960 after fifty-two years in service. Listed weight in working order of this locomotive was 48 tons 16 cwt and it was 36 ft 3 in from buffer to buffer. For more details see A History of W.A.G.R. Steam Locomotives, by A. Gunzburg, ARHS(WA) 1984, p. 56–58.

During the period when the DD class tender locomotives were under construction at the Newport Workshops, the need arose for a new, powerful tank locomotive for use on the longer hilly lines. The DD class design was modified to produce the DDE tank locomotive. From 16 June 1908 when No 702, the first DDE entered service, a total of fifty-eight were built, with No 749 the last to enter service on 28 June 1913.

While five were built as shunters, the remainder were used for both passenger and goods work on the Dandenong, Frankston, Williamstown, Lilydale, Kew, Darling and Upper Ferntree Gully lines. Two of the DDE class were converted to DD class tender locomotives; No 712 in 1922 and No 710 in 1923. Both were scrapped in the mid 1930s. Two DDEs were fitted with cow catchers; No 282 was

DDE CLASS (VIC)
WHEEL ARRANGEMENT: 4-6-2T
SUBURBAN TANK LOCOMOTIVE
58 IN CLASS
FINAL NOS: 250-287

based at Ballarat and was used on various lines, even out to Maryborough, and No 271 was used in the Mornington area on a variety of tasks.

With the electrification of the suburban lines, most of the DDE were used as shunters. By the mid 1940s thirty-two had been scrapped, and by 1960 only six were still in use. By mid year three of these had also gone, leaving only No 274, which was scrapped on 7 February 1961, and No 285 the last to go in February 1962, after fifty-three years in service. No 268 was moved to the ARHS Railway Museum in May 1961.

Builder: Newport Workshops 58

Preserved: No 268, at ARHS Railway Museum, Champion Rd, North Williamstown.

Above: Built by the Newport Workshop, No 702 was the first of the DDE class and entered service with Victorian Railways on 16 June 1908. It was scrapped on 26 June 1924, having travelled 429 868 miles during sixteen years in service. Listed weight in working order of this locomotive was 69 tons and it was 41 ft ½ in from buffer to buffer. For more details see The Tank Locomotives of the Victorian Government Railways, *M.H. Clark & A. Madden, ARHS Bulletin No 384, October 1969, p. 236–9.*

Built by R & W Hawthorn Leslie & Co in England in 1896, Nos 140 to 143 had all entered service as the Q class by early 1897. They were used for about ten years as shunters, until No 140 was converted to Qa class on 30 September 1905. The conversion involved a new boiler, a four wheel trailing bogie and increased fuel and water capacity. The conversion was a success, enabling loads nearly fifty percent heavier to be hauled over the steepest sections of the Kalamunda zig-zag on the Upper Darling Range line. During 1909 the other three locomotives were also converted; Nos 141 on 13 March 1909, 142 on 29 April 1909 and 143 on 30 June 1909.

QA CLASS (WA)
WHEEL ARRANGEMENT: 4-6-4T
PASSENGER GOODS TANK
LOCOMOTIVE
4 IN CLASS
FINAL NOS: 140-143

Builder: R & W Hawthorn, Leslie & Co 6
Preserved: Nil

In 1911 the Qa class was approved to haul both passenger and goods trains on the suburban network. The Qas also hauled branch line services to Mundaring, Mundaring Weir, Pinjarra-Holyoake and the Upper Darling Range railway, as well as the eastern railway to Northam and the south-west main line to Bunbury. All four locomotives were withdrawn from service by the mid 1920s; Nos 140 and 143 on 31 June 1924, and Nos 141 and 142 the last to leave service on 31 March 1925.

Above: Built by R & W Hawthorn Leslie & Co in 1896, No 143 entered service on 13 March 1897 as a Q class. It was converted to a Qa class on 30 June 1909. It was scrapped on 31 January 1924 after about twenty-seven years in service. Listed weight in working order of this locomotive was 52 tons and it was 35 ft 2 in from buffer to buffer. For more details see A History of W.A.G.R. Steam Locomotives, A. Gunzburg, ARHS(WA) 1984, p. 49–51.

A CLASS (TAS)
WHEEL ARRANGEMENT: 4-4-0
EXPRESS PASSENGER LOCOMOTIVE
8 IN CLASS
FINAL NOS: A2-A9

Built by Beyer Peacock & Co in England in 1892, the A class was intended for use on express passenger services. Six entered service in 1892, and a further two were delivered and in service by 1902. By 1908, the need for more power resulted in A2 and A4 being rebuilt with enlarged Belpaire boilers and extended smoke boxes. Over the period 1927 to 1932, five more were rebuilt, with A7 remaining in original condition until 1946.

Until early 1945 the A class was still in regular use on main line passenger services, and was doubled headed on heavier services which were usually hauled by the R class. In the north-west of the state they were used between Wynyard, Stanley and Smithtown.

They were also used in the Hobart area, working north to Brighton and west to Maydena. In the north, they worked from Launceston east to Herrick and south to Parattah. The use of diesel railcars on north-western lines in 1945 released two A class locomotives for other duties, such as the daily return goods service from Wynyard to Stanley. In 1950 an A class was used on the daily Devonport–Wynyard passenger service.

Between 1952 and 1954 all A class locomotives were withdrawn from service and stored at Turners Marsh, with seven sold for scrap in 1956. A4 was removed to Launceston in 1959, repainted and placed in the City Park in 1960. In August 1990, A4 was moved to the Don River Railway for possible restoration.

Builder: Tasmanian Government Railway Workshops 8

Preserved: No A4, at Don River Railway, Devonport.

Above: Built by Beyer Peacock & Co in 1891, No A4 entered service in 1892 and was one of the first to be fitted with a Belpaire boiler. After being withdrawn from service it was preserved in Launceston. Listed weight in working order of this locomotive and tender was 55 tons 4 cwt with a combined length of 46 ft 1½ in from buffer to buffer. For more details see The Decline of Steam Power on the Tasmanian Government Railways 1945–1965, H.J.W. Stokes, ARHS Bulletin No 347, September 1966, p. 193–202.

The first of a total of five locomotives of this class, No 928 entered service with N.S.W. Government Railways on 3 December 1909, after delivery from Eveleigh Workshops in Sydney. The final locomotive of the class entered service on 11 April 1910 as No 932. They were designed as a faster, more powerful version of the P(6) class, but were found to be unsuitable for most lines. After initial use on the Junee–Albury section, where they performed reasonably well, they were used in the Armidale and Taree areas. However, they were unsuitable for the steep grades and continuous curves, and were replaced by the (C)35 class and returned once again to the Junee area. In the late 1940s they worked the

N(928) CLASS (C)34 (NSW)
WHEEL ARRANGEMENT: 4-6-0
EXPRESS PASSENGER LOCOMOTIVE
5 IN CLASS
FINAL NOS: 3401-3405

south-west mail trains on the line between Junee and Narrandera, en route to Griffith, then hauled goods or mixed services to Hay.

In the early 1950s their boilers were condemned and they were scrapped, with No 3402 being the last withdrawn from service in August 1957. It had entered service in January 1910 as No 929, was superheated in November 1920, and scrapped in December 1962, after having travelled 892 820 miles during forty-seven years of service.

Builder: Eveleigh Workshops, Sydney 5

Preserved: Nil

Above: Delivered to N.S.W. Government Railways from Eveleigh Workshops, No 928 entered service on 3 December 1909, and was later renumbered 3401. It was withdrawn from service in February 1959 and scrapped on 7 August 1959, having travelled 917 180 miles during forty-six years of service. Listed weight in working order of this locomotive and tender was 113 tons 19 cwt with a combined length of 61 ft 5¼ in from buffer to buffer.
For more details see A Compendium of NSW Steam Locomotives, compiled by A. Grunbach, ARHS(NSW) 1989, p. 148–50.

The 0–6–0 goods locomotives designed by Kitson & Co, which were known as the 'New R' class, had entered service with Victorian Railways in 1889. Between 1889 and 1891 Robison Bros, Campbell and Sloss built twenty-five 'New R' class locomotives, based on the Kitson design, at their South Melbourne works. Once in service, most were sent to the north-west of Melbourne, especially to wheat growing areas. Between 1905 and 1909, new boilers and 18 inch cylinders were fitted. They were then known as the RY class, with the nickname of 'Slossies'.

After rebuilding, the RY locomotives were ranked second behind the V class as main line

RY CLASS (VIC)
WHEEL ARRANGEMENT: 0-6-0
GOODS LOCOMOTIVE
25 IN CLASS
FINAL NOS: 447–495
(ODD NUMBERS ONLY)

Builder: Robison Bros, Campbell and Sloss 25

Preserved: Nil

locomotives. Along with the Y class, they continued to handle the bulk of the wheat harvest. They regularly hauled suburban passenger trains on the Ringwood, Box Hill and Caulfield lines before these lines were electrified. By the mid 1930s fourteen of the class had been scrapped, with another nine meeting the same fate by April 1951. Only two remained in service, with No 481 the first to go on 10 September 1951. It was closely followed by the last of its class, No 467, on 12 April 1960, after about sixty-one years in service.

Above: Built in 1890 by Robison Bros, Campbell and Sloss at their South Melbourne works, No 126 entered service with Victorian Railways on 30 July 1890 as a Y class locomotive. After being rebuilt between December 1905 and 1909 it became No 465 of the RY class. It was scrapped on 24 June 1951 after sixty-one years in service. Listed weight in working order of this locomotive and tender was 71 tons 1 cwt with a combined length of 47 ft 4 in from buffer to buffer. For more details see The New R Class, ARHS Bulletin No 311, September 1963, p. 139–42.

The Oa class was built at the Midland Junction Workshops in 1909 by Western Australian Government Railways, using parts taken from ten O class locomotives which had been withdrawn from service during 1907 and 1908, and parts used to build ten N class tank locomotives. During the building process, a number of improvements were made, including new frames and larger diameter coupled wheels, as well as a sand dome mounted on the boiler to replace the boxes fitted beneath the running boards. The tender on the Oa class was also different. While the O class had carried 2000 gallons of water, the Oa carried only 1500 gallons, while the coal capacity was increased to 7½ tons compared with the 3½ tons carried by the O class.

OA CLASS (WA)
WHEEL ARRANGEMENT: 2-8-0
HEAVY GOODS TENDER TANK LOCOMOTIVE
10 IN CLASS
FINAL NOS: 24, 171-173, 175-179, 219

Builder: Midland Junction Workshops 10
Preserved: Nil

Both the O and Oa classes were used on the light agricultural lines which were expanding at that time, especially in wheat growing areas. Several Oa class locomotives were converted back to O class or to Oas, and then back to Oa class during their time in service. While two were withdrawn from service in the 1950s, the remainder of the class lasted until 25 July 1961, when six were withdrawn. Of the remaining two, No 171 was withdrawn on 19 December 1961, with No 179 the last to go on 30 May 1962, after fifty-two years in service.

Above: Built by Midland Junction Workshops as No 5, it entered service on 10 December 1910. It was renumbered No 172 on 22 August 1949. It was withdrawn from service on 25 July 1961 after fifty-one years in service. Listed weight in working order of this locomotive and tender was 62 tons 14 cwt with a combined length of 47 ft 4 in from buffer to buffer. For more details see A History of W.A.G.R. Steam Locomotives, *A. Gunzburg, ARHS(WA) 1984, p. 52–5.*

JR TURNER
004002829096

2ND I CLASS (SA)
WHEEL ARRANGEMENT: 0-4-0ST
SMALL SADDLE TANK LOCOMOTIVE
1 IN CLASS
FINAL NO: 161

Built by Beyer Peacock & Co in England, this locomotive arrived in Victoria in 1888 to work on a private railway. It was used by contractors Waring and Rawdon who were involved in the reclamation, development and construction work of Outer Harbour, on the coast some twelve miles to the north-west of Adelaide city centre. It was then acquired by the Engineer-in-Chief's Department, who in turn passed it on to South Australian Railways in 1910. It was given the number 161, which had become vacant when the G class tank engine 161 was condemned in December 1904.

Given the nickname 'Dirty Gert', it spent most of its life shunting around the Port Adelaide wharves and marshalling yards. It was fitted with a bell which was rung by the driver to clear the path ahead. It met the same fate as other small locomotives such as the G, Gd and Ge classes, which were scrapped in favour of larger engines and road tractors. It was classified as the only locomotive in the 2nd I class during 1918–19.

Builder: Beyer Peacock & Co, Manchester, England 1
Preserved: Nil

Above: Arriving in Victoria in 1888, No 161 was built in England by Beyer Peacock and Co. Initially used on a private railway and as a contractors engine, it entered service with South Australian Government Railways on 9 December 1910. It was condemned on 8 April 1929 and cut up on 10 May 1930, after forty-one years of service, nineteen of which were with South Australian Government Railways. Listed weight in working order of this locomotive was 22 tons 7 cwt and it was 21 ft 5½ in from buffer to buffer. For more detail see 'I' Class Locomotives, No 161 of the South Australian Railways, G.H. Eardley, ARHS Bulletin No 350, December 1966, p. 281–4.

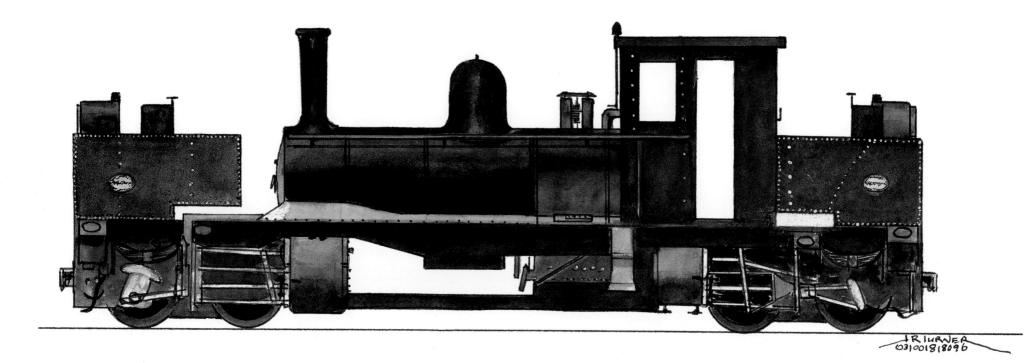

The first locomotives of their type in the world, the K class was built to H.W. Garratt's 1908 patented design. They arrived from Beyer Peacock & Co in England in late 1909, and following assembly at the Zeehan Railway Workshops they were put into service on the North-East Dundas Tramway in early 1910. They were used almost continuously, transporting sulphide ores and on goods services. The major problem with the K class was the placement of the cylinders under the floor of the cab. This resulted in the cab floor becoming extremely hot when in service, with obvious discomfort for the crews.

A 1913 timetable showed that a mixed train was provided each day, departing Zeehan at 7.15 a.m. and arriving at Williamsford, some twelve miles to the north-east, at 10.05 a.m. It then departed at 2.30 p.m., arriving back in Zeehan at 5.45 p.m. The construction of an aerial ropeway from Williamsford to

K CLASS (TAS)
WHEEL ARRANGEMENT: 0-4-0 0-4-0
GARRATT ARTICULATED
GOODS LOCOMOTIVE
2 IN CLASS
FINAL NOS: K1, K2

Rosebery caused the closure of the Nickel Junction to Williamsford section in 1929. Most other mining operations closed in the 1930s, the K class was withdrawn from service and placed in storage at Zeehan.

In 1947 Beyer Peacock & Co approached the Tasmanian government to have K1 placed on exhibition at their Gorton Works. Due to the poor condition of K1, parts of K2 were used to rebuild it, prior to shipping to England for display. It remained on display at the Beyer Peacock Museum until the late 1960s when Beyer Peacock closed down. Bought by the Festiniog narrow gauge railway in Wales, K1 was stored with plans to restore it to working condition. The remaining parts of K2 were gradually stripped and it was finally cut up for scrap.

Builder: Beyer Peacock & Co 2

Preserved: No K1, at Festiniog Railway, Wales, UK

Above: Built by Beyer Peacock & Co in England, K1 entered service with Tasmanian Government Railways in 1910 on the North-East Dundas Tramway, at Zeehan on the west coast of Tasmania. Withdrawn from service and stored in the 1930s after about twenty years in service, it was then rebuilt in the late 1940s, using parts from K2, and shipped to England. Listed weight in working order of this locomotive was 34 tons with a length of 31 ft 9 in from buffer to buffer. For more details see Railways of the Zeehan District, L.B. Manny, ARHS Bulletin No 313, September 1963, p. 165–7.

The need for a more powerful goods locomotive able to haul heavy loads up the ranges to Toowoomba, west of Brisbane, was discussed in January 1909. The prototype, B17, was built at the Ipswich Railway Works in 1911, and it entered service in May of that year as No 538. The final B17 was built in 1914, and entered service as No 691 in May of that year. It performed so well on both goods and mail trains that four more were ordered immediately. Nos 610 and 611 entered service in October 1911, No 612 in November, and No 613 in December. The new locomotives were used on the Sydney Mail run. A further order was placed for another sixteen locomotives and these entered service over the next three years.

Initially the use of the B17s was restricted, because of the need to rebuild or strengthen bridges on existing lines. They used more coal and water than a superheated locomotive which, when

B17 CLASS (QLD)
WHEEL ARRANGEMENT: 4-6-0
GOODS LOCOMOTIVE
21 IN CLASS
FINAL NOS: 538, 610-613, 676-691

these became available, were preferred on mail trains. The B17s were used on a wide variety of services, including goods and suburban passenger trains. The area they were able to serve expanded as bridges were strengthened, although they usually remained south of Rockhampton. They continued to be used on mail trains until the 1930s. Though No 678 had been superheated in October 1917, with dramatic savings in coal and water, the rest of the class were never superheated.

The first B17s were withdrawn in September 1950, with over half of the class written off by the mid 1950s. By 1960 only two remained in service, with Nos 689 and 690 both withdrawn in November 1, after about forty-six years in service.

Builder: Ipswich Railway Works, Ipswich 21
Preserved: Nil

Above: The prototype of the class was built by Ipswich Railway Works, and entered service as No 538 in May 1911. It was written off in May 1959 after about forty-eight years in service. The listed weight in working order of locomotive and tender was 82 tons 14 cwt with a combined length of 54 ft 1½ in from buffer to buffer. For more details see Locomotives in the Tropics Vol 2, *J. Armstrong, ARHS(QLD) 1994, p. 35–8.*

B13 BALDWIN (QLD)
WHEEL ARRANGEMENT: 4-6-0
GOODS LOCOMOTIVE
1 IN CLASS
FINAL NO: 5

Preserved: Nil

Being unable to purchase a B13 locomotive from Queensland Railways, which could only offer another B12, Cairns Shire Council ordered a new B13 from the Baldwin Locomotive Works of Philadelphia, USA. It was built in 1908. Although similar in performance to the British-built B13 locomotives then in service, it looked quite different. It had a low sided 8-wheel tender, which was U-shaped at the front, with the coal being shovelled up from floor level and a large cab from which a cord was attached to the bell, which was rung continuously as the train approached a level crossing. When the Cairns–Mulgrave Tramway was acquired by Queensland Government Railways in December 1911, No 5 was bought at the same time and used in the Cairns area until it was written off in October 1924, after 16 years in service.

Builder: Baldwin Locomotive Works, USA 1

Above: Built by the Baldwin Locomotive Co in February 1908, B13 was bought for use on the sugar cane harvest. It entered service with Queensland Government Railway in December 1911, and was scrapped in October 1924. While no details of the weight of this locomotive are available the combined length of locomotive and tender was 45 ft 5 in from buffer to buffer. For more details see Locomotives in the Tropics Vol 2, J. Armstrong, ARHS(QLD) 1994, p. 18–9.

E CLASS (WA)
WHEEL ARRANGEMENT: 4-6-2
HEAVY PASSENGER LOCOMOTIVE
65 IN CLASS
FINAL NOS: 291-355

During 1900, orders were placed for a total of forty-five E class locomotives, to be built by Vulcan Foundry Ltd in England, and Nasmyth, Wilson & Co also in England. No 291 was the first to enter service on 29 November 1902. A third order was placed with the North British Locomotive Co, with No 354 the last of its class to enter service on 24 February 1912. By the end of June 1903 there were thirty E class locomotives in use on passenger services. They were able to haul greatly increased loads, with savings in both time and costs. Some problems became apparent during 1905, but were quickly solved. With traffic increasing a final order for twenty locomotives was placed on 20 April 1911. They were almost identical to those then in service.

The whole class was then superheated, beginning with No 335 on 5 July 1924. The last to be

modified was No 353, on 7 September 1949. Several locomotives were converted to work on 45 lb rails, and were known as the Ea class.

From 1924 onward the introduction of the new P and later the Pr classes saw the E class relegated to branch line goods and passenger duties, with some main line work. Withdrawals began at the end of WW II, and by the late 1950s many had been taken out of service. Some were used to supply parts to build eight Dm class suburban tank locomotives. The last eight, Nos 299, 301, 304, 308, 324, 325, 326 and 329, were all withdrawn on 7 October 1963 after about sixty years in service with Western Australian Government Railways.

Builders: Nasmyth, Wilson & Co 15; Vulcan Foundry 30; North British Locomotive Co 20

Preserved: No 308, at ARHS Railway Museum, Bassendean.

Above: Built by the North British Locomotive Co in 1911, No 355 entered service with Western Australian Government Railways on 25 January 1912. It was superheated on 30 June 1928, converted to Eas class on 27 January 1934 and then back to Es on 29 July 1934. It was withdrawn from use on 19 September 1947 after 35 years in service. Listed weight in working order of this locomotive and tender was either 84 tons 12 cwt as Es or Eas class, or 83 tons 12 cwt as E class, with a combined length of 54 ft 10½ in from buffer to buffer. For more details see A History of W.A.G.R. Steam Locomotives, by A. Gunzburg, ARHS(WA) 1984, p. 82–6.

In 1909 the Western Australian Government needed a locomotive which could run on the lightly laid lines in remote areas. A number of designs were sent to Beyer Peacock in England, and plans were drawn up in April 1911. The six finished locomotives were shipped to Fremantle in November 1911, and assembled at the Midland Railway Workshops in early 1912. These were the first Garratts to have more than two axles on the motor bogies. No 388 was the first to enter service on 2 March 1912, and No 393 the last, on 6 April 1912.

On entering service the M class was the most powerful locomotive in use in Western

M CLASS (WA)
WHEEL ARRANGEMENT: 2-6-0 0-6-2
GARRATT ARTICULATED
LOCOMOTIVE
6 IN CLASS
FINAL NOS: 388-393

Builder: Beyer Peacock, England 6
Preserved: Nil

Australia, and could work on steep or curved, lightly laid branch lines of the South-Western and Eastern railways. They performed so well that the second order, placed in 1912, was for seven superheated locomotives known as the Ms class. No 389 was converted to Ms class in 1934. The remaining M class continued in service until the late 1940s, with No 393 the last to be withdrawn on 20 November 1951, after about thirty-nine years in service.

Above: Built by Beyer Peacock in 1911, No 388 was the first M class to enter service on 2 March 1912. It was withdrawn from service on 4 September 1947, after about thirty-five years in service. Listed weight in working order of this locomotive was 68 tons 16 cwt with a length of 53 ft 10½ in from buffer to buffer. For more details see A History of W.A.G.R. Steam Locomotives, A. Gunzburg, ARHS(WA) 1984, p. 89–92.

During 1901 a number of designs for new, more powerful goods and passenger locomotives were under consideration. The first C16, No 395, was built at the Ipswich Railway Works and entered service in November 1903. After evaluation it was found to perform well, though a bit short of steam on steep sections. Initially the class was restricted by the fact that the existing bridges were not able to handle the weight of the new engine, but the problem was solved after new bridges were built and others upgraded.

After further minor changes to improve the performance of the locomotive, including a larger boiler, an order was placed with the Ipswich Railway Works. Nos 414 to 433 entered service between 1907 and 1910. Originally the C16 class had been intended to haul

C16 CLASS (QLD)
WHEEL ARRANGEMENT: 4-8-0
GOODS LOCOMOTIVE
152 IN CLASS
FINAL NOS: 4–14, 19–22, 31, 34–39, 41, 43–44, 51, 63–5, 67, 69, 72–74, 96–99, 105–111, 118, 131–3, 139–142, 167–172, 176–178, 395, 414–433, 510–517, 614–675

Walkers Limited 45; Toowoomba Foundry 15

livestock trains and was painted black, but once in service they were assigned other duties. Three locomotives were used on the Sydney Mail run for which they were especially painted; No 427 was brown or chocolate, No 428 blue and No 429 green. While some were withdrawn from service in the 1930s, most continued working until the mid 1950s and 1960s. By 1970, only two remained on the books. No 38 was withdrawn in March and the last, No 133, was withdrawn in April after about fifty-five years in service.

Builders: Ipswich Railway Works 51; Evans, Anderson, Phelan & Co 41; Walkers Limited 45; Toowoomba Foundry 15

Preserved: No 106, at QR, (stored at present).

Above: Built by the Ipswich Railway Works in 1912, No 615 entered service in March 1912. It was withdrawn from service in December 1953 after almost forty-one years. Listed weight in working order of this locomotive and tender was 30 tons 9 cwt while the combined length of locomotive and tender was 52 ft 5½ in from buffer to buffer. For more details see Locomotives in the Tropics Vol. 1, J. Armstrong, ARHS(QLD) p. 83–5.

The first of a total of 190 locomotives of this class built by Clyde Engineering in Sydney, No 939 entered service with N.S.W. Government Railways on 26 April 1912. The final locomotive entered service on 2 November 1917 as No 1203. Designed by the N.S.W. Government Railways, the class was based on the earlier T(524) class, which had been well suited to a wide variety of conditions. But problems soon became apparent, and speed restrictions were imposed to avoid damage to the track. Known as 'total or terrible failures' the TF(939) class made headlines when a runaway locomotive pulling a heavy goods train ripped up five and a half miles of track between Lawson and Springwood in 1923. The

TF(939) CLASS (D)53 (NSW)
WHEEL ARRANGEMENT: 2-8-0
GOODS LOCOMOTIVE
190 IN CLASS
FINAL NOS: 5301-5490

locomotive, No 1122, was beyond repair.

After they were fitted with Standard Goods (superheated) boilers, the same as used on the (D)50, (D)53 or (D)55 classes, and the coupling rods were modified, the TF(939) class performed well right up to late December 1972, when the last few left in service were withdrawn and replaced by diesel locomotives.

Builders: Clyde Engineering, Sydney 160; Eveleigh Workshops, Sydney 30
Preserved: No 5353, at Dorrigo Steam Railway & Museum; No 5367, at Lachlan Valley Railway, Cowra; No 5461, at Rail Transport Museum, Thirlmere.

Above: Shown here as delivered to N.S.W. Government Railways, No 939 was built by Clyde Engineering and entered service on 26 April 1912. It was later renumbered 5301. It was withdrawn from service in March 1962 and scrapped on 2 November 1962, having travelled 1 241 131 miles during fifty years in service. Listed weight in working order of this locomotive and tender was 112 tons 13 cwt while the combined length was 60 ft 8 in from buffer to buffer.
For more details see A Compendium of NSW Steam Locomotives, *compiled by A. Grunbach, ARHS(NSW) 1989, p. 152–5.*

These locomotives were originally known as the W class. No 13 was delivered to South Australian Government Railways from Beyer Peacock & Co in England, and entered service in February 1878 on the Port Pirie to Jamestown line. There were forty-four locomotives in the class, and the final locomotive, No 56, entered service in October 1883 after a short time as a contractor's engine.

Seventeen of the W class locomotives were later rebuilt and renamed the Wx class. The first was No 19 on 14 May 1903. It was followed in order by Nos 20, 25, 40, 29, 15, 39, 37, 17, 26, 34, 28, 33, 18, 31, 56 and 55 over a period of eleven years. Fitting a new boiler extended their working life at least another twenty-five

WX CLASS (SA)
WHEEL ARRANGEMENT: 2-6-0
SMALL NARROW GAUGE
LOCOMOTIVE
17 IN CLASS
FINAL NOS: 15, 17-19, 20, 25-6, 28-9, 31, 33-4, 37, 39, 41, 55-6

Builder: Beyer Peacock & Co, England 17
Preserved: No 18, at Pichi Richi Railway, Quorn.

years. In the case of No 17, however, the new boiler exploded at Mount Gambier on 2 February 1914, with the dome landing sixty yards from the engine.

Used on most lines, the Wx class was gradually replaced by newer locomotives, with thirteen being withdrawn from service between 1928 and 1929. The remaining four were still in service until the 1950s, when No 18 was condemned on 17 March 1959, having been in service just over seventy-nine years.

Above: Shown here as it looked in later years, the original No 22 (1878) entered service with South Australian Government Railways in October 1883 as No 56, and was rebuilt as a Wx class on 13 May 1912. It was one of the last of its class to be withdrawn from service in March 1959. Listed weight in working order of this locomotive and tender was 31 tons 5 cwt with the combined length of locomotive and tender being 27 ft 3 in from buffer to buffer.
For more detail see Narrow Gauge Memories, The Locomotives, S. McNicol, Railmac Publications, 1993, p. 133–8.

D & DS CLASS (WA)
WHEEL ARRANGEMENT: 4-6-4T
PASSENGER GOODS TANK
LOCOMOTIVE
20 IN CLASS
FINAL NOS: 368-385, 387;
D CLASS NO 386

Built by the North British Locomotive Co, the D class entered service in 1912. The locomotives were used for suburban passenger services, as well as goods and mixed trains. During the early 1930s many locomotives of different classes were being superheated. On 18 April 1931 D class No 383 was converted, becoming the first of the Ds class. When superheated, the Ds locomotives were able to haul loads that were five percent heavier, with a reduction in coal consumption. They were found to be excellent in country areas, where they linked branch lines with the main line.

By the mid 1930s a total of fourteen D class had been superheated; nineteen were eventually converted to Ds class, (superheated). No 377, which was converted on 5 September 1935, was also given extended side tanks which increased its water capacity from 1600 to 1810 gallons. This locomotive was then used as a prototype for the later Dm and Dd class engines which entered service in 1945 and 1946. The extended tanks were removed from No 377 in May 1959 and were not fitted to any other Ds class locomotives.

Few changes were made to this class while in service, and they were still in use on suburban passenger and goods services until the early 1960s. No 371 was the last to go on 18 November 1965, after a total of fifty-three years in service.

Builder: North British Locomotive Co 20

Preserved: Nil

Above: Built by North British Locomotive Co in 1912, No 374 entered service with Western Australian Government Railways on 29 June 1912. It was superheated on 30 April 1934 to become a Ds class, and was withdrawn from service on 23 April 1963, after about fifty-one years in service, twenty-nine of those as a Ds class. Listed weight in working order of this locomotive was 69 tons 14 cwt with a length of 42 ft 6¼ in from buffer to buffer.
For more details see A History of W.A.G.R Steam Locomotives, A. Gunzburg, ARHS(WA) 1984, p. 93–5.

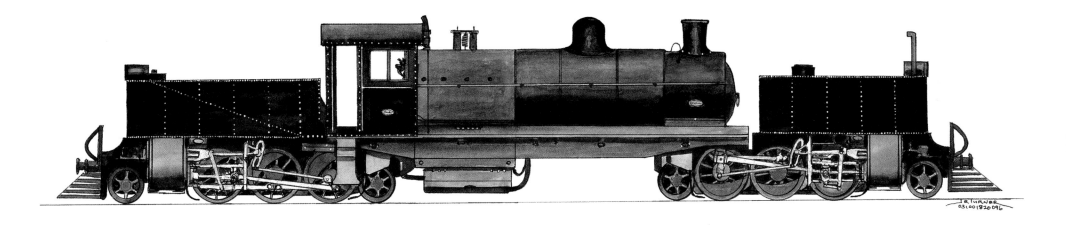

The need for new locomotives to be used on goods traffic resulted in two Garratt locomotives arriving from Beyer Peacock & Co in England in 1912. They supplemented the older E class then used on goods traffic. Both L class locomotives entered service in 1912 and were based in Launceston, where they were used on freight trains between Launceston and Hobart, a distance of about 123 miles. They were also used to haul passenger services on the north-eastern and western lines.

The introduction of new Q class locomotives, built by Clyde Engineering in 1936 and 1937, resulted in the L class being placed in storage. In 1943, the increased rail traffic brought about by

L CLASS (TAS)
2-6-2 2-6-2 GARRATT
ARTICULATED GOODS LOCOMOTIVE
2 IN CLASS
FINAL NOS: 1, 2

WW II saw the L class given a complete overhaul and returned to service. In 1944 they were in use on the north-eastern line and also on goods trains between Launceston and Devonport. By 1945 more Australian Standard Garratt locomotives were introduced, and the L class locomotive was finally withdrawn from service. They were stored at the locomotive graveyard at Launceston and gradually stripped of parts. They were sold in 1951 and cut up for scrap at Mowbray in 1953.

Builder: Beyer Peacock & Co 2

Preserved: Nil

Above: Built by Beyer Peacock & Co in England, L1 entered service with Tasmanian Government Railways in 1912 and was used mostly on goods services. Stored in the mid 1930s, it was overhauled and used during 1943 to 1945 and then withdrawn from service and finally scrapped in the early 1950s. Listed weight in working order of this locomotive was 89 tons 19 cwt 3 qtr with a length of 63 ft 1 in from buffer to buffer. For more details see The Decline of Steam Power on the Tasmanian Government Railways 1945–1965, *H.J.W. Stokes, ARHS Bulletin No 347, September 1966, p. 193–202.*

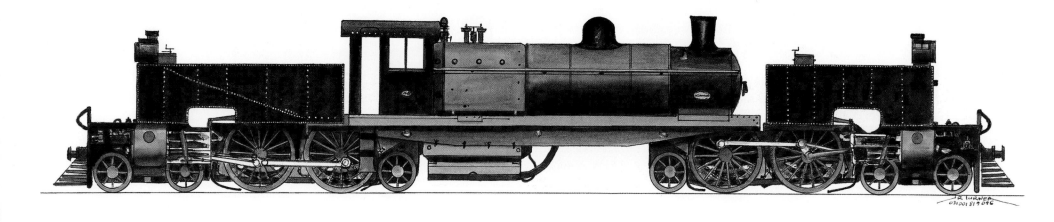

The success of the earlier Garratt locomotives resulted in the M class being ordered from Beyer Peacock & Co in England. The two locomotives were delivered in 1912. Built especially for use on passenger services, they were based at the Launceston Depot and on delivery they were used on the main expresses between Launceston and Hobart. With identical boilers to the L class, one of the M class is said to have reached a speed of 55 mph while in service. In later years they were used on the night mail trains to Antill Ponds, about 80 miles south of Launceston.

M CLASS (TAS)
WHEEL ARRANGEMENT: 4-4-2 2-4-4
GARRATT ARTICULATED PASSENGER LOCOMOTIVE
2 IN CLASS
FINAL NOS: M1, M2

Preserved: Nil

The M class was not very successful in service, and when the R class was introduced, they were both withdrawn. M1 was the first to go, followed by M2 in 1931. After withdrawal they spent many years lying derelict near the Launceston roundhouse, until they were sold in the early 1950s. The last to go was M2, with this locomotive finally being cut up for scrap in 1953.

Builder: Beyer Peacock & Co 2

Above: Built by Beyer Peacock & Co in England, No M1 entered service with Tasmanian Government Railways in 1912 and was withdrawn from service in the early 1930s. Listed weight in working order of this locomotive was 94 tons 11 cwt with a length of 68 ft 6 in from buffer to buffer. For more details see The Decline of Steam Power on the Tasmanian Government Railways 1945–1965, *H.J.W. Stokes, ARHS Bulletin No 347, September 1966, p. 193–202.*

Originally built for the Launceston and Western Railway Co by Robert Stephenson & Co, England in 1869, this locomotive was employed on construction of the line until it opened on 10 February 1871. By the end of 1880 it had travelled 252 942 miles. It was made redundant in 1883, and then sold in 1885 to the Great Victoria Colliery, where it was used for a short time on coal trains. It was then stored in a shed for almost twenty years. Acquired by contractors Smith and Timms, it was given a complete overhaul. The side tanks were removed and a short four-wheel tender permanently attached, with the name 'Gawler' painted on the side. Both tender and engine were painted green.

After use in the construction of the Gawler to Angaston line in 1912, the locomotive then

2ND O CLASS (SA)
WHEEL ARRANGEMENT: 4-4-0WT
WELL TANK LOCOMOTIVE
1 IN CLASS
FINAL NO: 204

entered service with South Australian Government Railways as No 204. It was given an O class boiler, but kept the tender, which carried extra water. The tender was seen standing derelict at the Islington Workshops in 1922, with 'Gawler' still painted in black on its sides. No 204, however, continued on, spending most of its time on work between the Mile End goods yard and the Port Adelaide goods sidings. It worked a variety of routes, pulling between 250 and 460 tons per trip depending on the line. It was withdrawn from service in 1929.

Builder: Robert Stephenson & Co, England 1

Preserved: Nil

Above: Built by Robert Stephenson & Co in 1869 and used in Tasmania and Victoria, it entered service with South Australian Government Railways in 1912 where it was used as a shunter. It was withdrawn from service on 1 November 1929, and cut up on 1 May 1930 after sixty years of varied service. Listed weight in working order of this locomotive was 37 tons 14 cwt and it was 29 ft 4 in from buffer to buffer. For more details see The Second O-Class Locomotive of South Australia, *G.H. Eardley, ARSH Bulletin No. 411, January 1972, p. 21–3.*

RX CLASS (SA)
WHEEL ARRANGEMENT: 4-6-0
BROAD GAUGE LOCOMOTIVE
84 IN CLASS
FINAL NOS 5, 9, 10, 15, 20, 25, 48, 55-6, 91-96, 102-107, 138-150, 155, 158, 160, 190-203, 206-235

When the R class entered service in early 1886, it was found to be an excellent locomotive, and a total of thirty were in service by the end of 1895. It was felt, however, that a larger boiler would make them even better. As the boilers came due for renewal between 1899 and 1913, all thirty were sent to the Islington Workshops and converted to Rx class. From 1909, the first batch of new Rx locomotives was built at the Islington Workshops, but due to Federal Government policy at the time, the next batch was built in England and delivered towards the end of 1913. The final three orders were filled locally by the Islington Workshops and Walkers of Maryborough. With increased traffic in the 1920s, the Rx class was double-headed to cope with longer and heavier trains.

By the mid 1920s the introduction of the 500, 600 and 700 classes saw the Rx locomotives relegated to secondary lines, where they continued to work until broad gauge steam operations ceased

on 30 June 1967. There were more than twenty of the class still in service. No 146, the first converted, was condemned on 24 August 1966 and cut up at Islington on 13 September 1966, having travelled 1 324 186 miles during seventy-one years in service.

Builders: Dubs & Co, Glasgow, Scotland 6; James Martin & Co, Gawler, SA 24; S.A.R. Islington Workshops 15; North British Locomotive Co, Scotland 15; Walkers, Maryborough, Queensland 25

Preserved: No 5, at Rotary Playground, Hill St, Kapunda; No 55, at Historical Village, Loxton; No 93, at Port Dock Railway Museum (SA) Inc, Port Adelaide; No 160, at Murray Bridge Wharf; No 191, at park near station, Victor Harbour; No 201, at Rotary Park, Railway Terrace, Tailem Bend; Nos 207 and 224, at Steamranger, Goolwa; No 217, at Barossa Valley Historical Trust, Nuriootpa; No 231, at children's playground, Ewing St, Kadina.

Above: Built by the North British Locomotive Company, of Hyde Park Works, Glasgow, No 195 entered service with South Australian Railways on 8 September 1913. It was written off on 7 September 1967 after fifty-four years in service. Listed weight in working order of this locomotive and tender was 88 tons 12 cwt while their combined length was 57 ft 11¾ in from buffer to buffer. For more detail see The RX-Class Locomotives of South Australia, *G. Eardley,* ARHS Bulletin No 456, October 1975, p. 230–45.

Built in 1913 by Beyer Peacock & Co, England, the Ms Class entered service in 1913. Nos 424 and 426 were the first, on 27 September. The last, No 430, had entered service in November at the State Saw Mills at Manjimup, but was found to be too large to use on bush tramways. It was then exchanged for two W.A.G.R. G class locomotives, Nos 57 and 59, and finally entered service on 11 June 1914. Another Ms, No 389, was originally an M class which was superheated on 12 April 1935.

While the M and Ms were similar in appearance and size, tests conducted in February 1914 showed a marked difference in performance, in favour of the superheated locomotive. A saving of 31 percent in coal and 19 percent in water was achieved. The M class also took up to half an hour longer to complete the tests, with steam problems and refilling water tanks. Both the M and Ms Garratts performed well and required little modification or maintenance.

By 1947 four of the eight had been withdrawn from service, with the remainder withdrawn in the early 1950s. No 429 was the last, on 13 January 1955, after forty-two years in service.

MS CLASS (WA)
WHEEL ARRANGEMENT: 2-6-0 0-6-2
GARRATT ARTICULATED
LOCOMOTIVE
8 IN CLASS
FINAL NOS: 389, 424-430

Builder: Beyer Peacock & Co, England 8
Preserved: Nil

Above: Built by Beyer Peacock in 1913, No 430 was initially used at the State Saw Mills at Manjimup from November 1913 until 11 June 1914, when it entered service with the W.A.G.R. It was withdrawn from service on 29 May 1953, after thirty-nine years in service. Listed weight in working order of this locomotive was 69 tons 16¼ cwt and it was 53 ft 10½ in from buffer to buffer. For more details see A History of W.A.G.R. Steam Locomotives, *A. Gunzburg, ARHS(WA) 1984, p. 89–92.*

Approval was given to build these locomotives in November 1911. They were all built by the Ipswich Railway Works in 1914, with No 692 entering service in February 1914. No 694 entered service in December 1914.

Superheated boilers were a success overseas, and it was decided to use these three locomotives to test its performance in Australia. With that in mind, No 692 was saturated, No 693 received a Schmidt superheater and No 694 a Robinson superheater. The superheated locomotives proved more efficient, and in December 1916, No 692 had a Robinson (M.L.S.) superheater fitted.

In July 1920, No 693 hauled ten coaches which formed the Royal Train from Wallangarra to

C18 CLASS (QLD)
WHEEL ARRANGEMENT: 4-6-0
GOODS LOCOMOTIVE
3 IN CLASS
FINAL NOS: 692-4

Brisbane and Maryborough during the visit to Australia of H.R.H. the Prince of Wales, later to become King Edward VIII. Though mostly used on the main and southern lines, No 694 was based at Toowoomba from 1939 onwards. In 1958 it hauled the last train on the old Gowrie–Wyreema line before it was closed. After years in service hauling passenger, fruit and wheat trains, No 694 was written off in September 1961. All three locomotives were scrapped, but the numbers and nameplates of Nos 693 and 694 have been preserved.

Builder: Ipswich Railway Works 3
Preserved: Nil

Above: Built by the Ipswich Railway Works in 1914, No 693 entered service with Queensland Government Railways in September 1914. It was written off in February 1960 after about forty-six years in service. The listed weight in working order of locomotive and tender was 93 tons with a combined length of 55 ft 10¼ in from buffer to buffer. For more details see Locomotives in the Tropics Vol 2, J. Armstrong, ARHS(QLD) 1994, p. 39–42.

The first of a total of 280 locomotives of this class entered service with N.S.W. Government Railways on 17 June 1896 as No 2nd 524, following its delivery from Beyer Peacock & Co in England. The final locomotive of the class, built by North British Locomotive Co, entered service in May 1916 as No 2nd 522.

These locomotives were found to be well suited for their primary task of hauling heavy goods trains on steep gradients and sharp curves. At times they were used to assist passenger trains on steep grades such as those found on the Blue Mountains line. The first 206 locomotives were delivered as saturated type, with the remaining seventy-four delivered superheated. One hundred and six were subsequently superheated, although others remained in their original

T524 CLASS (D)50 (NSW)
WHEEL ARRANGEMENT: 2-8-0
HEAVY GOODS LOCOMOTIVE
280 IN CLASS
FINAL NOS: 5001–5280

saturated form, including No 5069, which hauled the last non-air coal train from east Greta Junction to Port Waratah on 22 December 1972. For many years No 5112 was on display at Bathurst railway station, as it had been driven by Ben Chifley, who later became Prime Minister of Australia. This locomotive is being restored to operating condition along with six carriages.

Builders: Beyer Peacock & Co 151; Dubs & Co 5; Neilson & Co 10; North British Locomotive Co 84; Clyde Engineering, N.S.W. 30

Preserved: No 5096, at Rail Transport Museum, Thirlmere; No 5112, owned by Bathurst City Council under restoration, Orange, NSW; Nos 5069 and 5132, at Dorrigo Steam Railway & Museum.

Above: Shown here modified with a Laird crosshead and 5000 gallon turret type tender, No 1297 was delivered to N.S.W. Government Railways from the North British Locomotive Co. It was superheated when built, and entered service on 23 December 1914. It was later renumbered 5270, and was withdrawn from service in December 1968 and scrapped in February 1969, having travelled 1 199 667 miles during its forty-four years in service. Listed weight in working order of this locomotive and turret tender was 131 tons 14 cwt while the combined length was 67 ft 5⅝ in from buffer to buffer. For more details see A Compendium of N.S.W. Steam Locomotives, *compiled by A. Grunbach, ARHS(NSW) 1989, p. 129–35.*

CC CLASS (TAS)
WHEEL ARRANGEMENT: 2-6-0
GOODS LOCOMOTIVE
6 IN CLASS
FINAL NOS: CC16-19, CC26, CC27

Following the successful rebuilding of two A class locomotives in 1908, it was decided that six of the Beyer Peacock-built C class locomotives would also be rebuilt, with enlarged Belpaire boilers and extended smoke boxes. This work was carried out between 1912 and 1916 by Tasmanian Government Railway Workshops. The rebuilt locomotives were designated the CC class while retaining their original numbers. They were used for a wide variety of different tasks including shunting, the transportation of goods and mixed goods and passenger services.

Following the end of WW II it was decided that diesel locomotives should be bought, which resulted in the X class being brought into service. By the early 1950s those CC class locomotives still in service were mostly used on shunting or local goods services, with an occasional passenger service in the Hobart area. By 1957, the newer M and Q class locomotives had taken over the few passenger services which the CC class had previously hauled. The last three locomotives, CC18, CC26 and CC27, were all scrapped in 1965 after about fifty years in service.

Builder: Tasmanian Government Railway Workshops 6
Preserved: Nil

Above: Built by Beyer Peacock & Co in England, C27 was rebuilt by Tasmanian Government Railway Workshops to become CC27, and was one of the last of its class to leave service. Listed weight in working order of this locomotive and tender was 55 tons 14 cwt with a combined length of about 43 ft 3 in from buffer to buffer. For more details see The Decline of Steam Power on the Tasmanian Government Railways 1945–1965, H.J.W. Stokes, ARHS Bulletin No 347, September 1966, p. 193–202.

2ND F CLASS (SA)
WHEEL ARRANGEMENT: 4-6-2T
PASSENGER TANK LOCOMOTIVE
44 IN CLASS
FINAL NOS: 168-89, 240-55

Designed specifically for suburban passenger work, these locomotives were more powerful than the older P and G class tank engines they replaced. Built by South Australian Railways Workshops at Islington, the first locomotive entered service on 30 April 1902 as No 167. The final locomotive, No 255, entered service on 6 October 1922, after delivery from Perry Engineering at Mile End. They were used on all lines in the metropolitan area, but rarely went further due to their limited water supply. Though easily able to travel at 60 mph, the short distances between stations meant that they rarely got over 35 mph. In July 1920, No 181 was especially decorated for use as the locomotive on the Royal train.

By the late 1950s almost half of the class had been withdrawn from service and cut up.

During their time in service a number of F class engines were involved in collisions, and No 244 was condemned after an accident on 6 April 1956. A second No 244 was then constructed, using the frame of No 239 and the boiler of the first 244. When No 167 was withdrawn from service in October 1955, it had travelled 1 289 282 miles during fifty-three years of service. When No 255 was condemned in August 1969, it had travelled 905 627 miles during forty-seven years of service.

Builders: S.A.R. Islington Workshops 21; James Martin & Co, Gawler, S.A. 12; Perry Engineering, Mile End, S.A. 10

Preserved: No 245, at Rotary Park, Gawler; No 251, at Steamranger, Goolwa; No 255, at Port Dock Railway Museum, Adelaide.

Above: One of the second batch of F class locomotives, and shown here as it looked in early years, No 243 was delivered from James Martin & Co at Gawler, and entered service on 3 July 1915. It was condemned on 2 July 1958 and cut up at Islington on 16 August 1960, after about forty-three years in service. Listed weight in working order of this locomotive was 59 tons and it was 40 ft 7¼ in from buffer to buffer. For more details see Steam Locomotives and Railcars of the South Australian Railways, *R.E. Fluck, R. Sampson and K.J. Bird, Mile End Railway Museum 1986, p. 77–9.*

This locomotive was built by Hudswell Clark & Co in 1911, and purchased by the Engineer-in-Chief's department. It was employed on the South-East Drainage Scheme, where it hauled side-tipping wagons to and from the Woakwine Range Main Drainage Channel near Beachport, north-west of Mount Gambier. On completion of this work it was given the number 260 and began service with South Australian Railways. It was assigned to shunting duties at Wallaroo, on the coast of Spencer Gulf about 80 miles north-west of Adelaide. As well as yard duties, No 260 assisted the V class tank

NO 260 CLASS (SA)
WHEEL ARRANGEMENT: 0-4-0ST
SMALL SADDLE TANK LOCOMOTIVE
1 IN CLASS
FINAL NO: 260

Builder: Hudswell Clark & Co 1
Preserved: Nil

engines in shunting grain wagons on the jetty, and was said to be more powerful and easier to work than the V class.

When the gauge of the line was changed in the mid 1920s, No 260 was transferred to Peterborough, about 105 miles north-east of Wallaroo, where it was again employed as a shunter. It was sold again in 1936, with no further record of its movements.

Above: One of the smallest locomotives used on South Australian Government Railways, it was first used on construction work and given the number 260 on entering government service on 30 September 1916. Used as a shunter it was condemned in June 1936 and sold, its fate unknown. Listed weight in working order of this locomotive was 15 tons l8 cwt and it was 20 ft 2¼ in from buffer to buffer. For more detail see Narrow Gauge Memories, The Locomotives, *S. McNicol, Railmac Publications, 1993, p. 168–9.*

V(1217) CLASS (X)10 (NSW)
WHEEL ARRANGEMENT: 0-4-0T
SMALL SADDLE TANK LOCOMOTIVE
2 IN CLASS
FINAL NOS: 1022-1023

Two of these locomotives were built for the Public Works Department in 1916, by Vulcan Iron Works at Wilkes Barre, USA. They entered service on 31 December 1916, when the N.S.W. Government Railways took over the Public Works Department, and were allocated numbers 1217 and 1218. They were renumbered 1022 and 1023 in 1924. Although used in the construction of the Metropolitan Goods lines, they spent most of their working life shunting tenders and locomotives around the Enfield locomotive depot. From 1943 to 1945 they were hired to the US Army, and painted green for use at the US Quartermasters Corps store near Sandown.

In June 1964, No 1023 was withdrawn from service and scrapped on 29 April 1968, having travelled 277 728 miles during its forty-seven years in service. After No 1022 was withdrawn from service, it spent a fair amount of time on tourist operations with the NSW Steam Tram & Railway Preservation Society, at Parramatta Park, Sydney from October 1970 until June 1993. The locomotive is currently back with the Rail Transport Museum at Thirlmere.

Builder: Vulcan Iron Works, Wilkes Barre, USA 2
Preserved: No 1022, at Rail Transport Museum, Thirlmere.

Above: Originally delivered to the Public Works Department in 1916 and numbered PWD57, this locomotive entered service with N.S.W. Government Railways on 31 December 1916 as No 1217. It was later renumbered 1022.
It was withdrawn from service in June 1970 and condemned on 9 October, after forty-eight years of service. Listed weight in working order of this locomotive was 26 tons 18 cwt while its length was 25 ft from buffer to buffer.
For more details see A Compendium of NSW Steam Locomotives, compiled by A. Grunbach, ARHS(NSW) 1989, p. 167.

One of five of its class, this locomotive was built in 1916 by Manning Wardle & Co, England, especially for the Public Works Department. They were used for railway construction during the building of some sections of the North Coast line. Although all five locomotives were transferred to N.S.W. Government Railways on 31 December 1916, when the Public Works Department was taken over, nly PWD59 entered service. The other four locomotives were sold before they could be used in lway service.

F(1212) CLASS (X)10 (NSW)
WHEEL ARRANGEMENT: 0-4-0T
SMALL SADDLE TANK LOCOMOTIVE
1 IN CLASS
FINAL NO: 1021

Although it had been allocated the number 1212, the locomotive was renumbered 1021 in 1924. It spent most of its working life as a shunter at Cardiff Workshops, before being transferred to Broadmeadows as a depot shunter. Finally withdrawn from service in November 1970, it is now preserved at the Rail Transport Museum at Thirlmere, some distance south of Sydney.

Builder: Manning Wardle & Co, England 1
Preserved: No 1021, at Rail Transport Museum, Thirlmere.

Above: First delivered to the Public Works Department, PWD59 entered service with N.S.W. Government Railways at the end of 1916 as No 1212, and was renumbered 1021 in 1924. Withdrawn from service in November 1970, it was condemned on 30 March 1972 after about fifty-six years of service. Listed weight in working order of this locomotive was 21 tons 1 cwt and its length was 19 ft from buffer to buffer. For more details see A Compendium of NSW Steam Locomotives, compiled by A. Grunbach, ARHS(NSW) 1989, p. 164.

N o 1027 was the first of a total of thirty-five locomotives of this class to enter service with N.S.W. Government Railways on 4 August 1914. It was delivered on 4 August 1914 from Eveleigh Workshops in Sydney. The final locomotive entered service on 22 November 1923, as No 1323. These locomotives were intended to haul the heavier passenger carriages which had been introduced on main line express trains, and were used on the Sydney–Katoomba line from 1918. By the 1930s Nos 3506, 3526 and 3535 were painted Caledonian Blue and had a large silver star painted on their smoke box doors. They hauled the Caves Express, which carried tourists from Sydney to Katoomba in a six-car train, painted blue and cream to match the colour of the locomotive.

The introduction of newer, more powerful engines saw the (C)35s relegated to working north

NN(1027) CLASS (C)35 (NSW)
WHEEL ARRANGEMENT: 4-6-0
EXPRESS PASSENGER LOCOMOTIVE
35 IN CLASS
FINAL NOS: 3501-35

of Gosford. In the mid 1960s they were often seen hauling passenger trains on the lines north and west of Newcastle, as well as assisting more powerful locomotives such as the (AD)60 Garratt hauling goods trains. Some in their final years received modified turret tenders discarded from withdrawn standard goods locomotives.

A highlight for this class was when locomotives 1312 and 1315 were painted Royal blue and used to haul the Royal train which took the Prince of Wales (later King Edward VIII) from Sydney to Canberra and back, when he visited Australia in 1920. No 3526, along with its original tender are under restoration at the Rail Transport Museum, Thirlmere.

Builder: Eveleigh Workshops, Sydney 35
Preserved: No 3526, at Rail Transport Museum, Thirlmere.

Above: Delivered to N.S.W. Government Railways, this locomotive entered service on 8 May 1917 as No 1315, and was renumbered 3527 in 1924. It is shown here in original condition, painted Royal blue for the visit of the Prince of Wales in 1920. It was rebuilt in May 1938, withdrawn from service in October 1965 and scrapped in April 1966, having travelled 1 710 874 miles during forty-eight years in service. Listed weight in working order of this locomotive and tender was 124 tons 14 cwt while the combined length was 62 ft 9½ in from buffer to buffer. For more details see A Compendium of NSW Steam Locomotives, compiled by A. Grunbach, ARHS(NSW) 1989, p. 158–63.

The first of eight of these small 'Mogul' type locomotives entered service with the Public Works Department in February 1913. Built by the Hunslet Engine Co in England, the final locomotive entered service in May 1913. They had been built specifically for railway construction work, and when the Public Works Department was taken over by N.S.W. Government Railways in 1917, two of these engines were at Coffs Harbour–Glenreagh on North Coast construction, one each at the workshops at Tottenham and Burrowa–Tumbarumba, another two were at Telegraph Point on North Coast construction work, and two more on the Dubbo–Binnaway–Werris Creek construction.

Under NSWGR ownership, they saw use on the North Coast, Dorrigo, Tumbarumba,

G(1204) CLASS (Z)27 (NSW)
WHEEL ARRANGEMENT: 2-6-0
GOODS LOCOMOTIVE
8 IN CLASS
FINAL NOS: 2701-08

Merriwa and Binnerwa–Coonabarabran. However it quickly became apparent that they were unsuitable for use on lines with curves. As a result the locomotives were all soon based at Narrabri, where they were used on the long straight lines hauling stock and goods trains. All of them were rebuilt between 1930 and 1942 with a standard Z-25 class boiler. By the late 1950s most had been withdrawn from service, the last of the locomotives to go being Nos 2705 and 2708 in 1960.

Builder: Hunslet Engine Co, England 8

Preserved: No 2705, at Rail Transport Museum, Thirlmere. This locomotive was restored to working order and entered service hauling vintage trains in September 1995.

Above: Shown here in original condition, this locomotive entered service with NSWGR in 1917 as No 1211. It was later renumbered as 2708. Withdrawn from service in January 1960 and condemned on 10 April 1963, it was scrapped on 28 September 1963, having travelled 740 816 miles during forty-four years of service. Listed weight in working order of this locomotive and tender was 80 tons 7 cwt while the combined length was 54 ft 4⅞ in from buffer to buffer. For more details see A Compendium of NSW Steam Locomotives, compiled by A. Grunbach, ARHS(NSW) 1989, p. 165–6.

This locomotive was built as a prototype using coke as fuel instead of coal, the idea being to reduce the large amount of smoke and cinders, and in so doing improve passenger comfort when travelling through tunnels in Brisbane. After unsuccessful trials with a C16 and then a 6D16, another trial was conducted around 1914 in which two tank engines were also converted to burn fuel oil. The First World War intervened, and it was not until 1918 that the Ipswich Railway Works completed No 204. It entered service on 13 August of that year.

Being a prototype, it had some unusual features, such as Southern valve gear and a 'Prairie' 2–6–2 wheel arrangement It would appear that, as with other prototype locomotives built around this time, a variety of ideas were tried out. The gas works at South Brisbane and Wynnum supplied the coke, and a machine was installed at Ipswich to crush it ready for use. This locomotive immediately

B16½ CLASS (QLD)
WHEEL ARRANGEMENT: 2-6-2
PASSENGER LOCOMOTIVE
1 IN CLASS
FINAL NO: 204

came under fire, and the Commissioner's office was informed that two firemen could be needed to work the locomotive. Tests proved that more than twice as much shovelling was required with coke than with coal. After this, no more locomotives using coke were built.

A number of changes were made to the locomotive over the years. It was altered to burn coal in June 1927, and the tender was changed. It was used on coal trains and passenger services, where it would normally haul seven carriages. It was kept in service after WW II during the locomotive shortage, but was finally withdrawn from service in February 1950, and scrapped in September of that year after about thirty-two years of service.

Builder: Ipswich Railway Works 1

Preserved: Nil

Above: Built by the Ipswich Railway Works in 1918 and designed to use coke instead of coal for fuel, No 204 entered service in August 1918 and was written off in September 1950 after thirty-two years in service. Listed weight in working order of this locomotive and tender was 86 tons 8 cwt while the combined length was 57 ft 2 in from buffer to buffer. For more details see Locomotives in the Tropics Vol. 2, J. Armstrong, ARHS(QLD) 1994, p. 46–7.

The first of a total of 120 locomotives of this class was built by Clyde Engineering at Granville. It entered service with N.S.W. Government Railways on 20 November 1918, as No 1353. The final locomotive entered service on 13 March 1925 as No 5620, after the general reclassification and renumbering of August 1924. As delivered, the class were fitted with a 'Wampu' design tender, although in later years, as coal burners, many received turret tenders.

This class was similar to the TF(939) class, the major difference being the use of the Southern valve gear, which was rarely used outside the U.S.A. While the Southern valve gear required less maintenance, it was more expensive to repair if it did fail. These locomotives were also more sluggish when pulling heavy loads.

K(1353) CLASS (D)55 (NSW)
WHEEL ARRANGEMENT: 2–8–0
GOODS LOCOMOTIVE
120 IN CLASS
FINAL NOS: 5501-5620

During the coal shortage of the late 1940s, seventy of this class were converted to burn oil, with fifty continuing to burn coal. By 1953, the majority of the oil burners had been withdrawn from service, with most scrapped by the mid 1950s. Thirteen were subsequently reconverted to burn coal. The last oil burner was withdrawn from service in early 1959 and scrapped in September 1961, having travelled 750 707 miles during thirty-five years of service. The last coal burner was locomotive No 5597, which was withdrawn in July 1967 and scrapped the following month, having travelled 957 399 miles during forty-three years of service.

Builder: Clyde Engineering Co, Granville 120

Preserved: No 5595, with 'Wampu' tender, at Rail Transport Museum, Thirlmere.

Above: Delivered to N.S.W. Government Railways, No 1353 is shown as delivered, before electric headlights were fitted. No 1353 entered service on 20 November 1918, and was later renumbered 5501. It was withdrawn from service in November 1956 and scrapped in early 1957, having travelled 902 260 miles during thirty-eight years of service. Listed weight in working order of this locomotive and tender was 127 tons 9 cwt 1qtr with a combined length of 60 ft 10¾ in from buffer to buffer. For more details see A Compendium of N.S.W. Steam Locomotives, compiled by A. Grunbach, ARHS(NSW) 1989, p. 172–5, 182–3.

B ased on a Beyer Peacock & Co design which had been used in
three other states, the two locomotives designated AY and BY
were built by James Martin & Co of Gawler, S.A. They were
bought from Western Australian Government Railways in 1907 for use on
the Chilligoe Railway, and both entered service with Queensland
Government Railways in July 1919. In 1921 AY was listed as No 128, and
sold in 1923 to the Chilligoe State Smelters, where it remained in service until the smelter closed
down in 1942. After lying idle at Chilligoe, it was bought by timber merchants Bunning Bros. from

AY & BY CLASS (QLD)
WHEEL ARRANGEMENT: 2-6-0
GOODS LOCOMOTIVE
2 IN CLASS
FINAL NOS: 128, 159

Builder: James Martin & Co 2
Preserved: Nil

Western Australia and hauled to Stratford near Cairns in 1950 where it
was dismantled; however, only the boiler was shipped west.

The second locomotive, known as BY, became No 159. After being
shipped to Innisfail, it was used on the last stages of the construction of
the North Coast line, which was completed in 1924. By 1927 it was in
Townsville, where it was written off in November of that year.

Above: Built by James Martin & Co of Gawler, S.A. in 1896, AY entered service with Western Australian Government Railways in December 1896. It was withdrawn on 19 August 1907, and bought by the Chilligoe Mining & Railway Co.
It carried builder's plates dated that year but was out of use by 1912 and was dismantled. Sold to Queensland Government Railways, it re-entered service in July 1919, and was written off in late 1927. The listed weight in working order
of locomotive and tender was 47 tons 11 cwt with a combined length of 39 ft 3⅛ in from buffer to buffer. For more details see Locomotives in the Tropics Vol 2, J. Armstrong, ARHS(QLD) 1994, p. 22–3.

2ND M CLASS (SA)
WHEEL ARRANGEMENT: 2-4-2T
SIDE TANK LOCOMOTIVE
20 IN CLASS
FINAL NOS: 256-75

Built between 1889–1894, these locomotives were used on Victorian Government Railways and were designated E class. By 1920 the electrification of suburban lines made them redundant. They were put up for sale at £1000 each, and twenty were bought by South Australian Government Railways. The first entered service in June 1920, and the final locomotive in April 1925. A trial run on the north line established that they were too heavy for the bridges and culverts on that line, so they were mainly used on the Adelaide to Port Adelaide track. They were quiet-running locomotives, and moved half a dozen carriages without effort. As was the custom, the number was fixed to the front of the chimney and side tank, with the class letter fixed to the back of the chimney.

Several of the class were withdrawn from service within a couple of years, and parts from Nos 256 and 270 were combined to make No 256 2nd. During 1928–1929 all of this class were scrapped, except for No 257, which survived until May 1935 when it too was scrapped. Most met their fate in the yard of the Islington Workshops, at the hand of H. Morrell, scrap metal dealer.

Builders: Phoenix Foundry 15; David Munro 5; S.A.R. Islington Workshops 1 (built from 256 and 270)

Preserved: Nil

Above: Built by the Phoenix Foundry in December 1896, this locomotive was No 434 when in service as an E class with Victorian Government Railways. In service with South Australian Government Railways in June 1920 as No 258, it was condemned in March 1929 and scrapped in September 1929 after thirty-three years in service. Listed weight in working order of this locomotive was 53 tons 8 cwt and it was 33 ft 8 in from buffer to buffer. For more detail see The Second M-Class Locomotives of South Australia, *G.H. Eardley, ARHS Bulletin No 421, November 1972, p. 223–5.*

After the outbreak of WW I, the building program for a superheated version of the C16 was delayed until 1919, when material ordered in 1915 arrived from Britain. The initial ten C17 locomotives were built in 1920 at the Ipswich Railway Works, with the first, No 15, entering service in August. The last of the group, No 179, was built in 1921 and entered service in February 1922. Walkers Limited was also building the C17 at the same time and the first of their locomotives, No 182, was the second of the class to enter service in November 1920. A number of teething problems were soon apparent, but by late 1921, most had been solved and the locomotives were considered satisfactory. The required changes were then incorporated into those locomotives under construction, and those built later. When ordered, the C17 was seen as a superheated version of the C16, but when in service it was

C17 CLASS (QLD)
WHEEL ARRANGEMENT: 4-8-0
GOODS LOCOMOTIVE
169 IN CLASS
FINAL NOS: 2, 15, 17, 24, 25, 29, 32-3, 45-6, 55, 57, 62, 68, 121, 138, 145-147, 165-6, 179, 182, 187-8, 191, 226, 245-261, 263-4, 705-30, 752-67, 772-91, 802-26, 831-40, 859-63, 917-48, 955-960

found to have improved performance which enabled them to haul bigger loads. They were used on a variety of services including goods, livestock, mixed and passenger trains on main and secondary lines.

Between 1920 and 1929, 143 C17s were built, followed by a further 26 Nos 929–960 built between 1948–58. A few were written off in the early 1950s, but most were withdrawn over a two-year period in the late 1960s. The last few were written off in August 1970, including No 247 which had almost fifty years in service.

Builders: Ipswich Railway Works 10; Walkers Limited 86; Evans, Anderson Phelan & Co 28; Armstrong Whitworth & Co 25; Clyde Engineering 20

Preserved: No 251, at Charters Towers Historical Society; No 2, at QR in storage. More than twenty other locomotives have been preserved.

Above: *Built by Ipswich Railway Works in 1920, No 15 entered service in August 1920 and was withdrawn from service in July 1968, after nearly forty-eight years in service. Listed weight in working order of this locomotive and tender was 81tons 15 cwt with a combined length of 53 ft 5½ in from buffer to buffer. For more details see* Locomotives in the Tropics *Vol. 2, J. Armstrong, ARHS(QLD) 1994, p. 48–63.*

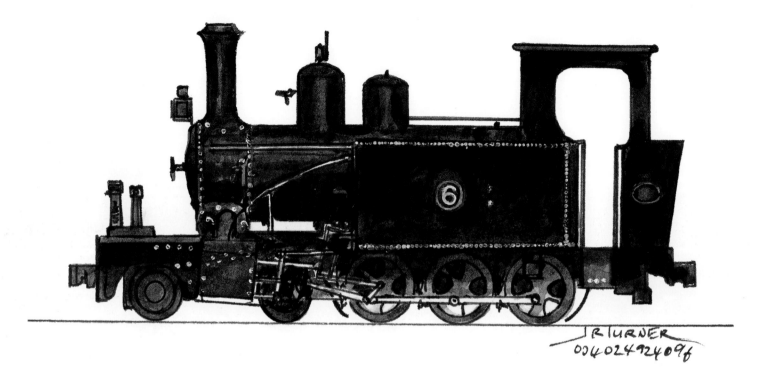

These locomotives were all built by the Hunslet Engine Co, Leeds, England in 1916, and were used for transporting goods on light railways during WW I. The first was bought from the Engineering Supply Co of Australia, and entered service in October 1920, as No 6 on the Innisfail Tramway. It was needed to fill the gap while No 5, the new 6D8½ locomotive, was in transit from England. Although similar in performance to the Fowler locomotives, No 6 was quite different in a number of ways. It had an enclosed steel cab and Walschaerts valve gear, and a four-wheel leading

6D9½ CLASS (QLD)
WHEEL ARRANGEMENT: 4–6–0T
SMALL NARROW GAUGE TANK
LOCOMOTIVE
3 IN CLASS
FINAL NOS: 1, 2, 6

Preserved: Nil

bogie. While only intended to be used for a short time, it eventually stayed in service for about seventeen years. Two other locomotives built by Hunslet were also bought, with No 2 entering service in August 1924, and No 1 in August 1925. All three remained in service until 1937, when Nos 6 and 1 were written off in July. No 2 was the last withdrawn from service in June 1938.

Builder: Hunslet Engine Co. Leeds, England 3

Above: Built in 1916 by Hunslet Engine Co, Leeds, England, No 6 entered service in October 1920. It was written off in July 1937, after nearly seventeen years in service. Listed weight in working order of this locomotive was 14 tons 4 cwt with a length of 20 ft 6 in from buffer to buffer. For more details see Locomotives in the Tropics *Vol. 2, J. Armstrong, ARHS(QLD) 1994, p. 28–9.*

After WW I, rail traffic increased, and the existing locomotives were unable to cope. It was obvious that more locomotives were needed. In 1921 six T class locomotives were bought second-hand from South Australian Railways, retaining their South Australian class and number. Built by Walkers of Maryborough in Queensland in 1914, some were based at Launceston. They worked goods trains and the daily mixed service on the north-eastern line, and main line goods trains south to Parattah. Some were also based at Devonport, hauling goods trains on the line west to Stanley. On 30 June 1955, four T class locomotives were based at Launceston, while two were based at Devonport.

In November 1957 the branch line to Roland was closed, leaving the T class little to do apart

T CLASS (TAS)
WHEEL ARRANGEMENT: 4–8–0
GOODS LOCOMOTIVE
6 IN CLASS
FINAL NOS: 219, 222–3, 230, 235, 237

followed by T230 in 1959. In 1962, T222 and T237 followed, with T235 the last when its boiler was removed in 1963.

Builder: Walkers Ltd 6
Preserved: Nil

from shunting and goods services west to Ulverstone. When the MA class arrived at Launceston the T class were withdrawn from service, with only T237 still used for shunting until September 1959.

T222 and T235 were based at Devonport. In April 1959, T222 was replaced by a diesel, but T235 was used for some shunting work until late 1961. The first two to be scrapped were T219 and T223 in 1958,

Above: Built by Walkers Ltd, T235 entered service with South Australian Railways on 8 September 1914. It was sold to Tasmanian Government Railways in November 1920, and entered service on 3 March 1921. It was superheated on 10 October 1927 and written off on 26 August 1963. Listed weight in working order of this locomotive and tender was 73 tons 5 cwt with a combined length of about 53 ft 6 in from buffer to buffer. For more details see The Decline of Steam Power on the Tasmanian Government Railways (1945–1965), H.J.W. Stokes, ARHS Bulletin No 348, October 1966, p. 217–29.

6D8½ CLASS (QLD)
WHEEL ARRANGEMENT: 0-6-0T
SMALL TANK LOCOMOTIVE
6 IN CLASS
FINAL NOS: 1–5, 8

A number of similar locomotives were grouped to form the 6D8½ class. The first two, Nos 1 and 2, had been built in 1900 by John Fowler & Co of Leeds, England. For a number of years they burned wood, but later burned coal. By the time they entered service with Queensland Government Railways in 1914, the boiler was in need of overhaul and the locomotive was sent to Ipswich for repair. In 1914 John Fowler & Co supplied two new engines, Nos 3 and 4, both entering service in August 1915. No 5 entered service in June 1921. By 1923 another Fowler had arrived, with No 8 entering service in March 1923. In June 1924 No 2 was written off, followed by No 1 in October 1925.

A typical load varied on different sections of the line, but the class was allowed to haul twelve wagons totalling 143 tons on one section, and they often hauled up to 156 tons on the harbour line. In 1919 No 4 hauled 249 tons on one section of the line. Nos 3, 4 and 5 were withdrawn from service in September 1957 after more than forty years in service. No 8 continued in service until January 1962, when it was the last steam locomotive used as a shunter on the Mourilyan wharf.

Builder: John Fowler & Co, Leeds, England 6
Preserved: Nil

Above: Built by John Fowler & Co in England in 1921, No 5 entered service in June 1921. It was withdrawn from service in June 1957 after thirty-six years in service. Listed weight in working order of this locomotive was 13 tons 5 cwt and it was 18 ft 6¾ in from buffer to buffer. For more details see Locomotives in the Tropics Volume 2, J. Armstrong, ARHS(QLD) 1994, p. 26–7

On the 9 March 1918 the first of the C Class Heavy Goods Locomotives entered service with Victorian Railways. It was built at Newport Workshops and numbered C1, the last being C26, which began its service on 20 December 1926. During its first year in service, C1 completed 31 615 miles, which included hauling regular goods services between Melbourne and Seymour. Compared with the DD and A2 locomotives, it was superior to both in the load it could haul and in economy of use. The success of C1 resulted in an order being placed in 1919 for ten more locomotives.

Because of the weight of the locomotive it was necessary to strengthen both track and bridges on routes to be used by the C Class. A number of changes were made over the years, with improvements to superheaters, new headlights and automatic couplers. On 28 August 1929 C13 hauled the first 1100 ton coal train from Nyora to Melbourne. During WW II the C class was often

C CLASS (VIC)
WHEEL ARRANGEMENT: 2-8-0
HEAVY GOODS LOCOMOTIVE
26 IN CLASS
FINAL NOS: 1-26

used on heavy passenger trains, including at times the *Spirit of Progress*. Though speed was usually restricted to 50 mph, this was increased to 60 mph on passenger services. Between August 1946 and February 1949 all C class locomotives were converted to burn heavy fuel oil, which in turn created a problem with smoke. As a result German pattern smoke deflectors were fitted.

During the early 1950s the first of the class was scrapped, and by 1960 only eleven remained in service. By 1962 only three remained, with C 7 scrapped on 10 May 1962 and C13 on 15 May 1962. C10 was withdrawn for preservation on 18 May 1962, having travelled 1 160 856 miles during forty years in service.

Builder: Newport Workshops 26

Preserved: C10, at ARHS Railway Museum, Champion Rd, North Williamstown.

Above: *Built at Newport Workshops, C5 entered service with Victorian Railways on 5 December 1921. In May 1933 it was the first locomotive used by Victorian Railways to be fitted with a modified front end which included the loss of its curved chimney for the stovepipe model. Withdrawn from service on 1 August 1958, it was scrapped a week later on 7 August, having travelled 1 045 905 miles during thirty-seven years in service. Listed weight in working order of this locomotive and tender was 128 tons 4 cwt with a combined length of 65 ft 3 in from buffer to buffer. For more details see* The Era of the C & X Class Locomotives in the Victorian Railways, *S. Watson.*

B uilt in 1922–23 by Perry Engineering in South Australia, the four R class locomotives were designed to haul passenger services, and took over most main line passenger services when introduced in 1923. Working from Hobart north to Launceston, Devonport and Burnie, they were also used on the Derwent Valley line from Hobart to National Park, and Maydena to the west during the summer months. The R class was also used at times on main line goods services, which continued until 1953 when they were mainly restricted to working the western line, hauling the daily all-stations passenger service from Launceston to Wynyard. They were also used on goods services from Launceston to Western

R CLASS (TAS)
WHEEL ARRANGEMENT: 4-6-2
PASSENGER LOCOMOTIVE
4 IN CLASS
FINAL NOS: R1–R4

Junction and Deloraine, and sometimes went as far west as Smithton.

On 30 June 1955, three of the R class locomotives were based at Launceston, with the other based to the west at Wynyard. In September 1957 the second-division passenger train from Launceston to Wynyard was cancelled, and R3 was withdrawn from service, followed by R1 in October. These were the last of the R class, R2 and R4 having been withdrawn from service the previous year.

Builder: Perry Engineering 4
Preserved: Nil

Above: Built by Perry Engineering in South Australia in 1923, R4 entered service with Tasmanian Government Railways in 1923. It was withdrawn from service in 1956 after thirty-three years in service. Listed weight in working order of this locomotive and tender was 97 tons 15 cwt 3 qtr with a combined length of about 59 ft 2 in from buffer to buffer. For more details see The Decline of Steam Power on the Tasmanian Government Railways 1945–1965, H.J.W. Stokes, ARHS Bulletin No 347, September 1966, p. 193–202.

In the early 1920s the need for a new express locomotive was evident, with delivery needed before the 1924–5 wheat harvest. After problems calling tenders for supply, the North British Locomotive Co of Glasgow built a total of ten locomotives, which arrived in two groups. Nos 441 to 446 all entered service between 13 and 27 December 1924. The second group entered service in early 1925, with Nos 447 and 450 on 14 February, and Nos 448 and 449 on 21 February.

All ten were exclusively used on express passenger services between Perth and Kalgoorlie. With a 30 percent saving on fuel, and savings on water, it meant fewer stops and reduced travel times. During the mid 1920s, boiler problems were caused by the high salt content in water coming from Mundaring Weir, the water supply for the Goldfields. Apart from this the locomotives had few problems and were popular with crews.

P CLASS (WA)
WHEEL ARRANGEMENT: 4-6-2
EXPRESS PASSENGER LOCOMOTIVE
25 IN CLASS
NO ENTERING SERVICE: 441–465
FINAL NOS: 501–517

The success of the P class resulted in an order for ten more to be built by the Midland Railway Workshops, with the first, No 451, in service on 28 February 1927 and the last, No 460, on 1 October 1927. The final batch of these locomotives was delivered in 1929, with Nos 461 to 465 all in service between January and May. During their time in service, the P class had the lowest running costs of any locomotive, with over 100 000 miles travelled between overhauls. They continued working the main line passenger services between Perth, Kalgoorlie, Albany and Bunbury until the late 1930s. After being renumbered in 1949, they remained in service until the late 1960s. The last five were all withdrawn on 6 October 1969, after about forty-five years in service.

Builders: North British Locomotive Co 10; Midland Junction Workshops 15

Preserved: No 508 (first numbered 448), at ARHS Railway Museum, Bassendean.

Above: Built by North British Locomotive Co Glasgow in 1924, No 443 entered service on 27 December 1924. It was renumbered 503 on 2 May 1947, and was withdrawn from service on 6 October 1969 after forty-five years in service. Listed weight in working order of this locomotive and tender was 102 tons 5 cwt with a combined length of 62 ft 2 in from buffer to buffer. For more details see A History of W.A.G.R. Steam Locomotives, *A. Gunzburg, ARHS(WA) 1984, p. 102–7.*

The first of its class, No 3601 entered service with N.S.W. Government Railways on 7 January 1925. The final locomotive entered service on 19 June 1928 as No 3675. Nicknamed 'Pigs', the class was designed by N.S.W. Government Railways for long journeys using the same locomotive, with up to a hundred miles between stops. The basic design was also used in 1938 to construct C class locomotives for the Commonwealth Railways, which required them to work the Port Pirie–Kalgoorlie line. However the C class was equipped with much larger 12-wheel tenders.

Initially there were many problems with the (C)36 class, but once solved these locomotives were found to be excellent. They replaced the (C)32 and (C)35 classes on the heavier services, and cut travelling time by eliminating water stops. During the early 1930s these locomotives set numerous record times, hauling passenger trains on the southern, western and northern lines.

(C)36 CLASS (NSW)
WHEEL ARRANGEMENT: 4–6–0
EXPRESS PASSENGER LOCOMOTIVE
75 IN CLASS
FINAL NOS: 3601–3675

By the late 1930s the increasing size of express trains made it necessary to use two locomotives per train. By the late 1940s the new (C)38 class replaced the (C)36 on many of the heaviest express and mail services. Between 1953 and 1957, all but two of the class had new Belpaire-type boilers fitted.

From 1958 they began to be withdrawn from service. In the 1960s some were used for a time hauling goods trains, several of the class being fitted with power reverse equipment taken from withdrawn 57 and 58 classes, which assisted in shunting or pickup goods work. The last of the class in regular service was No 3642, withdrawn on 30 September 1969.

Builders: Eveleigh Workshops 10; Clyde Engineering Co 65.

Preserved: Nos 3609, 3616 and 3642, at Rail Transport Museum, Thirlmere. No 3642 is in working order and used to haul heritage trains.

Above: The class leader, shown without headlight as originally introduced, was delivered to N.S.W. Government Railways and entered service on 7 January 1925 as No 3601. It was rebuilt with the Belpaire boiler in early 1954. Withdrawn in February 1962, it was scrapped on 14 May 1963, having travelled 1 570 079 miles during thirty-seven years of service. Listed weight in working order of this locomotive and tender was 159 tons 9 cwt while the combined length of locomotive and tender was 67 ft 11½ in from buffer to buffer. For more details see A Compendium of NSW Steam Locomotives, compiled by A. Grunbach, ARHS(NSW) 1989, p. 184–94.

The need for a new heavy goods locomotive for main line use resulted in the N class, designed by A.E. Smith and built by the Newport Workshops. The first of the N class, No 110 (later No 419) entered service with Victorian Railways on 25 May 1925, with No 432 the last on 25 July 1951. The class was built in two groups. The first, from Newport Workshops, entered service between 1925 and 1931 (Nos 110–139 were all renumbered in 1950), and the second, built by North British Locomotive Co, between 1950 and 1951. Newport Workshops built Nos 430, 431 and 432 in 1950 and 1951.

On entering service the N class was assigned to haul freight, relieving the DD class which was hard pressed at that time to keep up with demand. During the 1930s No 110 was used for experimental modifications, including auto couplers, electric lights, a modified front end and smoke deflectors.

N CLASS (VIC)
WHEEL ARRANGEMENT: 2-8-2
GOODS LOCOMOTIVE
33 IN CLASS
FINAL NOS 400-432

In later the years the N class made headlines for different reasons. No 430 was painted hawthorn green with yellow and black trim, and hauled the Centenary Jubilee train on a 6000 mile journey to 200 centres, with 535 250 people inspecting the display between February and June 1951. In 1952, No 408 made history of the worst kind when, whilst hauling a heavy wheat train, it collided with a tourist bus on a level crossing at Horsham. Twelve people were killed.

On 1 December 1958, No 419 was the first to be scrapped, having travelled 676 235 miles. The last to go on 15 July 1966 was No 428, having travelled 613 764 miles in thirty-five years in service.

Builders: Newport Workshops 33
Preserved: No 432, at ARHS Railway Museum, Champion Rd, North Williamstown.

Above: Built by Newport Workshops, No 110 entered service on 23 May 1925. In July 1936 a modified front-end conversion was carried out. It was scrapped on 1 December 1958, having travelled 676 235 miles in thirty-three years in service. Listed weight in working order of this locomotive and tender was 120 tons 13 cwt with a combined length of 66 ft 6⅛ in over couplers. For more details see The Era of the N Class Locomotives in the Victorian Railways, *S. Watson.*

In order to cope with increased suburban traffic it was decided that more tank engines should be built. They were to be superheated and have larger cylinders. While approval for their construction was given in late 1920, changes in the design meant another two years passed before work got under way. It was March 1924 before No. 26 and No. 47, built by Walkers Ltd, entered service. No. 886, built by Ipswich Railway Workshops, was the last into service in August 1942. A number of modifications were made to later locomotives as they were being built, and the earlier locomotives were also modified.

6D17 CLASS (QLD)
WHEEL ARRANGEMENT: 4-6-4T
SUBURBAN TANK LOCOMOTIVE
30 IN CLASS
FINAL NOS: 26, 47, 53, 56, 60, 75–7, 85, 112–4, 122, 137, 260, 262, 266–269, 853–857, 882–886

Used on passenger services in the Brisbane metropolitan area, they were known as the Black Tanks, and had a distinctive panting and puffing sound. A typical seven carriage train weighed about 160 tons, while the Brisbane to Ipswich goods service hauled a load of 420 tons. Withdrawals began in the early 1960s, with No. 47 the first to go in late 1961. Most were taken out of service in 1967, with Nos 53 and 75 the last to go in December 1968.

Builders: Walkers Ltd. 10; Ipswich Railway Workshops 20

Preserved: No. 855, at ARHS Queensland Division Kunkala, Queensland.

Above: Built by Ipswich Railway Workshops, No. 85 entered service with Queensland Government Railways in May 1925; shown here as it looked after 1951. It was written off in April 1963 after thirty-eight years. The listed weight in working order of this locomotive was 58 tons 8 cwt and it was about 40 ft in length from buffer to buffer. For more details see Locomotives in the Tropics Vol. 2, *J. Armstrong, ARHS(Qld) 1994, p. 71–7.*

J R TURNER
011002 854 096

Built by Vulcan Foundry, England in 1903, this locomotive entered service with Western Australian Government Railways on 15 February 1904. It had been ordered for use as a shunter and mobile crane at the Midland Junction Workshops which were then under construction, with work completed in January 1905.

A typical locomotive of its type, it had a 14 ft long fixed jib and could lift 3 tons, using one of two small twin-cylinder steam engines to lift and the second to slew the crane. The locomotive had side tanks and a rear fuel bunker which formed part of the support for the crane. It was confined to operating within the Workshop yard and carried a sign on its tanks which read 'Loco Crane—Must Not Leave Workshops Yard'. The workshop staff were responsible for its

U CLASS (WA)
WHEEL ARRANGEMENT: 0-6-0T
CRANE TANK LOCOMOTIVE
1 IN CLASS
FINAL NO: 7

repairs and maintenance during this time.

On 30 June 1925 it re-entered service again as the Workshops' shunter. The crane had been removed and the fuel bunker increased in size by half a ton, while the water capacity had been increased by 360 gallons. In January 1939 No. 7, which was the third locomotive to use this number, was replaced by a B class shunter, No. 14, and it was intended to convert No. 7 to a B class. However it was withdrawn from service on 15 June 1940 and scrapped after thirty-six years in service.

Builder: Vulcan Foundry, England 1

Preserved: Nil

Above: Built by Vulcan Foundry, England in 1903, No. 7 entered service with Western Australian Government Railways on 15 February 1904. The crane was later removed and it re-entered service on 30 June 1925 as shown here. It was withdrawn from service in January 1939 and scrapped on 15 June 1940. The listed weight in working order of this locomotive was 35 tons 4 cwt without the crane and it was 27 ft 8¼ in from buffer to buffer. For more details see A History of W.A.G.R. Steam Locomotives, *A. Gunzburg, ARHS(WA) 1984, p. 87–8.*

By 1924 the B15 locomotives were widely used on many branch lines. As new lines opened, tenders were called for the construction of a new batch of PB15 locomotives, and eventually an order was placed with Walkers Limited for six engines. This was followed by a second tender for 24 engines which Walkers won in November 1924. The first of these, No. 5, entered service in October 1925 and the last, No. 751 in July 1926.

One of the major changes made was to use Walschaerts valve gear instead of the Stephenson link motion previously used. Fitting larger tenders meant the B13s could travel long distances without taking on water, which was an important factor when in the west of the state. They worked mail trains

PB15 (1924) CLASS (QLD)
WHEEL ARRANGEMENT: 4-6-0
PASSENGER LOCOMOTIVE
30 IN CLASS
FINAL NOS: 5, 103, 126, 128, 143, 220, 286, 339, 340, 731–751

in inland Queensland, from Chinchilla and Roma to Charleville and Cunnamulla, Cloncurry to Mount Isa, even Innisfail to Cairns. In some cases the trains were given nicknames. The service connecting Charleville and Quilpie was known as the 'Flying Flea', its small size and few stops making it one of the fastest trains in Queensland. No. 744, which was used on tourist trains to Kuranda, was known as 'Miss Cairns'. The class was withdrawn from service between 1967 and August 1970, after forty-five years in service.

Builder: Walkers Limited, Maryborough 30

Preserved: No. 732, at Queensland Rail; No. 738, at ARHS, Freeman Rd, Kunkala.

Above: Built by Walkers Limited, No. 5 entered service in October 1925 and was withdrawn from service in June 1968 after about forty-three years in service. The listed weight in working order of locomotive and tender was 62 tons 1 cwt with a combined length of 47 ft 6 in from buffer to buffer. For more details see Locomotives in the Tropics Vol. 2, by J. Armstrong, ARHS(Qld) 1994 p. 79–83.

By 1922 new locomotives were needed that were suitable for use on the 2400 miles of 45 lb track in rural areas, and in 1923 the L class locomotives were approved. They were built at Midland Junction Workshops using some parts from the old Ec class, mainly the bar frames and wheels along with the original cabs and tenders, but with new boilers, simple expansion cylinders and Walschaerts valve gear. The first to enter service was No. 250 on 19 January 1924 with the last, No. 240, on 19 December 1925. All these locomotives carried old Ec class numbers when in service.

The cost of building the L class was recovered in four years, as they were cheaper per mile to operate than the Ec class they replaced. They were said to be popular with crews due to

L CLASS (WA)
WHEEL ARRANGEMENT: 4-6-2
GOODS LOCOMOTIVE
20 IN CLASS
NOS ON ENTERING SERVICE: 236-55
FINAL NOS: 471-90

improvements in the cab, and became the standard locomotive used on agricultural main line tracks.

During the 1930s a number of the engine frames developed serious cracks and between 1934 and 1948 a total of fourteen locomotives were fitted with new frames. With a few minor changes they operated until the late 1950s when many were withdrawn from service, with No. 484 the last to go on 7 May 1958 after about thirty-four years in service. They were superseded by the W class on the light lines.

Builder: Midland Railway Workshops 20

Preserved: Nil

Above: Built by Midland Junction Workshops, No. 241 entered service on 12 December 1925. It was re-framed on 13 November 1935, re-numbered No. 476 on 2 November 1948 and was withdrawn from service on 14 March 1957 after thirty-two years of service. The listed weight in working order of this locomotive and tender was 77 tons 12 cwt with a combined length of 56 ft 8 in from buffer to buffer. For more details see A History of W.A.G.R. Steam Locomotives, A. Gunzburg, ARHS(WA) 1984, p. 100–1.

Designed by F.J. Shea and built in England by Sir W.G. Armstrong-Whitworth & Co, the 700 class was intended for use on light lines. The first to enter service was No. 700 which was unloaded from the steamer *Beldis* on 20 March 1926. It made a test run on the North Line on 27 April 1926 and had covered over 1500 miles by the time the remaining nine 700 class locomotives arrived on the steamer *Belday* on 29 June 1926. Several problems were evident with bearings and springs, but after modification these were solved and the class performed well and the locomotives required very few changes throughout their time in service. They were used on almost every broad gauge line

700 CLASS (SA)
WHEEL ARRANGEMENT: 2-8-2
GOODS LOCOMOTIVE
10 IN CLASS
FINAL NOS: 700-709

throughout the state hauling both goods and passenger services.

Following WW II five of the class were converted to burn oil, but in the 1960s they were converted back to coal until withdrawn from service, with No. 703 and No. 707 both condemned on 9 June 1959. In the mid 1960s there were still five in service, but three were condemned in October 1966. No. 700 was the last to go on 18 September 1967, having travelled 781 660 miles during forty-one years in service.

Builder: Sir W.G. Armstrong-Whitworth & Co. 10

Preserved: No. 702, at Port Dock Railway Museum (SA) Inc, Port Adelaide.

Above: Built by Sir W.G. Armstrong-Whitworth & Co in England, No. 700 entered service in June 1926. In 1949 it was converted to burn a coal-oil mixture. In 1958 it became an oil burner but was converted back to coal in 1964. It was withdrawn from service in April 1967. The listed weight in working order of this locomotive and tender was 171 tons 3 cwt with a combined length of 73 ft 1½ in from buffer to buffer. For more detail see The 700 Series of Locomotives of the South Australian Railways, D. Colquhoun, R. Stewein and A. Thomas, ARHS (SA Division) Inc, 1979, p. 7–19.

G CLASS (VIC)
WHEEL ARRANGEMENT: 2-6-0 0-6-2
NARROW GAUGE LOCOMOTIVE
2 IN CLASS
FINAL NOS: 41-42

With increasing traffic on the series of narrow gauge railways, NA class locomotives were finding it difficult to maintain the service, often having to double-head as loads increased. To overcome this problem two Garratt articulated locomotives were ordered from Beyer Peacock & Co in England. They arrived in Australia during April 1926 on the *SS Ferndale*, and were assembled and painted black at Newport Workshops. They were numbered G41 and G42.

G41 was transported to Colac for use on the seventy-kilometre line to Crowes, where the Garratt was able to haul a load of 255 tons. The NA could only haul 68 tons on the same section. G42 was sent to Moe to replace NA 12A on the Moe–Walhalla line, where a similarly dramatic increase was noted. Where 12A could haul only 55 tons on this line, G42 could haul 180 tons. Notwithstanding the increased loads, the Garratts used 40 percent less water and fuel.

The increased use of road transport gradually closed lines, and on 31 March 1944 G42 hauled the last train on the Platina–Walhalla line. In October 1952 it hauled the last train on the Erica–Platina line. On 26 June 1954 the Erica–Moe line closed and G42 was transferred to Colac to replace G41. On March 8 1961 G42 made the last run to Crowes, recovering rails. On 30 June 1962 it hauled the last train between Colac and Beech Forest, with the Colac–Weeaproinah line also closing on that day. On 10 July 1962, G42 was transported to Newport Workshops and stored.

In July 1964 it was bought by the Puffing Billy Preservation Society and is undergoing restoration for return to service.

Builder: Beyer Peacock & Co 2
Preserved: No. G42, at Puffing Billy Preservation Society, Belgrave.

Above: Built by Beyer Peacock & Co in England in 1926, G42 was the second of its class. It entered service on 28 June 1926 and after 36 years was withdrawn from service on 10 July 1952. The listed weight in working order of this locomotive was 69 tons 1 cwt and was 52 ft 6 in from buffer to buffer. For more details see Steam on the Two Foot Six Vol. 1—Locomotives, *P. Medlin, 1992.*

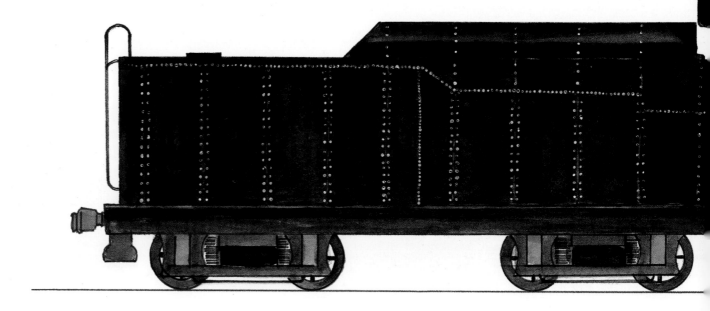

In 1923 tenders were called for a new Express Passenger locomotive to replace the Rx, Q and S classes then used on passenger services. In late 1923 Sir W.G. Armstrong-Whitworth & Co were instructed to build ten 600 class locomotives. During April 1926 they began to arrive in Adelaide from England on the steamers *Beldis* and *Belday*, which were built especially to carry railway locomotives. The first into service was No. 601 on 10 May 1926, while No. 609 was the last on 21 August 1926.

Built for use on express passenger services between Murray Bridge and Serviceton, the 600 class was almost three times as powerful as the S class and over seventy percent more powerful than the Rx class then in use on that line. As broad gauge lines were extended, the 600s were used as far as Port Pirie

600 CLASS (SA)
WHEEL ARRANGEMENT: 4-6-2
EXPRESS PASSENGER LOCOMOTIVE
10 IN CLASS
NOS: 600-609

after 1937, then on the Wolseley to Mount Gambier line and sometimes south to Victor Harbour. When used for hauling goods trains the 600 class was able to take a load of 1200 tons between Tailem Bend and Serviceton, or 1000 tons on the Port Pirie line. These powerful locomotives never reached their full potential, with speed restricted due to the standard of the track. They were the first to go when diesels were introduced. Nos 601 and 605 were the first to be condemned on 26 March 1958, while No. 603 was the last, condemned on 6 July 1961 after having travelled 1 071 961 miles in about thirty-five years in service.

Builder: Sir W. G. Armstrong-Whitworth & Co 10
Preserved: Nil

Above: Built by Sir W.G. Armstrong-Whitworth & Co in England, No. 600 entered service with South Australian Government Railways on 14 August 1926. It was condemned on 9 June 1959 and was cut up at Islington on 26 September 1961 after having travelled 1 512 812 miles during thirty-five years in service. The listed weight in working order of this locomotive and tender was 199 tons 11 cwt 2 qtr with a combined length of 79 ft 33¼ in from buffer to buffer. For more details see Steam Locomotives and Railcar of the South Australian Railways, R.E. Fluck, R. Sampson and K.J Bird, Mile End Railway Museum 1986, p. 91–2

The need for a locomotive able to haul heavy passenger and goods services over the steep grades of the Mount Lofty ranges resulted in the design of the 500 class by F.J. Shea, Assistant Chief Mechanical Engineer. Built by Sir W.G. Armstrong-Whitworth & Co in England, No. 502 was the first to enter service on 22 May 1926, the last being No. 505 on 28 October 1926. Each of these locomotives was given the name of a well-known person from South Australia.

The most powerful two cylinder locomotives to be used in Australia and the largest and most powerful used by the South Australian Government Railways, they spent most of their time in service on the Main South Line hauling heavy goods loads over the Mount Lofty ranges. They were also used

500 CLASS (SA)
WHEEL ARRANGEMENT: 4-8-2
PASSENGER, HEAVY GOODS
LOCOMOTIVE
10 IN CLASS
NOS: 500-509

on the Melbourne Express, which had previously been hauled by two Rx locomotives with a third pushing to climb the Mount Lofty ranges.

After nearly three years in service, No. 507 was the first to be converted to a 500B class on 17 April 1929. This conversion involved the removal of the two wheel trailing truck and replacing it with a four wheel Delta trailing truck and booster, which increased the tractive effort of the locomotive from 51 000 lb to 59 000 lb. During 1929 and 1930 all but two were converted and these, Nos 503 and 508, were converted in 1936.

Builder.: W. G. Armstrong-Whitworth & Co 10

Preserved: Nil

Above: Built by Sir W. G. Armstrong-Whitworth & Co. in England No. 507 entered service with South Australian Government Railways on 12 October 1926. Named Margaret Murray it was used to haul the Royal Train on 4 April 1927.
It was converted to a 500B class on 17 April 1929 and scrapped on 26 March 1958. The listed weight in working order of this locomotive and tender was 218 tons 13 cwt with a combined length of 83 ft 11 in from buffer to buffer.
For more details see Steam Locomotives and Railcars of the South Australian Railways, R.E. Fluck, R. Sampson and K.J. Bird, Mile End Railway Museum 1986, p. 95.

These three locomotives were built by John Fowler & Co in England. The first, No. 9, was built in 1924 and entered service in December of that year. Though the 0–6–0 Hudswell Clarke locomotives at the CSR mills were larger, these were some of the biggest 2 ft gauge locomotives built for Australian customers by Fowler & Co. They were employed on the steep Nerada line of the Innisfail tramway, where their load of cane trucks to the South Johnstone sugar mill was limited to fifty tons. However they could haul 192 tons when used on the harbour line. Until 1959, sugar was shipped in jute bags on open bogie wagons. Bulk containers were then used from 1960. At first the old bogie wagons were used but these were soon replaced by specially built wagons.

B9½ CLASS (QLD)
WHEEL ARRANGEMENT: 0–6–2
NARROW GAUGE GOODS
LOCOMOTIVE
3 IN CLASS
FINAL NOS: 9, 10, 11

The first withdrawal from service was No. 9 in June 1961, with Nos 10 and 11 being withdrawn in June 1963. Local interest resulted in No. 11 being placed in Fitzgerald Park at Innisfail in 1964. After a number of moves in succeeding years it eventually ended up with the Australian Narrow Gauge Railway Museum Society headquarters at Woodford, near Caboolture in Queensland, where there are a number of cane industry locomotives on display. The boiler from another of this class ended its life as a steam plant for a sawmill.

Builder: John Fowler & Co England 3
Preserved: No. 11, at Australian Narrow Gauge Railway, Woodford.

Above: Built in England by John Fowler & Co in 1924 No. 9 entered service in 1924. It was withdrawn from service in June 1961. The listed weight in working order of locomotive and tender was 22 tons 12 cwt, and the combined length was 33 ft 6 in over the centre couplers. For more details see Locomotives in the Tropics Vol. 2, J. Armstrong, ARHS(Qld) 1994, p. 29–30.

RA CLASS (WA)
WHEEL ARRANGEMENT: 4-4-2
PASSENGER LOCOMOTIVE
14 IN CLASS
FINAL NOS: 148, 150, 153-4, 174-5,
177-8, 227-32

Builder: Dubs & Co (converted by Midland) 14
Preserved: Nil

Built by Dubs & Co in two batches in 1896 and 1898, the R class was used on express passenger and main line mail trains. Although the light rail lines were gradually being replaced with 60 lb rails some bottlenecks still existed, with sections of 45 lb rail which could not be replaced as there were no funds available. To overcome the problem, twelve R class locomotives were converted from 4-4-0 to a 4-4-2 wheel arrangement. This, with other modifications, reduced the load on the driving wheels so that they could operate on the 45 lb track.

By the mid 1920s a number of R and Ra class locomotives had been withdrawn from service, although six Ra class were still in use. These were used on the 45 lb sections of the South-Western and Northern railways.

On 30 September 1933 the Ra class was re-classified R but remained as 4-4-2. Nos 175 and 232 were withdrawn in the early 1940s, while three of the remaining four—Nos 148, 174 and 228—were withdrawn on 4 September 1947. No. 150 was the last to go, on 19 October 1948 after about fifty-two years in service.

Above: Built by Dubs & Co in 1896, No. 148 entered service with Western Australian Government Railways on 5 March 1897 and was converted to Ra class on 18 February 1928. After 50 years, it was withdrawn from service on 4 September 1947. The listed weight in working order of this locomotive and tender was 57 tons 1 cwt with a combined length of 48 ft 6 in from buffer to buffer. For more details see A History of W.A.G.R. Steam Locomotives, A. Gunzburg, ARHS(WA) 1984, p. 63–5.

esigned by A.E. Smith, the Chief Mechanical Engineer with Victorian Railways, the S class locomotives were built between 1919 and 1928 by Newport Workshops. S300 was the first to enter service on 14 March 1928, and S303 was the last in service on 15 November 1930.

On entering service S300 proved to be very reliable and able to run for long periods at high speed. It was put in service hauling the Sydney Limited, and immediately reduced travelling times by thirty minutes in each direction. Until that time Sydney Limited was hauled by a pair of A2 locomotives. The fame of the S class spread worldwide, with the reliability and high speed of the service they provided giving Victorian Railways an inestimable amount of publicity and prestige.

The combined mileage of the four S class locomotives from April 1928 until they were streamlined on 23 November 1939 was 2 243 949 miles, on runs between Melbourne and Albury.

S CLASS (VIC)
WHEEL ARRANGEMENT: 4-6-2
EXPRESS PASSENGER LOCOMOTIVE
4 IN CLASS
FINAL NOS: S300-S303

Builder: Newport Workshops 4

Preserved: Nil

Above: Built by Newport Workshops, No. S300 was the first of its class to enter service on 14 March 1928. It was used on the Sydney Limited express passenger service between Melbourne and Albury, as shown here, until it was streamlined. It then entered service with the Spirit of Progress which began service from Melbourne to Albury return on 23 November 1937. The listed weight in working order of this locomotive and tender was 194 tons 13 cwt with a combined length of 78 ft 6¾ in from buffer to buffer. For more details see The Era of the S Class and H220 Locomotives in the Victorian Railways, S. Watson.

Following the rebuilding of six of the C class to form the CC class, it was decided that four more of the Beyer Peacock-built C class would be rebuilt. The work was carried out between 1924 and 1928, and the locomotives were fitted with superheating and Walschaerts valve gear. They were then known as the CCS class, while still retaining their C class numbers. These locomotives were used for the same work as the C and CC classes including goods, mixed goods and shunting. On some occasions they were used on passenger trains.

Most of the CCS class were used at Devonport and Launceston in north Tasmania, but following WW II one worked on both freight and passenger services in the Hobart area. Another was

CCS CLASS (TAS)
WHEEL ARRANGEMENT: 2-6-0
GOODS LOCOMOTIVE
4 IN CLASS
FINAL NOS: CCS 21, 23-25

based at Zeehan and was used on goods and mixed services.

As more X class diesels came into use, the CCS class was used only when needed, or for special tours such as those of the Australian Railway Explorers Association in 1964 and 1965. One locomotive ran the Mole Creek Line service. By April 1965 only CCS 23 and CCS 25 remained in service. When they were withdrawn, both were preserved by the Van Diemen Light Railway Society, at Don Village, Devonport.

Builder: Tasmanian Government Railway Workshops 4
Preserved: CCS 23 and CCS 25, at Van Diemen Light Railway Society, Don Village, Devonport.

Above: Built by Beyer Peacock & Co in England, C23 entered service in 1902 and was rebuilt by Tasmanian Government Railway Workshops in 1928 to become CCS 23. Withdrawn from Tasmanian Government Railway service in the mid 1970s, it was used to haul tourist trains with the Van Diemen Light Railway Society at Don Village, Devonport, but has been out of use for several years. The listed weight in working order of this locomotive and tender was 56 tons 4 cwt, with a combined length of 42 ft 11 in from buffer to buffer. For more details see The Decline of Steam Power on the Tasmanian Government Railways 1945–1965, *H.J.W. Stokes, ARHS Bulletin No. 347, September 1966, p. 193–202.*

The problems created by having different railway gauges in different states were investigated by a Royal Commission in 1921, which recommended that from 1923, all new Victorian Railways locomotives should be built so that they could be converted from broad to standard gauge if required. In 1925 the need for a new heavy goods locomotive resulted in the X class being built at Newport Workshops.

The first, No. 27, entered service on 19 March 1929. No. 55 was the last in service on 24 October 1947. The X class were the most powerful goods locomotive used in Victoria until the introduction of the H class in 1941. When double heading with a C class it was not uncommon for the X class to haul it

X CLASS (VIC)
WHEEL ARRANGEMENT: 2-8-2
HEAVY GOODS LOCOMOTIVE
29 IN CLASS
FINAL NOS 27-55

as well as the load, especially on long grades. The introduction of diesel locomotives resulted in an order which had been placed with Clyde Engineering for fifteen more X class being cancelled in 1952.

No. 43 was withdrawn on 31 August 1955 and scrapped on 12 April 1957, the first of the class to go. The last was No. 29; it was withdrawn on 6 December 1960 and scrapped on 6 February 1961, having travelled 821 819 miles during thirty years in service.

Builder: Newport Workshops 29
Preserved: No. 36, at ARHS Railway Museum, Champion Rd, North Williamstown.

Above: Built by Newport Workshops, X 28 entered service with Victorian Railways on 20 March 1929. It was withdrawn from service on 27 May 1959 and scrapped on 27 July 1957, having travelled 782 020 miles during thirty years in service. The listed weight in working order of this locomotive and tender was 185 tons 6 cwt, with a combined length of 77 ft 4¼ in from buffer to buffer. For more details see
The Era of the C & X Class Locomotives in the Victorian Railways, S. Watson.

With the success of the 700 class it was decided in late 1927 to build ten more of these locomotives at the Islington Workshops, and although a few modifications were made they were basically identical to the 700 class. The first to enter service was No. 710 on 25 October 1928, and the last No. 719 on 1 August 1929. They were all built with a booster fitted to the trailing truck, but due to weight limits it was removed from No. 714 in early 1931. This alteration was made to another five locomotives in 1932, and the remaining four in 1938 and 1939. They were used on main and secondary broad gauge

710 CLASS (SA)
WHEEL ARRANGEMENT: 2-8-2
GOODS LOCOMOTIVE
10 IN CLASS
NOS: 710-719

Builder: South Australian Railways Islington Workshops 10
Preserved: Nil

lines for both freight and passenger services.

The first to be withdrawn from service was No. 712 on 6 July 1961. It was cut up at Islington on 24 October 1962. By late 1965 only two remained in service. No. 717 was withdrawn in 1967, with No. 718 the last to go on 2 June 1968. It was cut up at Islington on 5 October 1968, having travelled 617 082 miles during thirty-nine years in service.

Above: Built at the Islington Workshops, No. 719 entered service on 1 August 1929. It was the only locomotive used in South Australia to be fitted with a Worthington Type BL2 feed-water heater, but this was removed in 1943. Withdrawn from service on 16 July 1963, No. 709 was cut up at Islington on 21 October 1964, having travelled 611 805 miles in about thirty-four years in service. When in use the combined weight of locomotive and tender was 175 tons 16 cwt, with a combined length of 75 ft 7¼ in from buffer to buffer. For more details see The 700 Series of Locomotives of the South Australian Railways, D. Colquhoun, R. Stewien and A. Thomas, ARHS(SA) 1979, p. 21–3.

Imported from England by contractor E.H.V. Keane, this locomotive was one of four built for him by Hudswell Clarke & Co in 1891. It was originally named *Perth*, but this was removed soon after delivery. After use on railway construction it was sold to the Perth Metropolitan Waterworks Board, and then sold again to Hendrickson & Knutson and shipped to Tasmania for use on the construction of breakwaters at East Devonport. It was later bought by J.S. Lee of Smithton for his sawmill, and used to transport timber on the Marrawah Tramway. When the Public Works Department bought the tramway, the locomotive was hired to them by Mr. Lee. On 6 November 1915 the department bought the locomotive from him for 450 pounds, and it was renamed *Six-Wheeler*.

SIX-WHEELER (TAS)
WHEEL ARRANGEMENT: 0-6-0ST
SADDLE-TANK LOCOMOTIVE
1 IN CLASS
FINAL NO: 2

Following an overhaul in Launceston in 1916, the locomotive returned to service on the tramway in January 1917. In August 1929 *Six-Wheeler* was transferred to the Tasmanian Government Railways. It was written off in 1938–39 but was not sold until 1947, when F. Jaeger, a sawmiller from Salmon River near Smithton, bought the locomotive and later rebuilt it with a diesel engine. Finally abandoned near Hayes timber mill on the Marrawah road, it was removed for preservation in January 1973 and combined with the boiler from another locomotive. It was placed at Marrawah Hall, but was later scrapped.

Builder: Hudswell Clarke & Co 1

Preserved: Nil

Above: Built by Hudswell Clarke & Co. in 1891 and known as Perth, it was shipped to Tasmania from Western Australia in 1901. Bought by the Tasmanian Public Works Department in 1915, it was renamed Six-Wheeler. It was sold again to the Tasmanian Government Railways in August 1929, and was written off in 1938–39. While its weight is not recorded this locomotive was about 19 ft in length. For more details see The Midland Railway Company Locomotives of Western Australia, *A. Gunzburg, Light Railway Research Society of Australia 1989, p. 9–10, 12.*

Big Ben was built by the Baldwin Locomotive Co of Philadelphia, in 1919. It was bought by Mr. Ford, the manager of the Marrawah Tramway to move the increasing volume of timber from Mr Lee's sawmill. *Big Ben* was shipped from New York and arrived in Hobart probably in January 1920. It had a large number 3 on the smokebox door, possibly due to numbers assigned to the other tramway locomotives with *Spider* No. 1 and *Six-Wheeler* No. 2. The only new locomotive to be used on the tramway was *Big Ben*.

Following an overhaul at Launceston in 1948, *Big Ben* was sent south to work goods trains on

BIG BEN (TAS)
WHEEL ARRANGEMENT: 0–6–0ST
SADDLE-TANK LOCOMOTIVE
1 IN CLASS
FINAL NO: 3

Builder: Baldwin Locomotive Co 1
Preserved: Nil

the Parattah to Oatlands branch line just prior to its closure. This line was not able to take a locomotive larger than a 2–6–0 which, if used on the line, would not have been fully employed while locomotives were needed on other branch lines.

After the line closed, *Big Ben* was sent to Launceston and withdrawn from service. It was sold for scrap in October 1951.

Above: Built by the Baldwin Locomotive Co in 1919, Big Ben entered service with Tasmanian Government Railways in August 1929 and was withdrawn from service around 1950. The listed weight in working order of this locomotive was 14 tons 16 cwt and was 19 ft 11 in long. For more details see Locomotives of the Marrawah Tramway, H.J.W. Stokes, In Light Railways, Spring 1972, p. 4–6.

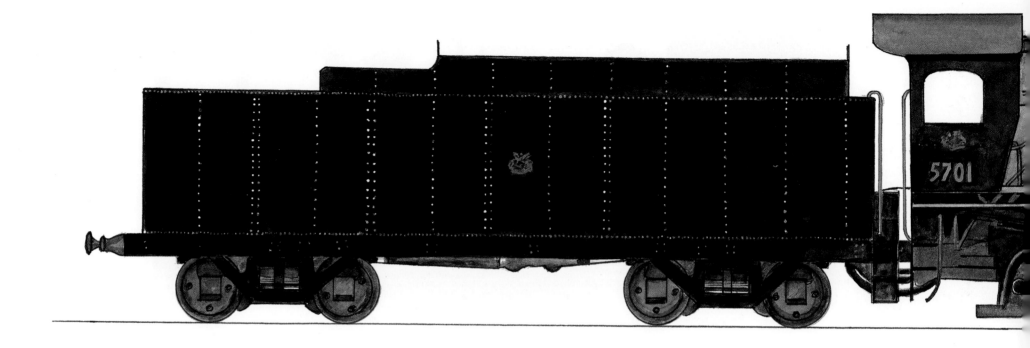

The first of a total of 25 locomotives of this class, No. 5701 entered service with N.S.W. Government Railways on 6 September 1929. The last entered service on 8 December 1930. The locomotives were built by the Clyde Engineering Co at Granville, but the tenders came from Mort's Dock & Engineering Co in Newcastle.

The first 'Mountain' type locomotive to be used in NSW, it was designed by the N.S.W. Government Railways and included many improvements which gave an increase in tractive effort of 67 percent over the standard goods (D50/53/55) classes. By the standards of the time, some very heavy loads were hauled, including a record 2000 ton load down the Blue Mountains by No. 5712 in November 1934.

(D)57 CLASS (NSW)
WHEEL ARRANGEMENT: 4-8-2
HEAVY GOODS LOCOMOTIVE
25 IN CLASS
FINAL NOS: 5701-5725

An early problem with the air compressor was solved by moving it from the middle of the boiler to the side of the smoke box. Because of their weight and width, the (D)57s were restricted to working between Enfield and Thirroul (Illawarra), Junee (south) and Lithgow (west). Electrification of the line to Lithgow in 1957 caused many (D)57s to be withdrawn, the remainder ending their days on the Illawarra and southern lines.

In October 1961 No. 5711 was the last of its class withdrawn from the southern line, having travelled 1 017 354 miles during thirty-one years of service.

Builder: Clyde Engineering Co Sydney 25

Preserved: No. 5711, at Rail Transport Museum, Thirlmere.

Above: *Delivered to N.S.W. Government Railways from Clyde Engineering Co, No. 5701 entered service on 6 September 1929. It was withdrawn from service in November 1960 and was scrapped on 15 November 1963, having travelled 1 012 198 miles during its thirty-one years of service. The combined weight of locomotive and tender was 226 tons 3 cwt, with a combined length of 87 ft 6⅛ in from buffer to buffer. For more details see* A Compendium of NSW Steam Locomotives, *compiled by A. Grunbach, ARHS(NSW) 1989, p. 201–5.*

The first of this class began life in 1915 as DD 953, then on 19 December 1929 it was rebuilt with a larger boiler and superheater to become D3 685. It was the first of a total of ninety-four to be built. DD 533 was the last, and in April 1947 it was renumbered D3 604. Popular with crews and the public, the D3 was a reliable locomotive. Able to handle goods trains as well as passenger services, it was also employed at times to assist mainline passenger and goods locomotives, including on one occasion H220 the largest locomotive ever used on Victorian Railways.

During its long period in service the D3 class was changed; the front end was modified although the original cast-iron, flanged chimneys were retained. One problem was the sudden collapse of the main steam pipe. Replacing this pipe was most easily achieved by fitting a new boiler, but as none were available the locomotives were condemned although otherwise in excellent condition.

D3 CLASS (VIC)
WHEEL ARRANGEMENT: 4–6–0
PASSENGER LOCOMOTIVE
94 IN CLASS
FINAL NOS: 606–699

In 1977 only one D3 remained with Victorian Railways. It was No. 639 which had been built as DD 586 in 1903.

Builders: Beyer Peacock & Co 3; Baldwin Locomotive Co 6; Ballarat North 6; Ballarat 1; Bendigo North 7; Newport Workshops 58; Thompson & Co 8; Walkers Ltd. 5

Preserved: No. 608, at VR Locomotive Depot, Ballarat East; No. 619, at VR Workshops, Bendigo; No. 635, at ARHS Railway Museum, North Williamstown; No. 638, at Peninsula Gardens, Rosebud; No. 639, at Steamrail Victoria Ltd; No. 640, at Folk Museum, Swan Hill; No. 641, at Wotherspoon Reserve, Beaufort; No. 646, near Ballarat station, Maryborough; No. 653, at VR Workshops, Ballarat North; No. 666, at children's playground, King St, Bayswater; No. 671, at park alongside Hamilton Highway, Lismore; No. 677, at Steamrail Victoria Ltd, Newport; No. 684, at Seymour Steam Loco Preservation Group; No. 688, at Flinders Naval Base, Crib Point, as No 640.

Above: Built in 1915 by Newport Workshops as DD 953, it was rebuilt to become D3 685 in December 1929 and was the pattern engine for the class. It was scrapped on 15 June 1962. The listed weight in working order of this locomotive and tender was 99 tons 11 cwt with a combined length of 58 ft 3⅜ in from buffer to buffer. For more details see Metamorphosis of an Ugly Duckling: The D3-Class Locomotives of Victoria, *J.L. Buckland and M.H.W. Clark, ARHS Bulletin No. 475, May 1977, p. 97–111.*

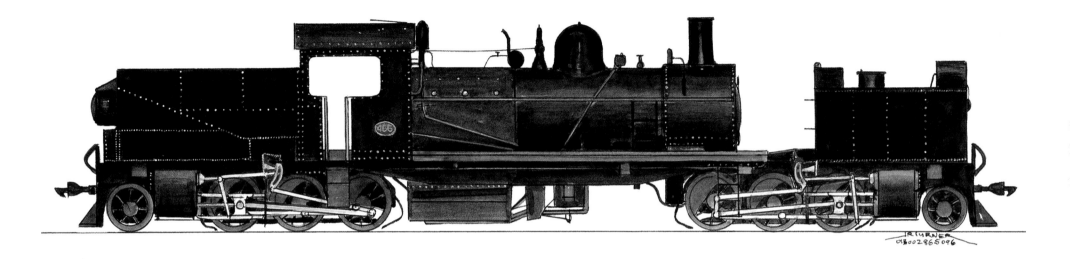

Based on the Ms class Garratt, the Msa class was built by Midland Junction Workshops, the first Garratts to be built in the southern hemisphere. With the rapid increase of wheat growing areas, more locomotives were needed for the 1930 harvest. Work began on the Msa locomotives in February 1929, with Nos 466 and 467 in service on 22 February 1930. No. 475 was the last in service, on 1 November 1930. During the design stage changes were made to the Msa Class, and parts from other locomotives were used to reduce the need for special spare parts.

During trials the locomotive was found to operate well, though it did use more coal than the Ms class because the grate area was too large. Because of higher boiler pressure, the Msa class was able to haul heavier loads, and during the first year in service hauled in a record harvest. Able to haul

MSA CLASS (WA)
WHEEL ARRANGEMENT: 2-6-0 0-6-2
GARRATT ARTICULATED
LOCOMOTIVE
10 IN CLASS
NOS ENTERING SERVICE: 466–475
FINAL NOS: 491–500

heavy traffic anywhere on the system except for two isolated district railways, the locomotives were all re-numbered between 1947–49.

They continued in service until the early 1960s, and were last used on the Bunbury–Boyup Brook and Pinjarra–Boddington lines, both located between 60 and 120 miles south of Perth. By this time a number were in storage. No. 498 was the first to be withdrawn from service on 6 September 1962. The remaining nine were all withdrawn from service on 7 October 1963. It had been planned to preserve one of the Msa class, but it was cut up by accident while stored at Midland Junction Workshops.

Builder: Midland Junction Workshops 10
Preserved: Nil

Above: Built by the Midland Junction Workshops, No. 466 was the first of its class to enter service on 22 February 1930. It was renumbered No. 491 on 22 September 1947, went into storage on 3 April 1962 and was withdrawn from service on 7 October 1963, 32 years in service. The listed weight in working order of this locomotive was 74 tons 2½ cwt, with a length of 55 ft 5¼ in from buffer to buffer. For more details see A History of W.A.G.R. Steam Locomotives, A. Gunzburg, ARHS(WA) 1984, p. 108–10.

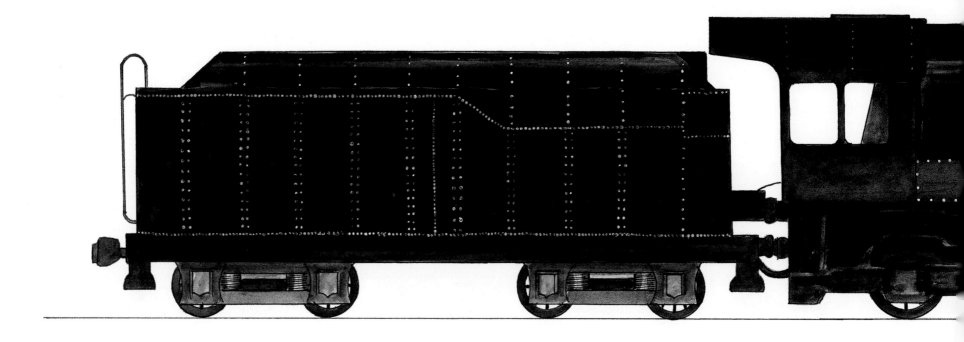

Designed by F.J. Shea and built in England by Sir W.G. Armstrong-Whitworth & Co, the 500s were all in service in 1926. By mid 1929 the first locomotive was converted from the 4–8–2 500 to the 4–8–4 500B class. The conversion involved the removal of the two-wheel trailing truck and installation of a four-wheel Delta trailing truck with booster. This raised the tractive effort from 51 000 lb to 59 000 lb. No. 507 was the first converted on 17 April 1929, followed by another seven in late 1930. The final two, Nos 503 and 508, were converted in late 1936.

They continued to haul the heavy goods and passenger services over the Mount Lofty Ranges on the Main South Line, and were used on the Overland Express between Adelaide and Tailem Bend.

500B CLASS (SA)
WHEEL ARRANGEMENT: 4–8–4
PASSENGER, HEAVY GOODS
LOCOMOTIVE
10 IN CLASS
NOS: 500–509

Builder: Sir W. G. Armstrong-Whitworth & Co 10
Preserved: No. 504, known as 'Tom Barr Smith', at Port Dock Railway Museum (SA) Inc, Port Adelaide.

From the late 1930s they were used north to Port Pirie, Terowie and Angaston, and south to Victor Harbour

In the early 1950s, after 25 years of hauling the Overland, the 500 class was replaced by diesels and confined to goods services. Nos 501 and 507 were the first to be condemned on 26 March 1958. The last to go was No. 500 on 12 May 1963, having travelled 912 730 miles during thirty-seven years in service.

Above: *No. 501 was built by Sir W. G. Armstrong-Whitworth & Co in England. It entered service as a 500 class with South Australian Government Railways on 2 July 1926, and was converted to a 500B class on 10 April 1930. The first of its class used on the Melbourne Express on 27 September 1926, it was named* Sir Henry Barwell *in 1927. Condemned on 26 March 1958, it was cut up at Islington on 29 March 1961, having travelled 1 029 926 miles during thirty-two years in service. The listed weight in working order of this locomotive and tender was 222 tons 6 cwt with a combined length of 84 ft 2 in from buffer to buffer. For more details see* Steam Locomotives and Railcars of the South Australian Railways, *R.E. Fluck, R. Sampson and K.J. Bird, Mile End Railway Museum, p. 91–4.*

In March 1927 the Railway Construction Branch of the Public Works Department called for tenders for the supply of two tender locomotives, with that of Andrew Barclay, Sons & Co of Kilmarnock, Scotland being accepted on 4 November 1927. The locomotives both entered service on 31 July 1928 with the railway construction branch of the Public Works Department. They had placed the order because of the ageing condition of the four G class and one L class then in use.

On entering service they were named *Wiluna* and *Nornalup*, after current construction projects. Similar to the G class, they had a larger-capacity bogie tender, able to carry three times the coal and slightly more water than the G class. A few years later, on 5 January 1931, the Railway Construction Branch was merged into the Railway Department. The locomotives then became

(2ND) Q CLASS (WA)
WHEEL ARRANGEMENT: 4-6-0
TENDER LOCOMOTIVE
2 IN CLASS
FINAL NOS: 62, 63

Nos 62 and 63 respectively of the Q class, and had their large cast name plates removed from the sides of their cabs; these were located above the builders' plates.

When new construction work ceased they were used as shunters, with No. 62 sent to the Railway Department sawmill at Banksiadale for a time in March 1935. Only minor changes were made during their time in service with new safety valves fitted and the position of the whistle changed. No. 62 was withdrawn from service on 25 October 1949. No. 63 lasted until 9 October 1953, when it was withdrawn after twenty-five years in service

Builder: Andrew Barclay, Sons & Co 2

Preserved: Nil

Above: Built in 1928 by Andrew Barclay, Sons & Co of Kilmarnock, Scotland, this locomotive entered service with the Public Works Department on 31 July 1928 named Wiluna. On entering service with Western Australian Government Railways on 5 January 1931 it became No. 62 and was withdrawn from service on 25 October 1949. The listed weight in working order of this locomotive and tender was 60 tons with a combined length of 49 ft 3⅜ in from buffer to buffer. For more details see, A. Gunzburg, ARHS(WA) 1984, p. 111–12.

Between 1903 and 1917, 145 saturated tank locomotives with 4–6–4 wheel arrangement were constructed (Beyer Peacock 95; Eveleigh Works, NSWR 50) for suburban passenger operations. Following the completion of the initial stage of Sydney suburban electrification (1926–1932), a total of 77 of the class were deemed surplus and were rebuilt as 4–6–0 light tender engines for country branch lines. They retained their 1924 series road numbers, but were known as the (C)30T class.

The first to be converted was delivered by Clyde Engineering in August 1928, retaining its number 3088T—the T being added to indicate tender. The final locomotive converted was No. 3020T, which entered service in July 1933 from Eveleigh Workshops. Twenty-seven of the converted engines were fitted with superheaters between 1930 and 1957, including 3090 (illustrated). The

(C)30T CLASS (NSW)
WHEEL ARRANGEMENT: 4-6-0
LIGHT LINE MIXED TRAFFIC
LOCOMOTIVE
77 IN CLASS
FINAL NOS: 3001-3145

Conversion by: Clyde Engineering Co 10; Eveleigh Workshops 65
Preserved: No. 3001TS, at Rail Transport Museum, Thirlmere; Nos 3102T and 3016TS, at Canberra Railway Museum, Canberra; No. 3026T, at Lachlan Valley Railway, Cowra; Nos 3028T and 3090TS, at Dorrigo Steam Railway and Museum; No. 3075TS, at Kelly Reserve, Parkes (static display).

(C)30T class used a variety of tenders from earlier locomotives and could travel on most lines at the maximum permitted speed of 50 mph.

The (C)30T class continued working on most light lines hauling stock, goods, mixed passenger and mail trains until they were gradually replaced by diesels. Merriwa was the last line to use them until the early 1970s. They continued to be used as shunters at most major centres throughout the state, until the last was withdrawn from service in 1972.

Above: Originally built as a 4–6–4 tank engine by the NSWGR, 3090 entered service as S1011 on 21 October 1912. It was renumbered 3090 in August 1924 and rebuilt as a tender engine in April 1931 at Eveleigh Workshops. It was superheated in March 1950 and withdrawn from service in July 1970, having travelled 1 382 232 miles during fifty-eight years in service. Finally it was sold to the Hunter Valley Railway Museum (now the Dorrigo Steam Railway and Museum) on 22 October 1974. When in use as depicted, the listed weight of the locomotive and bogie tender was 99 tons 13 cwt 3 qtr, with a combined length of 57 ft 7½ in from buffer to buffer. For more details see A Compendium of NSW Steam Locomotives, *compiled by A. Grunbach, ARHS(NSW) 1989, p. 196–200.*

The need for more locomotives was outlined in a report in 1920. New lines were planned to open, and existing services were being cancelled due to lack of locomotives. An order was placed for thirty-five Cl9s, but none of the quotes submitted were acceptable, so it was decided to build ten at Ipswich Railway Works. The first, No. 695, was built in 1922 and entered service in October of that year. No. 801, the last built by Ipswich, entered service in January 1928.

A second batch was built by Walkers Limited and all entered service in 1935. They were numbered 196–201. When No. 695 entered service it was found to be overweight, and following locomotives were examined for ways to reduce weight before delivery. It appears that weight was reduced on the frames, which resulted in cracked frames later on. Due to the slow rate of production, later locomotives had smaller domes. Other changes included fitting electric lights to replace the oil

C19 CLASS (QLD)
WHEEL ARRANGEMENT: 4-8-0
PASSENGER LOCOMOTIVE
26 IN CLASS
FINAL NOS: 196-201, 695-801

lights used on earlier locomotives.

The C19s were widely used throughout southern and central coastal Queensland, with some of the first batch sent to Toowoomba and others to Roma Street. Initially two were used at Maryborough, but this was later increased to four. They worked to Rockhampton, Gympie, Miles, Roma, Ipswich, Toowoomba, Mackay, Bundaberg, Warwick, Stanthorpe and Chinchilla on wheat and fruit trains. Two were used on Royal trains; No. 699 with the Duchess of York in April 1927 and No. 700 with the Duke of Gloucester in December 1934.

Over twenty of the class were withdrawn in the late 1950s. No. 700 was the last, withdrawn in February 1962.

Builders: Ipswich Railway Works 20; Walkers Limited 6
Preserved: No. 700, at QR, in storage.

Above: *Built by Walkers Limited in 1935, No. 196 entered service in July of that year. The first of six C19s built by Walkers, it was withdrawn from service in May 1962 after about twenty-seven years in service. The listed weight in working order of this locomotive and tender was 97 tons 2qtr while the combined length was 56 ft 10¼ in from buffer to buffer. For more details see* Locomotives in the Tropics Vol. 2, J. Armstrong, ARHS(Qld) 1994, p. 66–70.

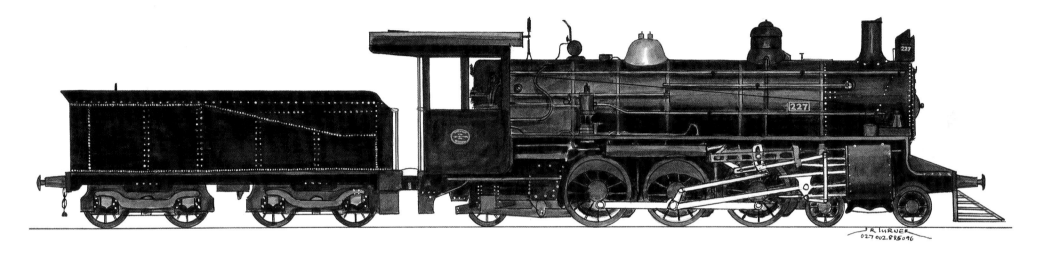

The need for a new locomotive for use on mail trains was discussed in 1922 with the building of a prototype approved in September of that year. Delays in completion of plans and estimates delayed building. The prototype, No. 84, which was built at the Ipswich Railway Workshops, did not enter service until 16 July 1926. Following use on mail, passenger and mixed services it was decided that eight more of these locomotives should be built. The first two entered service in December 1928, with the remainder all in service by August 1929. Eighty-three were eventually built, the last being No. 916 in November 1947.

Modifications and improvements were made with succeeding locomotives, and when

B18¼ CLASS (QLD)
WHEEL ARRANGEMENT: 4-6-2
PASSENGER LOCOMOTIVE
83 IN CLASS
FINAL NOS: 16, 18, 27, 28, 30, 40, 50, 52, 84, 227–32, 768–71, 827–30, 841–52, 864–82, 888–916

Builders: Ipswich Railway Workshops 59; Walkers Ltd 24

Preserved: No. 771, at QR Railway Museum, opposite station, Redbank.

compared with other locomotives then in use the combination of more power, free steaming and a smooth ride made it the most popular class on the system until the 1950s. On passenger services they hauled loads of up to 315 tons on the Sunshine Express—more on some sections—while on goods services they hauled up to 650 tons. This was later increased to 735 tons in 1958.

In March 1967, No. 910 was the first withdrawn from service and by July 1970 the last two in service, Nos 770 and 881, were written off.

Above: Built by Ipswich Railway Workshops in 1935, No. 227 entered service in August of that year and was written off in June 1968 after about thirty-three years in service. The listed weight in working order of this locomotive and tender was 89 tons 15 cwt with a combined length of 58 ft 8½ in from buffer to buffer. For more details see Locomotives in the Tropics Vol. 2, J. Armstrong, ARHS(Qld) 1994, p. 86–96

620 CLASS (SA)
WHEEL ARRANGEMENT: 4-6-2
PASSENGER LOCOMOTIVE
10 IN CLASS
NOS: 620-629

By the mid 1930s the economy had begun to pick up after the depression. Rail traffic increased, and a new locomotive was needed on secondary lines to replace the Rx and S class locomotives then in use. Designed by F.J. Shea, the 620 class was built at the Islington Workshops, with No. 620 the first into service on 26 June 1936. No. 629 was the last, on 22 March 1938.

South Australia celebrated its centenary year in 1936, and No. 620 was put on show. It was streamlined and painted green, and hauled remodelled carriages which were also painted green with cream lines. The centenary train toured broad gauge lines with a series of excursion trips.

From 1937 the 620s were used to provide a fast passenger service between Adelaide and Port Pirie, enabling passengers to connect with Alice Springs and Perth services. They also hauled passenger services to Renmark and Pinnaroo in the east, south to Victor Harbour and north to Port Pirie and Terowie. By the 1950s passenger traffic had declined in country areas with rail cars and diesels being introduced on more services. The 620 class locomotives were gradually withdrawn from regular service. The first condemned was No. 620 on 6 July 1961, with most of the class withdrawn from service in late 1967. Nos 621 and 624 were the last to go on 21 August 1969.

Builder: Islington Workshops 10

Preserved: No. 621, at Steamranger, Goolwa; No. 624, at Port Dock Railway Museum (SA) Inc.

Above: Built by Islington Workshops, No. 621 entered service with South Australian Railways on 7 September 1936. It was used on the centenary train in 1936 and named Duke of Edinburgh on 6 April 1971 when it was used for ARHS tours. In May 1994 it travelled to Bacchus Marsh on the western outskirts of Melbourne before returning to Adelaide. The listed weight in working order of this locomotive and tender was 140 tons 15 cwt with a combined length of 69 ft 7¾ in from buffer to buffer. For more details see Steam Locomotives and Railcars of the South Australian Railways, *F.E. Fluck, R. Sampson and K.J. Bird, Mile End Museum 1986, p. 103–4.*

Originally built at the Ipswich Railway Works in 1904 as tank engines the B13s were rebuilt as tender engines between 1932–1938. No. 397 was the first converted by having its tanks and bunker removed, after which it was given a B13 tender. No. 398 followed in May 1937, No 400 and No. 401 in October, No. 396 in October 1938 and finally, No. 399 in November 1938.

After their conversion a weight distribution problem was found, but it was corrected by moving the engine jacks from the front platform to a position over the centre wheel. The sand box was also

B13½ CLASS (QLD)
WHEEL ARRANGEMENT: 0–6–0
SMALL TENDER LOCOMOTIVE
6 IN CLASS
FINAL NOS: 396–401

relocated behind the steam dome. These changes resulted in the B13½ being known as 'Pigs'. They spent their days on shunting duties. Withdrawals from service began in the early 1950s, but the B13s continued in use as shunters, with No. 400 used at Mayne until June 1961. No. 398 continued working as workshop shunter at Ipswich with the nickname of 'Pompey'. It is now preserved in the grounds of the QR Workshops at Ipswich.

Builder: Ipswich Railway Works 6
Preserved: No. 398, at QR Workshops, Ipswich.

Above: Originally built at the Ipswich Railway Works in 1904, No. 398 entered service in October 1904 as a tank engine. It was converted to a tender engine in May 1937, and though withdrawn from service in December 1953, continued in use until the late 1960s when it hauled two ARHS tour trains. The listed weight in working order of locomotive and tender was 49 tons 10 cwt with a combined length of locomotive and tender of 42 ft 10 in from buffer to buffer. For more details see Locomotives in the Tropics *Vol. 1, J. Armstrong, ARHS(Qld), p. 89.*

Designed by A.E Smith and built at the Newport Workshops, the S class entered service in March 1928. After extensive trials they were used to haul the Sydney Limited between Melbourne and Albury, from 1928 to 1937. They were found to be fast and reliable and became known worldwide for the service they provided.

On 23 November 1937 an upgraded service was introduced, with the new streamlined S class painted royal blue with gold lining for the inaugural run of the *Spirit of Progress*. As well as streamlining the locomotive, the tender was enlarged and fitted with two six-wheel bogies to handle almost thirty tons of extra fuel and water. With the larger tender the *Spirit of Progress* was able to do the 190-mile run from Melbourne to Albury without stopping. Prior to the first run

S CLASS (VIC)
WHEEL ARRANGEMENT: 4–6–2
STREAMLINED EXPRESS PASSENGER
LOCOMOTIVE
4 IN CLASS
FINAL NOS: S300–S303

of the *Spirit of Progress*, No. 302 with its royal blue and gold paint was put on public display at Spencer St station and some country centres, and over 55 000 people came to see it. The *Spirit of Progress* was the first all steel, streamlined, air conditioned express in Australia and also included the first stewardess—later called a hostess—to serve on Australian railways.

S301 was the first of the class to be scrapped, on 16 October 1953. It was followed on 28 May 1954 by S303, and S302 on 2 July. The last to go was S300 on 17 September 1954.

Builder: Newport Workshops 4
Preserved: Nil

Above: *Built by Newport Workshops, No. 302 entered service with Victorian Railways on 23 April 1929, and was used on the Sydney Limited passenger express service. In 1937 it was streamlined and used on the* Spirit of Progress, *until withdrawn from service and scrapped on 2 July 1954, having travelled a record total mileage for a steam locomotive of 1 446 468 miles, during twenty-five years in service. The listed weight in working order of this locomotive and tender was 222 tons 17 cwt with a combined length of 85 ft 6 in from buffer to buffer. For more details see* The Era of the S Class and H220 Locomotives in the Victorian Railways, *S. Watson.*

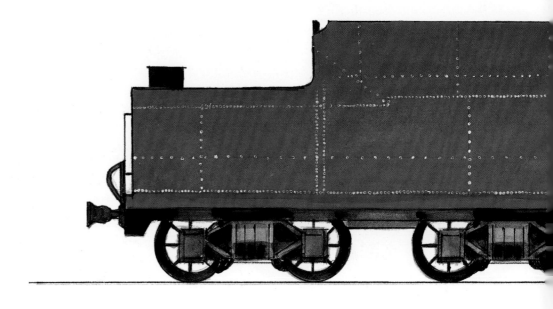

Ten Pr class locomotives were built at the Midland Junction Workshops, with the first, No. 138 named *Ashburton*, entering service on 28 January 1938. The last to enter service was No. 147, named *Murchison*, on 16 June 1939. The locomotives were named after Australian rivers with a brass nameplate situated mid-way along the running board, with 5-inch raised brass letters on a signal-red background. They had long-travel valve gear and a boiler designed for higher boiler pressure than the P class.

With the upgrading of bridges between Perth and Kalgoorlie, the Westland Express was introduced in 1938, and was hauled almost exclusively by the Pr class. The boiler pressure of the Pr class was increased to its designed value and train loads increased. Between 1941 and 1944, eight P class locomotives were upgraded to Pr class, each named after a river. A number of changes were

PR CLASS (WA)
WHEEL ARRANGEMENT: 4-6-2
EXPRESS PASSENGER LOCOMOTIVE
18 IN CLASS
NOS ENTERING SERVICE: 138-147,
453-457, 459, 461, 464
FINAL NOS: 521-538

made over the years, the most obvious being the swapping of long and short tenders. During the coal strikes of the late 1940s, ten Pr locomotives were modified to burn oil. One of these, No. 528, was destroyed by fire when leaking oil ignited at Kalgoorlie. In the early 1950s the old black and grey colours were changed to the green and black livery (as illustrated above).

The Pr class continued to work the Westland express until the X class diesels took over in 1954. They were then assigned to other passenger goods work, with most being withdrawn from service in the late 1960s. No. 521 *Ashburton* was the last to be withdrawn on 10 September 1970 after thirty-two years in service.

Builder: Midland Junction Workshops 18
Preserved: No. 521, at ARHS Railway Museum, Bassendean.

Above: Built by Midland Junction Workshops in 1938 No. 141, Fitzroy, entered service on 29 August 1938 and was renumbered No. 524. It was twice converted to burn oil between 1947–49 and was withdrawn from service on 11 September 1967 after twenty-nine years in use. The listed weight in working order of this locomotive and tender was 102 tons 10 cwt with a combined length of 62 ft 6⅛ in from buffer to buffer. For more details see *A History of W.A.G.R. Steam Locomotives, A. Gunzburg, ARHS(WA) 1984, p. 102–7.*

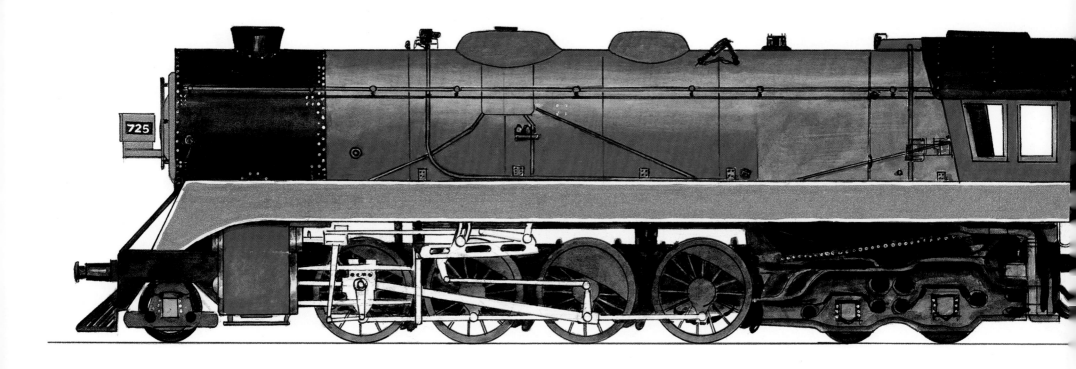

It was intended to build another batch of 710 class locomotives at Islington, but fitting a booster increased weight and caused problems. The design was modified further, and named the 720 class. While it was intended that the 720's should be used on light lines, they were found to be suitable only for the same lines used by the 500 and 600 classes.

The first to enter service was No. 720 on 26 November 1930, with Nos 721 to 724 entering service the following year. It was 1938 before No. 725 entered service, with the last, No. 736, in service on 7 August 1943. As well as being used on the main south and north lines, in 1937 they were able to reach Port Pirie using the east-west connection via Red Hill.

720 CLASS (SA)
WHEEL ARRANGEMENT: 2-8-4
HEAVY GOODS LOCOMOTIVE
17 IN CLASS
NOS: 720-736

replaced by new diesel locomotives.
Builder: Islington Workshops 17
Preserved: Nil.

While Nos 720, 721 and 723 only used coal, all the others were either coal/oil or oil burners when in service. Although they were able to haul heavy loads of up to 1600 tons between Mile End and Gawler, they did not perform as well as the 700 and 710 classes. The first to be withdrawn were Nos 729 and 734 on 26 March 1958, and by late 1959 only six of the class remained in service. All were condemned on 14 April 1960 and

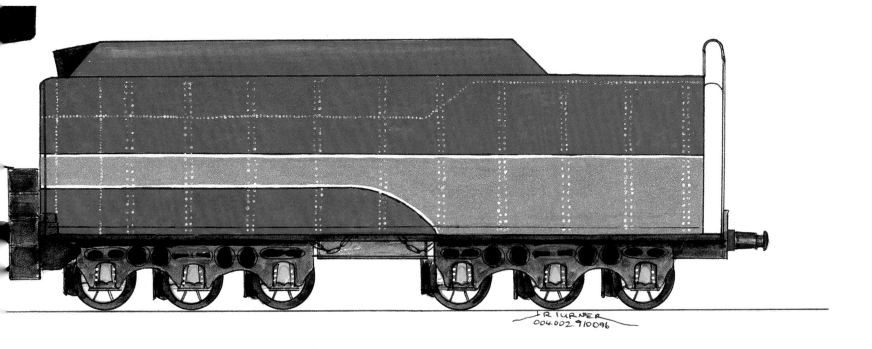

Above: *Built by South Australian Railways Islington Workshops, No. 725 entered service on 15 October 1938. It is shown here with a silver and green livery, although this was not typical of the class. It was oil and coal fired during its time in service. No. 725 was condemned on 30 September 1958 and cut up at Islington on 30 October 1958, having travelled 433 043 miles during twenty years in service. The listed weight in working order of this locomotive and tender was 227 tons 8 cwt with a combined length of 83 ft 6 in from buffer to buffer. For more details see* The 700 Series Locomotives of the South Australian Railways, *by D. Colquhoun, R. Stewien and A. Thomas, ARHS(SA) 1979, p. 24–35.*

A total of forty-one Wf class locomotives were built in New Zealand for New Zealand Government Railways between 1904 and 1928. Eight of these locomotives were bought by Tasmanian Government Railways and became the DS class, the first four arriving in 1939, with four more in 1944. Six were stationed at Hobart and used on suburban passenger services to Risdon, Cadburys and Brighton, and shunting in the Hobart yard. One was based at Launceston for shunting, and one at Devonport was used on goods traffic on the Melrose line as well as shunting duties.

The introduction of new locomotives resulted in less work for the DS class and DS2, DS3, DS5 and DS6 were placed in storage in 1949. The remaining four were replaced by diesels in 1951.

DS CLASS (TAS)
WHEEL ARRANGEMENT: 2-6-4T
GOODS, PASSENGER TANK
LOCOMOTIVE
8 IN CLASS
FINAL NOS: DS1-DS8

Builders: Addington Workshops Christchurch 2; Hillside Workshops Dunedin 5; A.&G. Price Ltd Thames 1

Preserved: Nil

DS2 was sold for scrap, followed by DS3, DS6 and DS8 in 1953. The Mount Lyell Railway bought DS4 in January 1952 and then DS1 a few months later for shunting, but they were replaced by diesels in 1953. The Emu Bay Railway hired DS5 from Tasmanian Government Railways in 1953 for shunting work, after which it was stored and then scrapped in 1956. The last to go was DS7, which was used as a steam cleaner at Devonport until 1957 and then scrapped in 1958.

Above: Built in New Zealand at the Addington Workshops in 1904 as a Wf class for New Zealand Government Railways, DS2 was bought by Tasmanian Government Railways and entered service in February 1939. It was used on passenger and shunting duties and was withdrawn from service in October 1951. The listed weight in working order of this locomotive was 43 tons 10 cwt with a length of 34 ft 3¼ in from buffer to buffer. For more details see The Decline of Steam Power on the Tasmanian Government Railways 1945–1965, *H.J.W. Stokes, ARHS Bulletin No. 347, September 1966, p. 193–202.*

K CLASS (VIC)
WHEEL ARRANGEMENT: 2-8-0
GOODS LOCOMOTIVE
53 IN CLASS
FINAL NOS: 140-192

With both the weight of trains and traffic increasing on light lines a new, more powerful locomotive, which was able to fit on the 53 ft turntables then in use, was needed. Designed by A.E. Smith for use on light lines, the first of the K class No. 140 entered service with Victorian Railways on 22 August 1922, with No. 192 the last in service on 31 October 1946.

The first group of ten locomotives were all in service in 1923, with the remainder built between 1940 and 1946. Over the years a number of modifications and additions were made, which included fitting electric lights, smoke deflectors, staff exchanger and a modified front end with stove-pipe chimneys.

By 1958 the first of the class were scrapped, with another twenty-five following in the 1960s. During the 1970s the last four were scrapped; No. 173 on 21 October 1970, No. 187 on 3 February

1971, No. 164 on 12 August 1971. The last to go was No. 158 on 23 June 1978, having travelled 430 211 miles during thirty-three years in service.
Builder: Newport Workshops 53
Preserved: Nos 151, 153, 183, 184 and 190, at Steamrail Victoria Ltd, Newport; No. 154, at Old Gippsland Folk Museum, Princes Hwy, Moe; Nos 157 and 160, at Castlemaine and Maldon Railway Preservation Society; No. 159, Apex Drive, Hamilton; No. 162, near station, Yarragon; Nos 163 and 177, at Flinders Naval Base, Crib Point; No. 165, at ARHS Railway Museum, North Williamstown; No. 167, at park on level crossing, Calder Hwy, Wycheproof; No. 169, at Coal Creek Historical Park, Korrumburra; No. 174, Brunswick St, Fitzroy; No. 175, at park near river, Mildura; No. 176, at locomotive depot, Seymour SLPS; No. 181, at Park, Nurmurkah; No. 191, Sisley Ave, south of station, Wangaratta; No. 192, at Wonthaggi Station, Wonthaggi.

Above: Built by Newport Workshops, No. 152 was one of the second group of K class and entered service with Victorian Railways on 23 August 1940. It spent most of its working life at Seymour until transferred to Bendigo on 27 June 1965, following a major overhaul the previous year at Ballarat North Workshops. It was withdrawn from service on 21 April 1967 with a defective boiler, and was scrapped on 30 August 1967. The listed weight in working order of this locomotive and tender was 104 tons 2 cwt 2 qtr with a combined length of 60 ft 3⅜ inches from buffer to buffer. For more details see The Era of the K & J Class Locomotives in the Victorian Railways, S. Watson, 1983.

Designed by the engineers of Victorian Railways in 1938, it was proposed that three H class locomotives would be built by Newport Workshops, to eliminate the need for double-heading on heavy passenger and heavy goods services. The only one of its class to be built, H220, or 'Heavy Harry' as it was known, entered service with Victorian Railways on 7 February 1941. It was used on heavy goods services and also at times on the *Spirit of Progress*, where it easily maintained the times set by the streamlined S class which usually hauled it.

During the year from 30 June 1943 to 30 June 1944, H220 covered 72 000 miles with ten trips per week between Melbourne and Wodonga, hauling 800 tons per trip. It had previously taken two

H CLASS (VIC)
WHEEL ARRANGEMENT: 4–8–4
HEAVY GOODS LOCOMOTIVE
1 IN CLASS
FINAL NO: H220

locomotives to haul this weight. In May 1945 H220 went back to Newport Workshops for its first major overhaul, having covered a total of 269 000 miles since entering service.

One problem which did affect the performance of a number of Victorian locomotives was the use of Lithgow coal in place of the Maitland coal which they usually used. The Lithgow coal meant that two or three stops of 20 to 45 minutes were required during a trip to clean the fires. Finally withdrawn from service on 30 April 1958, 'Heavy Harry' had during its seventeen years in service travelled a total of 821 860 miles.

Builder: Newport Workshops 1
Preserved: No. H220, at ARHS Railway Museum, North Williamstown.

Above: *Built by Newport Workshops, H220 was the only one of its class and entered service on 7 February 1941. It was the largest, heaviest and most powerful locomotive used on Victorian Railways and hauled both heavy goods and express passenger services. Withdrawn from service on 30 April 1958 after seventeen years in service, it was handed over to the ARHS Railway Museum for preservation on 10 April 1962. The listed weight in working order of this locomotive and tender was 260 tons 1 cwt with a combined length of 92 ft 5¼ in from buffer to buffer. For more details see* The Era of the S Class and H220 Locomotives in the Victorian Railways, *S. Watson.*

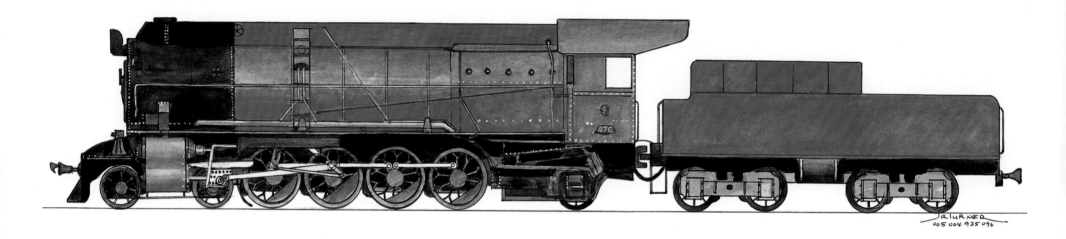

S CLASS (WA)
WHEEL ARRANGEMENT: 4-8-2
MIXED TRAFFIC LOCOMOTIVE
10 IN CLASS
FINAL NOS: 541-50

Designed in the late 1930s by WAGR Chief Draftsman Mr F Mills, the S class was developed from earlier drawings which had probably been based on the smaller Pr class locomotives. While it had been planned that construction would begin following completion of the Pr class, a lack of funds and then wartime restrictions and material shortages meant that even a revised completion date for the first locomotive of October 1941 was not met. Finally on 11 February 1943, No. 476 (later 541) named *Bruce* entered service with Western Australian Government Railways. Another two locomotives followed later that year, while the last, No. 550 named *Hardie*, entered service on 10 November 1947. Some modifications were required but the locomotives performed well.

Designed for both goods and passenger services, they were used on the eastern and Eastern Goldfields lines in early years. They then moved on to heavy goods services on the eastern and south-western lines, before being used on lines around Bunbury in the south-west of the state. In the late 1950s five locomotives were fitted with rebuilt tenders which had reduced coal and increased water capacity. On 17 June all of the class were withdrawn from service except for No. 549, which followed on 14 August 1972 after twenty-five years in service.

Builder: Midland Junction Workshops 10

Preserved: No. 542 named *Bakewell*, at East Perth Railway Terminal, Perth; No. 547 named *Lindsay*, Bellarine Peninsular Railway, Queenscliffe, Vic; No. 549, at ARHS Railway Museum, Railway Parade, Bassendean, WA.

Above: Built by Midland Railway Workshops in 1943, No. 476 (later 541) named Bruce *entered service with Western Australian Government Railways on 11 February 1943. It was withdrawn from service on 17 June 1971 after twenty-eight years in service. The listed weight in working order of this locomotive and tender was 119 tons 6 cwt with a combined length of 69 ft 3½ in from buffer to buffer. For more details see* A History of W.A.G.R. Steam Locomotives, *A. Gunzburg, ARHS(WA) 1984, p. 117-20.*

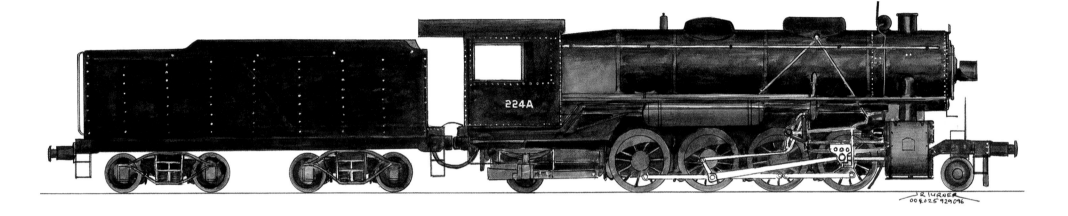

AC16 CLASS (QLD)
WHEEL ARRANGEMENT: 2–8–2
GOODS LOCOMOTIVE
20 IN CLASS
FINAL NOS: 216A–235A

With the Japanese advancing southwards and the Queensland railway system pushed to the limit, more locomotives and rolling stock were needed. Negotiations to purchase supplies from the United States were begun in 1941. The design of a locomotive for use by the Allies was approved in mid 1942, even though it was not suitable for use on Queensland's branch or secondary lines. In May 1943 the first five locomotives were delivered from the Baldwin Locomotive Works, unloaded in Sydney and railed to Clapham for assembly, the others following a short time later. On 26 June 1943 No. 223A was first to enter service with the last, No. 235A, in November 1943.

Once in service a number of problems were found, one being that the coal bunker floor was at floor level and not at knee level as with other Queensland locomotives. The tender bounced badly at higher speeds. In July 1943 the locomotives were banned from hauling passenger trains, and their speed was limited to 30 mph. A number of modifications were made during their time in service, and they retained the A after their number to distinguish them from other Queensland locomotives.

Having performed so well during the war years, most of the AC16s were due for an overhaul when hostilities ceased. In most cases they were stored, with preference being given to other types then in use. By the early 1950s they were back in service and in 1958 the first one was fitted with a B17 tender. By 1963 all nineteen in service had them. The new tenders solved the problem of bouncing and allowed the AC16s to be used on passenger services in country areas for a short period. In March 1964 No. 219A was written off, with No. 218A the last to go in June 1969.

Builder: Baldwin Locomotive Works 20
Preserved: No. 218A, at Zig Zag Railway Co-operative Ltd, Lithgow; No. 221A, at QR, in storage.

Above: Built by the Baldwin Locomotive Co in 1943, No. 224A entered service with Queensland Government Railways in July 1943, and was written off in September 1968 after twenty-five years in service. The listed weight in working order of this locomotive and tender was 94 tons 3 cwt 2 qtr with a combined length of 54 ft 3 in from buffer to buffer. For more details see Locomotives in the Tropics Vol. 2, J. Armstrong, ARHS(Qld) 1994, p. 102–8.

The first of a total of thirty locomotives of this class, No. 3801 entered service with NSW Government Railways on 22 January 1943, with the last, No. 3830, entering service on 27 September 1949. Designed by NSW Government Railways to replace the (C)36 class, only the first five were streamlined, the remaining twenty-five being of conventional external design. The first 'Pacific' type locomotives used in NSW, they were nicknamed the 'Grey Nurse' because of their grey paint scheme when they first entered service.

After WW II the class was painted green with yellow lining, but commencing in the early 1950s they were gradually repainted black, except for 3813 which remained green until its withdrawal.

First used on the Newcastle Express, the C38s performed well over many years on many lines before being replaced by diesels. They were then used on fast goods trains. The last official steam passenger service into Sydney was the Southern Highlands Express in October 1969. However, on 29

(C)38 CLASS (NSW)
WHEEL ARRANGEMENT: 4–6–2
EXPRESS PASSENGER LOCOMOTIVE
30 IN CLASS
FINAL NOS: 3801–30

December 1970, No. 3820 was the last of its class to be withdrawn from regular service after it hauled the *Newcastle Flyer* through to Sydney, without the usual change to electric traction at Gosford.

No. 3801 was withdrawn from service on 19 October 1965, but was restored on 27 October 1966 with financial contributions from the NSWRTM and RTS. However on 19 December 1976, boiler problems made it completely unserviceable.

Restored to working order again it was officially completed on 15 November 1986, and has since visited every mainland state—the only steam locomotive ever to do so.

Builders: Clyde Engineering Co. 5; Eveleigh Workshops 13; Cardiff Workshops 12

Preserved: No. 3801, at 3801 Limited, Eveleigh; No. 3813, dismantled remains shared between DSRTM and NSWRTM; No. 3820, at Rail Transport Museum, Thirlmere; No. 3830, at Powerhouse Museum, Eveleigh, on loan to 3801 Limited.

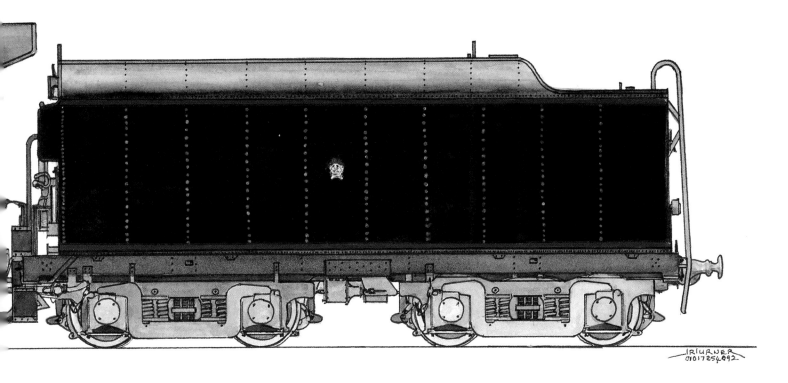

Above: *Delivered to NSW Government Railways from Clyde Engineering Co, No. 3803 entered service on 9 September 1943. It was withdrawn from service in October 1965 and scrapped in March 1966, having travelled 1 510 967 miles during twenty-five years of service. The listed weight in working order of this locomotive and tender was 201 tons 4 cwt, while the combined length was 76 ft 4⅝ in from buffer to buffer. For more details see* A Compendium of NSW Steam Locomotives, *compiled by A. Grunbach, ARHS(NSW) 1989, p. 211–23.*

Though a strong case was put forward to obtain more C17 locomotives which could work on all Queensland Railways lines, the Commonwealth Land Transport Board said that Queensland would get the Garratt locomotives whether it wanted them or not. Built at Victorian Railways' Newport Workshops, the first to enter service was G1 in September 1943. G53, built by Clyde Engineering, was the last to enter service in September 1944. Although G9 was sent to Brisbane, it never entered service with Queensland Railways. The ASG locomotives had several faults and though some of the problems were fixed, they were still restricted to a maximum load of 650 tons and were thus never used to their full potential.

ASG CLASS (QLD)
WHEEL ARRANGEMENT: 4-8-2 2-8-4
GARRATT ARTICULATED
LOCOMOTIVE
23 IN CLASS
FINAL NOS: G1–G5, G9, G11–G19,
G21–G25, G51–G53

The AFULE put a total ban on all ASG locomotives in September 1945. They were all placed in storage, and in 1948 Queensland Railways wrote them off and handed Nos 9, 11, 14, 18, 19, 25, 51 and 53 back to the Commonwealth Government. Several were sold to Tasmania, with G16, G17 and G23 going to the Emu Bay Railway in June 1948. The remaining fourteen locomotives were all scrapped in 1954 and 1955, with all but one having less than two years in service.

Builders: Victorian Railways Newport (G1–5 and G9) 6; South Australian Railways (G11–G19) 9; Clyde Engineering (G21–25, G51–53) 8

Preserved: Nil

Above: *Built by Victorian Railways' Newport Workshops in 1943, G1 entered service with Queensland Railways in September 1943. It was placed in storage when all ASG locomotives were banned in September 1945, and was scrapped in 1955. The listed weight in working order of this locomotive was 119 tons and it was 85 ft 9½ in from buffer to buffer. For more details see* Locomotives in the Tropics *Vol. 2, John Armstrong, ARHS(Qld) 1994, p. 109–113.*

By the early 1920s Tasmanian Government Railways were in need of new and more powerful locomotives. The Q class was designed by Mr. M.E. Deeble, the Chief Mechanical Engineer with Tasmanian Government Railways at the time, and six were built by Perry Engineering of South Australia. Designed as a heavy goods locomotive, they included a mixture of British and American features and were the first goods locomotives in Australia with a 4–8–2 wheel arrangement. The first batch of six locomotives, numbered 1 to 6, entered service between August 1922 and March 1923. Further Q class locomotives were delivered in 1929, 1936–37 and 1943–44, and the last two entered service in February and May 1945.

The best heavy goods locomotives to be used on Tasmanian Government Railways during the 1930s and 1940s, the Q class locomotives often travelled more than 40 000 miles in a year. Initially

Q CLASS (TAS)
WHEEL ARRANGEMENT: 4–8–2
HEAVY GOODS LOCOMOTIVE
19 IN CLASS
FINAL NOS. 1–19, 117

used on the main line between Hobart and Launceston and on the western line east of Devonport, their range was extended as tracks were upgraded to handle their weight. By the late 1920s they were used on the Fingal branch line, by 1937 on the Devonport–Wynyard section of the western line and in the Derwent Valley by about 1940.

In July 1956 Q9 was the first to be withdrawn from service; it was scrapped along with Q7, 8, 16, 17 and 18 in 1961. Others were scrapped at regular intervals, until by mid 1965 only Q5 remained. It was then bought by the Tasmanian Transport Museum for $700 and is now on display at Glenorchy. During its time in service Q5 travelled 955 876 miles in thirty-nine years in service.

Builders: Perry Engineering 6; Walkers Ltd 3; Clyde Engineering 10
Preserved: Q5, at Tasmanian Transport Museum, Anfield St, Glenorchy.

Above: *Built by Clyde Engineering, Q16 entered service with Tasmanian Government Railways in December 1943. It was withdrawn from service in May 1959 and scrapped in 1961, having covered 372 960 miles during sixteen years in service. The listed weight in working order of this locomotive and tender was 103 tons 19 cwt with a combined length of 61 ft 8 in from buffer to buffer. For more details see* Locomotives of the Tasmanian Transport Museum, Glenorchy, Tasmania, *A. Dix, 1991, p. 3–5.*

With the outbreak of WW II the Australian railway system was unable to cope with the increase in traffic resulting from moving troops, supplies and ammunition around the country. In March 1942 the Commonwealth Land Transport Board proposed the construction of 65 Garratt articulated locomotives for use on the 3 ft 6 in gauge rail systems. Several hundred detailed drawings were done of every part of the locomotive and 105 sub-contractors were used to manufacture the parts needed. By 1943 construction had begun and G26 was the first to enter service on 22 November 1943, from Midland Junction Workshops in Western Australia. The final locomotive to enter service was G65 on 4 August 1945, after delivery from Clyde Engineering Co, Granville, NSW.

Initially seen as a great success on entering service, within a year problems had arisen. The crews found conditions unbearable when operating in tunnels designed for smaller locomotives and

ASG CLASS (WA)
WHEEL ARRANGEMENT: 4-8-2 2-8-4
GARRATT ARTICULATED
LOCOMOTIVE
25 IN CLASS
FINAL NOS: G10, G20, G26–G32,
G44–G50, G54–G59, G63–G65

complained about the steam brake and regulator. The flangeless leading coupled wheels were responsible for several derailments on curves.

When unions claimed the locomotive was unsafe, the Railway Department disagreed. A Royal Commission was set up in W.A., commencing on 18 October 1945. In November 1946 the union called all members out on strike, which halted all rail services for two weeks. The Garratts were banned from service until modified, with the last one back in service on 7 August 1948.

By 1951 the new W class replaced the Asg. Six were then sold to South Australian Railways as their 300 class. The last eight were withdrawn on 10 January 1957, after about twelve years in service.

Builders: Newport Workshops, Victoria 3; Islington Workshops, South Australia 3; Midland Junction Workshops, Western Australia 10; Clyde Engineering, Granville, NSW 9

Preserved: Nil

Above: Built by the Midland Junction Workshops in Western Australia in 1944, G28 entered service on 8 February 1944. It was converted to burn oil on 6 February 1948, and back to coal on 19 December 1950. It was withdrawn from service on 10 January 1957 after nearly thirteen years in service. The listed weight in working order of this locomotive was 115 tons 8 cwt with a total length of 85 ft 10 in from buffer to buffer. For more details see *A History of W.A.G.R. Steam Locomotives*, A. Gunzburg, ARHS(WA) 1984, p. 121–24.

Early in WW II the need for a new locomotive to move troops and supplies on the Port Pirie line resulted in the design of the 520 class by F.H. Harrison. Built at the Islington Workshops, No. 520 entered service on 10 November 1943. No. 531 was the last steam engine ever built at Islington, and it entered service on 19 December 1947. Nos 523 to 531 were fitted with an improved, streamlined nose. In order to reduce their weight, welded steel parts were used instead of castings in the cylinder block, tender water bottom and tender bogie frames. The cab was well ventilated and the driver and fireman had padded seats.

They were able to run non-stop from Adelaide to Port Pirie and were soon used on passenger services on many other lines, including the Broken Hill and East–West Expresses. Designed for use

520 CLASS (SA)
WHEEL ARRANGEMENT: 4-8-4
PASSENGER LOCOMOTIVE
12 IN CLASS
NOS: 520-531

on both main and secondary lines they were capable of high speeds and performed well.

In the early 1950s diesels began taking over passenger services, initially on the south lines and then the north as more diesels were brought into service. The first 520s to be condemned were Nos 525, 527 and 528, on 6 July 1961. More followed in 1962 and 1963. In 1968 two more followed, with the last three in service all condemned on 21 August 1969.

Builder: Islington Workshops 12

Preserved: No. 520, at Steamranger, Goolwa; No. 523, at Port Dock Railway Museum (SA) Inc, Port Adelaide, S.A.

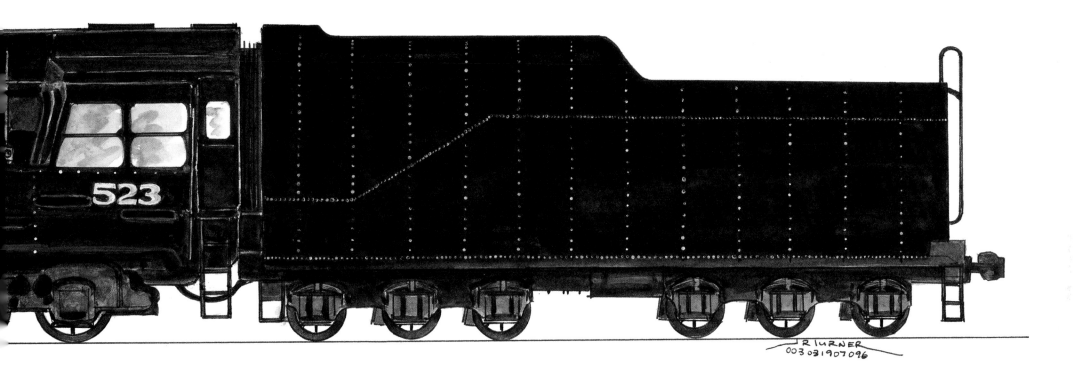

Above: Built by Islington Workshops, No. 523 entered service on 14 August 1944 and was named Essington Lewis. It was sent to the Mile End Railway Museum on 28 November 1968, and condemned on 21 August 1969. While in service it travelled 551 955 miles during twenty-four years. The listed weight in working order of this locomotive and tender was 200 tons 13 cwt 2 qtr with a combined length of 87 ft 4 in from buffer to buffer. For more details see Steam Locomotives and Railcars of the South Australian Railways, R.E Fluck, R. Sampson and K.J. Bird, Mile End Railway Museum 1986, p. 105–6.

G CLASS (TAS)
WHEEL ARRANGEMENT: 4-8-2 2-8-4
ARTICULATED GARRATT
LOCOMOTIVE
14 IN CLASS
FINAL NOS: G6-G9, G11, G12, G18, G19, G25, G37, G38, G60-G62

During WW II, the need for locally built locomotives resulted in the building of the Australian Standard Garratt, and in 1944 the first of those allocated for service in Tasmania arrived. They were used on goods services on the north-eastern line. The first group of three were numbered G6, G7 and G8. They were followed in 1945 by G60, G61 and G62, and then G37 and G38 in 1946. With more locomotives available they were then used on the main line between Launceston and Parattah in the south and Launceston and Stanley in the west. In 1949 four more Garratts arrived from Queensland. These were numbered G9, G11, G19 and G25, with G12 and G18 arriving in 1950. The additional locomotives also worked in the north of the state.

In 1954 six of the class were withdrawn from service, and then in 1957 the remaining eight were withdrawn. G6 went in April, followed by G7 and G25 in August, G12, G37 and G61 in September and G11 and G60 in October. In 1958 seven were scrapped, while the others were stored in pairs in the Launceston area and at various sidings between Launceston and Devonport.

In July 1961, G25 was bought and put in service by the Emu Bay Railway Co. It was destroyed in an accident and was replaced by G12 in July 1962. In 1963 it was replaced by a diesel and scrapped in 1964. By 1965 only G60 remained in storage at Relbia, near Launceston. All others of the class had been scrapped.

Builders: Victorian Railways Newport 6; South Australian Railways 4; Clyde Engineering 4

Preserved: Nil

Above: *Built by Newport Workshops in Victoria, G6 was the first to enter service with Tasmanian Government Railways in 1944. It was withdrawn from service in April 1957 and scrapped in 1958. The listed weight in working order of this locomotive was 119 tons with a length of 85 ft 4½ in from buffer to buffer. For more details see* The Decline of Steam Power on the Tasmanian Government Railways 1945–1965, *H.J.W. Stokes, ARHS Bulletin No. 348, October 1966, p. 217–29.*

At Midland Junction Workshops in 1944, work began on building eight tank engines similar to the earlier Ds class, but using parts from the 1902 E class tank engines combined with a new cab, bunker and four wheel bogie. The first of the Dm class entered service on 29 March 1945 using its E class number, 314. The next two also carried E class numbers 309 and 307. The next five were Nos 584 to 588, with No. 588 entering service on 23 November 1945. The boilers of the Ds and Dm classes were interchangeable and rated to haul the same loads, although the Dm carried a little more coal and water than the Ds.

During the locomotive shortage following the end of the war, the Dm class was used for a

DM CLASS (WA)
WHEEL ARRANGEMENT: 4-6-4T
SUBURBAN PASSENGER, GOODS
TANK LOCOMOTIVE
8 IN CLASS
FINAL NOS: 581-588

in operation.

Builder: Midland Junction Workshops 8

Preserved: Nil

variety of services. In the early 1950s a typical suburban train hauled by a Dm locomotive was limited to 200 tons, and this was reduced to 105 tons when required to work to diesel railcar schedules. By 1968 diesels took over suburban passenger services and the Dm was relegated to suburban goods traffic for the last few years of steam operation.

The last three Dm locomotives—Nos 586, 587 and 588—were all withdrawn from service on 17 June 1971, after about twenty-six years in operation.

Above: Built at Midland Junction Workshops in 1945, No. 309 was rebuilt using parts from Es 309 and entered service on 17 May 1945. It was renumbered No. 582 on 19 September 1945 and withdrawn from service on 10 September 1970 after twenty-five years in use. The listed weight in working order of this locomotive was 71 tons 18 cwt with a length of 43 ft 3¼ inches from buffer to buffer. For more details see A History of W.A.G.R. Steam Locomotives, *A. Gunzburg, ARHS(WA) 1984, p. l25–7.*

While the eight Dm class locomotives were being built at Midland Junction, plans were drawn up for a further ten locomotives which were almost identical, and called the Dd class. Also built at Midland Junction Workshops, the Dd locomotives were all built and in service in 1946. No. 591 was the first into service on 12 April, and No. 600 was the last, on 1 November. Though similar in appearance to the Dm, the Dd class used valve gear designed especially for this locomotive, which resulted in a free-running, economical engine. Other changes were made to the coupling rods, while the coupled wheels had Y-form spokes. The Dm, Ds and Dd class boilers

DD CLASS (WA)
WHEEL ARRANGEMENT: 4–6–4T
SUBURBAN PASSENGER, GOODS
TANK LOCOMOTIVE
10 IN CLASS
FINAL NOS: 591–600

were interchangeable and all three classes were rated to haul the same loads. The Dm and Dd both carried the same amount of coal and water.

By the late 1940s all three classes were being used on a variety of services, due to the shortage of locomotives at that time. By 1968 they were only used on suburban goods trains, as diesel railcars and locomotives took over on all suburban passenger services.

Builder: Midland Junction Workshops 10

Preserved: No. 592, at WAGR Diesel Depot, Forrestfield; No. 596, at Centrepoint Shopping Centre, Midland.

Above: Built at Midland Junction Workshops in 1946, No. 594 entered service with Western Australian Government Railways on 28 June 1946. It was withdrawn from service in February 1969 after twenty-three years in use. The listed weight in working order of this locomotive was 72 tons 12 cwt and it was 43 ft 3¼ in from buffer to buffer. For more details see A History of W.A.G.R. Steam Locomotives, A. Gunzburg, ARHS(WA) 1984, p. 125–7.

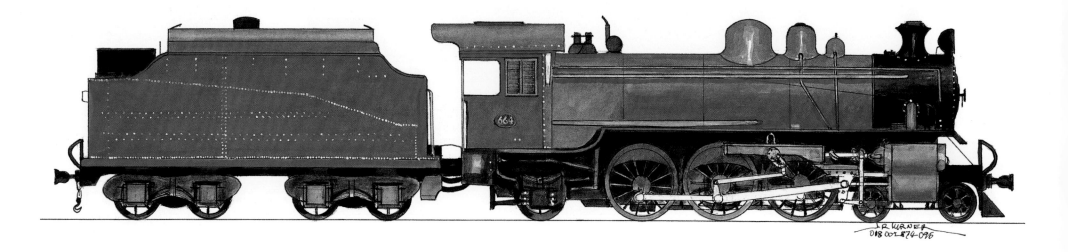

When advised by the Agent-General in England that fourteen war surplus 4–6–2 locomotives were available at 60 per cent of current prices, Western Australian Government Railways purchased them. Built by North British Locomotive Co in 1942, they had been stored unassembled at the Melbourne Military Depot in Derby England, and were shipped to Western Australia in 1946. No. 651 was the first to enter service on 30 November 1946 with the last being No. 664 on 4 April 1947.

Because of problems with coal supplies, they entered service using oil for fuel. Initially used on the express passenger services between Bunbury, Perth and Albany, they performed well. As a result a new express service, the Australind, was introduced on the main line to Bunbury. At that time it was the fastest 3 ft 6 in gauge passenger train in service in Australia.

U CLASS (WA)
WHEEL ARRANGEMENT: 4-6-2
EXPRESS PASSENGER LOCOMOTIVE
14 IN CLASS
FINAL NOS: 651–664

With the problems on the coal fields solved and the cost of oil rising, the U class became more expensive to run. By the mid 1950s they were 3½ times more expensive per mile to operate when compared to coal locomotives of similar power. In the mid 1950s diesel-electric locomotives were introduced, and the U class was assigned to goods services. By August 1957 twelve were in storage at Midland Junction, and one at Bunbury. No. 664 was still in service, having been converted to burn coal in December 1954.

The U class locomotives were all withdrawn in 1969, except for No. 655 which was the last to go on 10 September 1970, after about twenty-three years in use.

Builder: North British Locomotive Co 14

Preserved: No. 655, at ARHS Railway Museum, Bassendean.

Above: Built by the North British Locomotive Co in 1942, it was stored until 1946 and then shipped to Western Australia, where it entered service as No. 664 on 4 April 1947. It was converted to burn coal on 22 December 1954 and withdrawn from service on 6 November 1956. It was then rebuilt as a tank engine of the Ut class on 8 July 1957. The listed weight in working order of this locomotive and tender was 107 tons 15 cwt with a combined length of 60 ft 5⅛ in from buffer to buffer. For more details see A History of W.A.G.R. Steam Locomotives, A. Gunzburg, ARHS(WA) 1984, p.128–9.

F CLASS (TAS)
WHEEL ARRANGEMENT: 2–6–0
GOODS, PASSENGER LOCOMOTIVE
4 IN CLASS
FINAL NOS: 1–4

Following the end of WW II, the delay in delivery of new locomotives to Tasmanian Government Railways resulted in a stop-gap purchase of seven Commonwealth Government NFB class locomotives in 1948. Originally built as the Y class by James Martin in South Australia in the 1890s, they had been used on North Australian Railways between 1941 and 1944. Following their purchase they were hauled to Darwin and prepared for shipment to Tasmania. They left Darwin on the freighter *Barrigun* on 4 September 1948, and while the ship arrived in Hobart on 1 November it was not until the 16 November, when other cargo had been unloaded, that the ship was moved to Ocean Pier to unload the locomotives.

They were assembled at the Launceston workshops and painted black, with F1 the first into service on 21 February 1949. F4 was the last, on 23 May 1949. Initially all were used on goods services in Launceston and on the line west to Deloraine, but after a few months F2, F3 and F4 were sent to Hobart and used on goods, shunting and passenger services. With the introduction of new locomotives in 1951 they were used less, and F4 was sent back to Launceston.

By the mid 1950s withdrawals had begun, with F4 in 1954 and F2 in June 1955. F1 was sold in May 1956 to Emu Bay Railway, while F3 remained in use until 1957 and was written off in 1965.

Builder: James Martin & Co. 4
Preserved: Nil

Above: Built by James Martin & Co, F4 entered service with Tasmanian Government Railways on 23 May 1949. Originally entering service with South Australian Railways as Y class No. 138 on 7 November 1892, it was rebuilt as Yx class on 2 November 1923 and went to Commonwealth Railways on 5 February 1942. The listed weight in working order of this locomotive was and tender was 49 tons 19 cwt with a combined length of 39 ft 4⅞ in from buffer to buffer.
For more details see The F-class 2–6–0s of the Tasmanian Government Railways, *H.J.W Stokes, ARHS Bulletin No. 551, September 1983, p. 194–9.*

The first of a projected twenty-five locomotives of this class, No. 5801 entered service with N.S.W. Government Railways on 19 January 1950. The final locomotive, No. 5813, entered service on 31 October 1952. The remaining twelve were never completed.

Though approved to be built in 1943, it was seven years before this modified version of the (D)57 class entered service. It looked very similar to the (D)57, but had been modified to enable it to work the northern line. However only two return trips were made, apart from delivery workings. It was used mostly on the Illawarra, southern and western lines.

(D)58 CLASS (NSW)
WHEEL ARRANGEMENT: 4-8-2
HEAVY GOODS LOCOMOTIVE
13 IN CLASS
FINAL NOS: 5801-5813

Once the (D)58 was in service a number of problems became apparent, particularly with the valve gear. This required more frequent maintenance but was also less accessible. It was also found that they used more coal and water than the (D)57.

By July 1957 all had been withdrawn from service, with the last being cut up in 1964. With only five years in service, No. 5813 had travelled only 160 398 miles before being scrapped.

Builders: Eveleigh Workshop (NSWR) 11; Cardiff Workshop (NSWR) 2
Preserved: Nil

Above: *The first of 13 locomotives of this class, No. 5801 entered service with N.S.W. Government Railways on 19 January 1950. It was built by Eveleigh Workshops and withdrawn from service in February 1957 after only seven years, but was the longest in service of its class. It was scrapped in January 1964, having travelled only 241 280 miles whilst in service. In working order the combined weight of locomotive and tender was 227 tons 12 cwt 3 qtr with a combined length of 87 ft 6⅛ in from buffer to buffer. For more details see A Compendium of NSW Steam Locomotives, compiled by A. Grunbach, ARHS(NSW) 1989, p. 232–5.*

The C17 class originally entered service in the 1920s. In 1938 an updated version was introduced, which had a bigger sedan type cab and other changes. In June and November 1947 contracts were let to Walkers Ltd for a total of forty more C17 locomotives, with Timken roller bearings fitted on all axles. These locomotives began entering service in 1950. They were painted a medium brown colour with polished boiler bands, black smoke box with red buffer beams and willow green lining on tender sides and footboard edges. They were nicknamed 'Brown Bombers' after the world heavyweight boxing champion of the time, Joe Louis from America.

Most of their work was hauling goods and mixed trains on secondary lines, where they had a maximum speed of 45 mph. However they were also used to haul the Sunshine Express north of Bowen until the track was upgraded, the south-west passenger service between Dirranbandi and

C17 CLASS (1950 VERSION) (QLD)
WHEEL ARRANGEMENT: 4-8-0
MIXED TRAFFIC LOCOMOTIVE
40 IN CLASS
FINAL NOS: 961-1000

Builder: Walkers Ltd 40

Preserved: No. 965, opposite Joseph Banks Wharf, Gladstone; No. 966, at junction of Gregory and Matthew Flinders St, Cooee Bay, Yeppoon Parks; No. 967, at Ghan Preservation Society, Macdonnel Siding, Alice Springs; No. 971, at Historical Society, Chinchilla (restored as C17 921); No. 974, at QR; No. 980, at Blackwater Park, Blackwater; No. 988, at Bunda St (behind station), Cairns; No. 996, at Tuesleys Park, cnr North St and Esplanande, Southport; No. 1000, at QR in storage.

Warwick, and the Western Mail from Roma. Though the amount they hauled varied from line to line, on level track they were eventually permitted to haul a maximum of 695 tons.

In 1970 diesels took over on all Queensland Government Railway lines, and while quite a few C17 locomotives were still on record at the start of the year all were written off by August 1970.

Above: Built in 1950 by Walkers Ltd, No. 961 entered service in April 1950 and was written off the books in October 1969, after about nineteen years in service. Listed weight in working order of locomotive and tender was 82 tons 18 cwt with a combined length of 53 ft 5½ in from buffer to buffer. For more details see Locomotives in the Tropics Vol. 2, J. Armstrong, ARHS(QLD) 1994, p. 57–63.

The Cs class was made up of two different batches of locomotives. The first to enter service had a 4–6–0 wheel arrangement and was built by Baldwin Locomotive Works, U.S.A. in 1902. These were all converted to 4–6–2 between 1908 and 1918.

The second batch was built by Midland Railway Workshops as 4–6–2 and entered service in 1915. The first locomotive converted to Cs was No. 440 on 22 June 1929. It had been built at Midland and first entered service as a Ca class on 30 October 1915. After it was superheated, No. 440 was a complete success, which resulted in the gradual conversion of C and Ca class locomotives to Cs class.

By the mid 1930s metal fatigue was evident in the frames of some C class locomotives, and five new frames were built and fitted, the last in 1945. The introduction of the W class to light lines

CS CLASS (WA)
WHEEL ARRANGEMENT: 4-6-2
GOODS LOCOMOTIVE
16 IN CLASS
FINAL NOS: 264, 265, 268, 269, 270, 271, 275, 431–437, 439, 440

saw the C class removed from service by the mid 1950s. Four of the re-framed locomotives were transferred to the Western Australian Government Railway's Banksiadale sawmill in the early 1950s, where they hauled logs to the mill and shuttled the cut timber to Dwellingup. They were painted green and given the names of local native timber. No. 432 was named *Marri*, No. 439 *Banksia*, No. 440 was called *Jarrah* and No. 270 *Black Butt*. These four locomotives were sold, together with the timber mill, to Hawker Siddeley Building Supplies on 10 October 1961, and were scrapped on 6 May 1964 after the Banksiadale mill burnt down.

Builders: Baldwin Locomotive Works 7; Midland Railway Workshops 9

Preserved: Nil

Above: One of the C class locomotives built in 1902 by the Baldwin Locomotive Works, U.S.A., No. 270 entered service on 9 July 1902 and was converted to 4–6–2 on 10 September 1908. It was rebuilt on 22 June 1945 and converted to Cs class on 12 June 1950. Transferred to the WAGR Banksiadale sawmill on 18 January 1952, it was painted green and named Black Butt *on 4 September 1953. It was scrapped on 6 May 1964. The listed weight in working order of this locomotive and tender was 71 tons 9 cwt with a combined length of 55 ft 3 in from buffer to buffer. For more details see* A History of W.A.G.R. Steam Locomotives, *A. Gunzburg, ARHS(WA) 1984, p.72–5.*

In the years following the end of WW II there was not only a shortage of locomotives, but also a huge backlog of repairs which had been deferred. By mid 1948, one out of every three locomotives was out of service needing repair. As a result, an order placed in 1947 for ten Pr class locomotives was increased to thirty-five in 1949. Built by the North British Locomotive Co in 1949, the first Pm to enter service was No. 701 on 4 January 1950, with the last being No. 719 on 9 May 1950. The first Pmr into service was No. 722 on 20 June 1950, with No. 734 the last on 6 September 1950.

On entering service these locomotives were found to ride badly because the coupled wheels were not compensated, and so were not able to maintain passenger speed. As a result they were restricted to 40 mph and used on goods and fast freight services, where they performed well. They

PM AND PMR CLASSES (WA)
WHEEL ARRANGEMENT: 4-6-2
GOODS LOCOMOTIVE
35 IN CLASS
FINAL NOS: 701–735

were based at Northam and Merredin, and used on the Eastern Goldfields railways and their branch lines, and in the south from Bunbury to Perth and Collie. They continued in service until the end of the steam era. The first withdrawals of Pm and Pmr locomotives took place on 10 September 1970, with the remaining eighteen locomotives withdrawn on 14 August 1972 after about twenty-two years in service.

Builder: North British Locomotive Co 35

Preserved: No. 701, at ARHS Railway Museum, Bassendean; No. 706, at Allen Shepherd Memorial Park, Wickepin Rd, Narrogin; No. 720, at children's playground, caravan park, Grove St, Peterborough, SA; No. 721, at Old Station Museum, Fitzgerald St, Northam; No. 729, at Old Station, Coolgardie; No. 735, at Perth Electric Tramway Museum Society, Whiteman Park, Caversham.

Above: Built by the North British Locomotive Co in 1949, No. 713 entered service with Western Australian Government Railways on 28 September 1950. A Pm class locomotive, it had plain bearings on the coupled axles while the Pmr had roller bearings on all axles. After twenty-two years in service No. 713 was in the last group to be withdrawn from service on 14 August 1972. The listed weight in working order of this locomotive and tender was 109 tons 1 cwt with a combined length of 63 ft 7⅝ in from buffer to buffer. For more details see A History of W.A.G.R. Steam Locomotives, A. Gunzburg, ARHS(WA) 1984, p. 131–3.

Built by the North British Locomotive Co in 1949 and 1950, these locomotives were similar in appearance to the earlier N class which had entered service in the mid 1920s. Delivery of the first of the new locomotives was held up by a railway strike which lasted eight weeks. The first of these locomotives to enter service was No. 450 on 17 August 1950, while No. 499 was the last in service on 26 April 1951. A total of ten locomotives were sold to South Australian Government Railways within a few weeks of entering service, to become their 750 class with numbers 750 to 759.

Almost the same weight and length as the earlier N class, the new locomotives had alterations in the boiler and firebox which improved performance. They were used on the light country lines,

NEW N CLASS (VIC)
WHEEL ARRANGEMENT: 2-8-2
GOODS LOCOMOTIVE
50 IN CLASS
FINAL NOS: 450–499

replacing the DD and DDE class locomotives which were still in service. By the mid 1950s almost half of the class had been converted to burn fuel oil.

On 22 July 1965, No. 486 was scrapped after travelling only 190 949 miles. Others soon followed. The last to leave service was No. 475, which had been working at Serviceton until withdrawn from service on 14 October 1966. It had only travelled 160 276 miles in fifteen years in service.

Builder: North British Locomotive Co 50

Preserved: No. 477, at Port Dock Railway Museum (SA) Inc, Port Adelaide, (No 752 of 750 class).

Above: Built by North British Locomotive Co in Scotland, No. 455 entered service with Victorian Railways on 10 October 1950. It was scrapped on 15 December 1965, having travelled only 167 716 miles in fifteen years in service. The listed weight in working order of this locomotive and tender was 124 tons 13 cwt 2 qtr with a combined length of 67 ft 5¼ in from buffer to buffer. For more details see The Era of the N Class Locomotives in the Victorian Railways, by Stephen Watson.

Even though the Australian Standard Garratt had not been a success, the need for powerful locomotives resulted in an order being placed for ten Garratt locomotives with Beyer Peacock & Co on 3 October 1947. In June and August 1949 another twenty locomotives were ordered. The first ten were built by Beyer Peacock in Manchester, and arrived on the heavy lift ship *Peter Dal* on 3 September 1950. No. 1009 was the first to enter service on 22 September 1950. The second group of twenty locomotives was built by Société Franco-Belge de Materiel du Chemins de Fer, Raismes, France. Most entered service in 1951, with No. 1106 the last in January 1952.

After testing, they were used on all types of trains, from Brisbane north to Rockhampton and

BEYER GARRATT CLASS (QLD)
WHEEL ARRANGEMENT: 4-8-2 2-8-4
BEYER GARRATT ARTICULATED
LOCOMOTIVE
29 IN CLASS
FINAL NOS: 1001–1010, 1091–1109

west to Emerald. By 1953 diesels had replaced the Garratts on the north coast express trains, but they continued to haul trains to Emerald. As new coal mines were opened, the Garratts were moved to handle the increased traffic. By the mid 1960s more powerful diesels were taking over the coal trains. In June 1968 twenty-two of the class were written off, and sent to Ipswich and Redbank to be cut up. In June 1969 the last six in service were all withdrawn. No. 1009 was sent to Redbank for preservation, and in 1995 it was restored to working condition.

Builders: Beyer Peacock & Co 10; Société Franco-Belge de Materiel du Chemins de Fer 20

Preserved: No. 1009, as a QR Heritage locomotive.

Above: *Built by Beyer Peacock & Co in 1950, No. 1002 entered service with Queensland Railways in October 1950. It was written off in June 1968 and cut up for scrap after about eighteen years in service. The listed weight in working order of this locomotive was 137 tons with a length of 90 ft ⅜ in from buffer to buffer. For more details see* Locomotives in the Tropics *Vol. 2, J. Armstrong, ARHS(QLD) 1994, p. 122–31.*

The need for a locomotive to replace the Rx class still in use on country lines resulted in the purchase of ten N class locomotives from Victorian Railways in 1951. Built by North British Locomotive Co, they had only just entered service when they were sold to South Australian Railways.

Used mostly on goods services around Adelaide, they were also used in the south of the state at Tailem Bend and Mount Gambier, Truro to the east and Spalding in the north. The Rx locomotives they replaced were then used on the suburban lines. The 750 class had large smoke deflectors and were smaller in size than the 700 class, but though they looked different to

750 CLASS (SA)
WHEEL ARRANGEMENT: 2-8-2
GOODS LOCOMOTIVE
10 IN CLASS
NOS: 750–759

the locomotives then in use, they provided good service. Apart from removing the buffers, no other changes were made after they arrived in South Australia from Victoria.

With diesels being used on more lines they had only a short time in service, with No. 751 the first condemned on 6 July 1961. By late 1963, only two remained in service. Nos 752 and 755 were finally stored in October 1966, after about fifteen years in service.

Builder: North British Locomotive Co 10

Preserved: No. 752, at Port Dock Railway Museum (SA) Inc, Port Adelaide.

Above: *Built by North British Locomotive Co, No. 752 had been in service with Victorian Railways for only a few weeks when it was sold to South Australian Railways. It entered service there on 2 March 1951 and travelled a total of 262 593 miles during fifteen years in service. The listed weight in working order of this locomotive and tender was 124 tons 13 cwt 2 qtr with a combined length of 67 ft 5 in over the coupling points. For more details see Steam Locomotives and Railcars of the South Australian Railways, R.E. Fluck, R. Sampson and K.J. Bird, Mile End Museum 1986, p. 108–9.*

W CLASS (WA)
WHEEL ARRANGEMENT: 4-8-2
GOODS LOCOMOTIVE
60 IN CLASS
FINAL NOS: 901–960

The need for locomotives able to operate on light lines resulted in planning in early 1947 for the building of the W class. On 23 August 1948 thirty were ordered with Beyer Peacock & Co, with delivery due in 1950. On 10 May 1949, Beyer Peacock confirmed that a further ten locomotives had been added to the earlier order. In early 1950 the locomotive was redesigned to improve its operation. The crew were not forgotten, with adjustable cushioned seats, arm rests and a double cab roof with air space between.

On 17 January 1950 the changes had been agreed and the order was increased again from forty to a total of sixty locomotives. The first forty locomotives arrived from England partly assembled, while the last twenty were fully assembled when they arrived. No. 901 was the first to enter on 27 April 1951 with No. 960 the last on 27 June 1952. They introduced the modern larch green livery used on most of the post-war W.A.G.R. locomotives.

They performed well in tests and had none of the problems of the Pm and Pmr classes. The W class was mostly used on goods traffic, but at times hauled the Australind and other fast express trains with no problem keeping to the schedules. On 17 June 1971 over forty were withdrawn from service. The eighteen remaining were withdrawn on 14 August 1972, after twenty-one years in service.

Builder: North British Locomotive Co 60

Preserved: Nos 901 and 907, at Steamtown Peterborough RPS; Nos 903, 908, 920 and 945, at Hotham Valley Railway, Pinjarra; Nos 916, 931 ,933, and 934, at Pichi Richi Preservation Society, Quorn; No. 919, at Esperance Bay Historical Society, Esperance; No. 924, at Ghan Preservation Society, Macdonnel Siding, Alice Springs; No. 943, at Mining Museum, Collie; Nos 947 and 953, at ARHS Railway Museum, Bassendean.

Above: Built by North British Locomotive Co in 1951, No. 903 entered service with Western Australian Government Railways on 15 May 1951 and was withdrawn from service on 17 June 1971 after 20 years in service. The listed weight in working order of this locomotive and tender was 101 tons 2 cwt 1 qtr with a combined length of 61 ft 11 in from buffer to buffer. For more details see A History of W.A.G.R. Steam Locomotives, A. Gunzburg, ARHS(WA) 1984, p. 134–7.

DD17 CLASS (QLD)
WHEEL ARRANGEMENT: 4-6-4T
PASSENGER TANK LOCOMOTIVE
12 IN CLASS
FINAL NOS: 949-954, 1046-1051

The need for a more powerful tank locomotive to be used on suburban passenger services resulted in the building of the DD17 class locomotives. An initial order of six was then increased to twelve in 1946–47. During construction, a number of weight reduction techniques were used, and this enabled increased fuel to be carried. Built by Ipswich Railway Workshops, the first to enter service was No. 949, in December 1948. No. 1051 was the last in July 1952, and it was also the last new steam locomotive to be built at Ipswich Railway Workshops.

The first of the class to enter service was painted black with red trim, and the next five were dark blue. The following six were all painted Midway blue with red trim, and in 1951 all were re-painted Midway blue, resulting in the nickname 'Blue Babies'. Mostly used on the north side of Brisbane, they were reliable and performed well, while the diesels which replaced them, though cleaner, were sluggish by comparison.

When used on passenger services, the DD17 hauled eight carriages with a tare weight of about 210 tons during peak hours. They were also used on goods services during off-peak times and were able to haul up to 445 tons. In November 1966, No. 1048 was the first to be withdrawn from service; the rest of the class were gradually withdrawn, with Nos 1046 and 1047 being the last to go in October 1969.

Builder: Ipswich Railway Workshops 12

Preserved: Nos 1046, 1047 and 1049, at Zig Zag Railway Co-operative Ltd, Lithgow, NSW; No. 1051, in QR Heritage fleet.

Above: Built at Ipswich Railway Workshops in 1951 No. 1047 entered service with Queensland Government Railways in June 1951 and was withdrawn from service in October 1968. It is now in use at the Zig Zag Railway at Lithgow in NSW. The listed weight on working order of this locomotive was 62 tons with a length of 39 ft 7⅜ in from buffer to buffer. For more details see Locomotives in the Tropics Vol. 2, J. Armstrong, ARHS(QLD) 1994, p. 114–121.

Designed in 1948 by the engineers' department of the Victorian Railways, the R class was built by the North British Locomotive Co in Scotland. It was designed to replace the A2 class on main line passenger services. Except for H220—*Heavy Harry*—these locomotives were one of the most powerful to be used on Victorian Railways. The first to enter service was R700 on 24 July 1951, the last being R769 on 23 September 1953. A special crane was imported from England and installed on Nelson Pier where it unloaded all the R and N class locomotives which had been sent as deck cargo on ships from England.

Once in service, the R class proved its superiority over the ageing A2 locomotives. One major advantage was the ability to use inferior grade coal, and while the A2, H and S class locomotives required frequent stops to clean their fires, the R class could run non-stop. This gave a dramatic reduction in passenger train times and improved freight services. Used on both fast passenger and goods trains, the R class was used on all main lines north-east to Wodonga, west to Dimboola and also on the south-eastern and main lines. With the introduction of diesels, No. 715 was the first of the class to be withdrawn from service on 4 May 1956, having travelled 95 518 miles during four years in service.

By 1968 only two of the class remained. No. 766 was the first of these to go, on 1 April, after fourteen years in service and having travelled 137 664 miles. Using wood for fuel and with cars being directed around it, No 766 slowly reversed into Railway Reserve in Bendigo. When in position in the park, the wheels were welded to the rails, as blasts from its whistle rang out and crowds of people stood and watched.

The last to go was R707. It was withdrawn from service on 25 November 1968, having travelled 123 572 miles during fourteen years in service.

Builder: North British Locomotive Co. 70

Preserved: Nos 700, 761 and 766, at Steamrail Victoria Ltd, Champion Rd, Newport; No. 704, at ARHS Railway Museum, Champion Rd, North Williamstown; Nos 707 and 753, at Operations Newport Workshops; No. 711, at West Coast Railway, Ballarat East Locomotives.

Above: *Built by the North British Locomotive Co, No. R701 entered service with Victorian Railways on 20 July 1951 and worked for several months. It was then was transferred to Ballarat, where it spent most of its working life. It was withdrawn from service on 22 January 1965, having travelled 188 469 miles during fourteen years in service. The listed weight in working order of this locomotive and tender was 187 tons 8 cwt with a combined length of 77 ft 3¼ in from buffer to buffer. For more details see* The Era of the R Class Locomotives in the Victorian Railways, *S. Watson.*

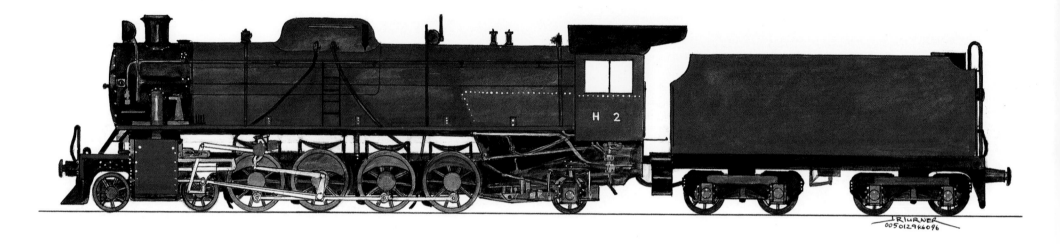

Following the end of WW II, orders had been placed for eight heavy goods locomotives. Vulcan Foundry was eventually given the job of building them. They arrived as deck cargo on the freighter *Belpareil*, which docked in Hobart on 12 October 1951. After unloading they were towed to Launceston workshops, from where they entered service between 7 November and 4 December 1951. They mostly hauled goods trains on the main line north of Parattah and the western line east of Wynyard, and also on the Fingal line.

Painted emerald green instead of black when they entered service, H2 and H6 were repainted red in September 1956 and assigned to haul the daily afternoon passenger service from Launceston to Wynyard. However this train was cancelled when a new timetable was introduced in 1957.

Beginning in January 1960, H8 was the first to be overhauled and its boiler retubed, followed by H6, H3, H5 and H7. The work was completed by August 1961, but by this time new diesel

H CLASS (TAS)
WHEEL ARRANGEMENT: 4-8-2
HEAVY GOODS LOCOMOTIVE
8 IN CLASS
FINAL NOS: H1-H8

locomotives were entering service, and no further overhauls were carried out on the H class until H2 was overhauled in 1967.

By June 1962 three of the class were stored, but steam-hauled excursion trains became increasingly popular with the public from the mid 1960s, and some goods work kept other class members in traffic, until further withdrawals in 1966 and 1968. Two were kept in service until the railway centenary celebrations in February 1971. With H5 withdrawn in mid 1971, H2 was the last to go in September 1975.

Builder: Vulcan Foundry 8

Preserved: H1, at Tasmanian Transport Museum, Glenorchy; H2, at Derwent Valley Railway, New Norfolk; H5, at Hillwood Strawberry Farm, Tamar Valley; H6, at Perth Lions Park, Midland Highway, Tasmania; H7, at Van Diemen Light Railway Society, Don Village, Devonport.

Above: Built by the Vulcan Foundry in England in 1951, H2 entered service with Tasmanian Government Railways on 23 November 1951 and last ran in September 1975. It is now at the Derwent Valley Railway, New Norfolk. The listed combined weight in working order was 110 tons 14 cwt with a combined length of 62 ft 9 in from buffer to buffer. For more details see Locomotives of the Tasmanian Transport Museum, Glenorchy, Tasmania, *A. Dix, 1991, p. 8–10.*

The M class were ordered from Great Britain following the end of WW II, and built by Robert Stephenson & Hawthorns Ltd in 1951. They arrived from England as deck cargo on the heavy lift ship *Christen Smith*, which docked in Hobart on 12 March 1952. After being unloaded, the locomotives were towed to Launceston where they were prepared to enter service. They were the last steam locomotives bought by Tasmanian Government Railways, and entered service between 7 April and 6 October 1952. Used on passenger and mixed trains in the north of the state, they were designed for use on light lines and replaced the old A and B class locomotives then in use.

As diesels were introduced on more lines, steam services were reduced, and on 21 December 1961 M6 hauled the last regular daily steam passenger service between Devonport and Burnie. In the late

M CLASS (TAS)
WHEEL ARRANGEMENT: 4-6-2
PASSENGER LOCOMOTIVE
10 IN CLASS
FINAL NOS: M1-M6

1960s some M class locomotives were used on excursion trains, and in February 1971 four M class were used in the railway centenary celebrations. However in June 1971 all were withdrawn from service and used as steam cleaners, except for M3, which was overhauled in March 1972 and remained in service until it was withdrawn in October 1975. Three members of the class, M4, M5 and M6, have since been restored to service.

Builder: Robert Stephenson & Hawthorns Ltd 10

Preserved: M1, off Midland Hwy on road leading to caravan park, Ross; M2, at Tyneside Locomotive Museum, Newcastle, UK; M3 and M4, at Van Diemen Light Railway Society, Don Village, Devonport; M5, at Tasmanian Transport Museum, Glenorchy. M6, at Bellarine Peninsula Railway, Queenscliffe, Vic.

Above: *Locomotive M6 was originally M9 until renumbered in 1958. It was painted green for most of its life but then painted red for the railway centenary celebrations in February 1971. The listed weight in working order of this locomotive and tender was 96 tons 12 cwt 3 qtr with a combined length of 59 feet 2¼ in from buffer to buffer. For more details see* Locomotives of the Tasmanian Transport Museum, Glenorchy, Tasmania, *A. Dix, 1991, p. 11–13.*

Prior to WW II a number of narrow-gauge Garratt locomotives had been used in Australia. During the war, the need for a powerful narrow-gauge locomotive to handle the increased traffic resulted in this Australian-designed and built Garratt, known as the Australian Standard Garratt. They were not popular with crews because of many problems, and were only used to haul ore trains until the new 400 class Beyer Garratts arrived from England. All six locomotives had been withdrawn from service on Western Australian Government Railways by 1951.

The first to enter service with South Australian Railways was No. 300, on 19 March 1952. No.

300 CLASS (SA)
WHEEL ARRANGEMENT: 4-8-2 2-8-4
ARTICULATED GARRATT
LOCOMOTIVE
6 IN CLASS
NOS: 300-305

305 was the last, on 5 November 1952. Based at Peterborough, they were used to haul ore trains from Cockburn to Belalie North, and soon lived up to their past reputation with a variety of problems and many complaints from their crews as a result. The arrival of the 400 class in mid 1953 saw them taken out of traffic. All of the locomotives were condemned by late 1954 but they were not officially withdrawn from service until 24 February 1956.

Builders: Newport Workshops Victoria 2; Midland Workshops Western Australia 4
Preserved: Nil

Above: Built by Midland Workshops in Western Australia as G26, it entered service with Western Australian Government Railways on 22 November 1943. It was withdrawn from service on 7 November 1951 and entered service with South Australian Government Railways as No 305 on 5 November 1952. It was finally withdrawn from service on 24 February 1956. The listed weight in working order of this locomotive was 119 tons with a length of 85 ft 10 in from buffer to buffer. For more details see Narrow Gauge Memories: The Locomotives, S. McNicol, Railmac Publications 1993, p. 169–74.

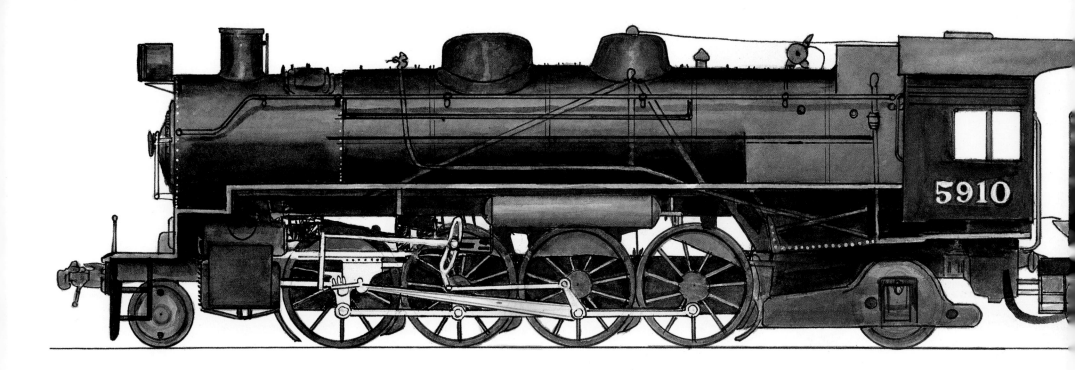

The first of a total of twenty locomotives of this class, No. 5901 entered service with N.S.W. Government Railways on 30 August 1952. The final locomotive, No. 5920, entered service on 31 March 1953. They were the only class to be delivered as oil-fired. These light Mikado-type locomotives were ordered following the end of WW II, but needed an especially shortened tender to fit on the 60-foot turntables then in use. It was not until 1952 that Baldwin-Lima-Hamilton Co in the U.S.A. could fill the order.

The (D)59 class was initially used on the northern and western lines, but this was restricted

(D)59 CLASS (NSW)
WHEEL ARRANGEMENT: 2–8–2
GOODS LOCOMOTIVE
20 IN CLASS
FINAL NOS: 5901–5920

due to the fact that they burnt oil. With the high cost of oil and the need to provide special storage facilities, it was decided in 1961 to convert most of the class to burn coal, with seventeen of the twenty locomotives converted between 1962 and 1966. By 1970 diesels began to replace them, with No. 5910 the last withdrawn from service in December 1970.

Builder: Baldwin-Lima-Hamilton Co 20

Preserved: Nos 5908, 5910 and 5916, at Rail Transport Museum, Thirlmere; No. 5917, at Lachlan Valley Railway, Cowra; No. 5920, at Dorrigo Steam Railway and Museum.

Above: *One of twenty locomotives of this class, No. 5910 entered service with N.S.W. Government Railways on 21 November 1952 and was converted to burn coal in February 1966. It was condemned on 11 August 1972 and withdrawn from regular service in December 1972. Restored to operating condition by the N.S.W. RTM, it is often used to haul heritage trains. The listed weight in working order of this locomotive and tender was 151 tons with a combined length of 67 ft 5½ in from buffer to buffer. For more details see* A Compendium of N.S.W. Steam Locomotives, *compiled by A. Grunbach, ARHS(NSW) 1989, p. 236–9.*

The first of a projected fifty locomotives of this class, No. 6002 entered service with N.S.W. Government Railways on 30 July 1952. The final locomotive, No. 6040, entered service on 2 January 1957. Only forty-two were delivered, with a further five in knocked-down condition as spare parts. One other locomotive was assembled from available spare parts at Cardiff Workshops and numbered 6010. It was withdrawn in August 1968.

The first Beyer Garratt type locomotive to be used on N.S.W. Government Railways, the (AD)60 class was introduced to haul goods along secondary lines for transfer to main line locomotives. Initially they were found to carry insufficient coal, so the bunker was modified to carry an additional four tons. It became evident that they were more suitable for main line work, but a number of problems needed to be solved, with the brakes, the need for dual controls and the problem of the crew being unable to hear detonators on the track. High cab temperatures prohibited them from working single-track tunnels with curves.

(AD)60 CLASS (NSW)
WHEEL ARRANGEMENT: 4-8-4 4-8-4
BEYER GARRATT HEAVY GOODS LOCOMOTIVE
42 IN CLASS
FINAL NOS: 6001–6042

From 1957, thirty of the class were modified to improve performance. They were known as 'Super Garratts' and identified by the double plus sign after their number. Because of their size, special 105 foot turntables were installed at Enfield, Broadwater and Werris Creek, with triangles used at other locations to turn the locomotive around. From 1966 onward, double-headed Garratts were a common sight in the Gosford area. The official last run for steam locomotives was done for politicians on 4 March 1972, but the final trip by a steam locomotive was on 24 February 1973, when No. 6042 did three trips to Wangi. Thus ended the regular use of steam on New South Wales Government Railways although No 6029 made a number of ARHS trips to Cooma in July 1976.

Builder: Beyer Peacock 42

Preserved: No. 6029, at Canberra Railway Museum, Canberra (for National Museum); No. 6039, at Dorrigo Steam Railway and Museum; No. 6040, at Rail Transport Museum, Thirlmere; No. 6042, at Dorrigo Steam Railway and Museum (at Forbes).

Above: After entering service with N.S.W. Government Railways on 27 November 1952, No. 6006 was converted to dual control in February 1960. It was withdrawn from service in May 1968 and was scrapped in October 1968, having travelled 478 601 miles during sixteen years of service. The listed weight in working order of this locomotive was 260 tons with a length of 108 ft 8 in from buffer to buffer. After rebuilding with extended bunker, dual controls and adjusted axle load, the weight increased to 264 tons 5 cwt. For more details see A Compendium of NSW Steam Locomotives, compiled by A. Grunbach, ARHS(NSW) 1989, p. 240–7.

740 CLASS (SA)
WHEEL ARRANGEMENT: 2-8-2
GOODS LOCOMOTIVE
10 IN CLASS
NOS 740-749

Built by Clyde Engineering in Sydney, the 740 class was part of an order of fifty locomotives which were intended for use in China. In 1948 the Communist takeover of China was partly responsible for the order being cancelled. The twenty locomotives which had been built were then used within Australia, with ten going to Commonwealth Railways as the L class, and the other ten becoming the 740 class in South Australia. After conversion to 5 ft 3 in gauge, the 740 class locomotives were sent from Sydney to South Australia on flat cars, and assembled on arrival. Once in service they were mostly used on goods trains. However they did haul passenger trains to Tailem Bend 60 miles east of Adelaide and to Gawler, 25 miles to the north of Adelaide.

As more diesels entered service, the 740s spent their last years as shunters in the Port Pirie area. They were the last new steam locomotives to enter service in South Australia. On 16 July 1963, seven of the class were condemned. By July 1964, two more had met the same fate, leaving only No. 747. This was later condemned on 25 November 1965, having travelled 200 754 miles during twelve years in service.

Builder: Clyde Engineering Sydney 10
Preserved: Nil

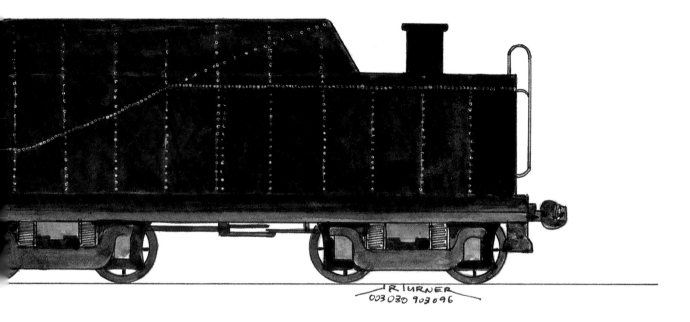

Above: Built by Clyde Engineering in Sydney, No. 746 entered service with South Australian Railways on 13 February 1953. It was condemned on 16 July 1963, having travelled 194 775 miles during ten years in service. It was cut up at Islington on 5 March 1964, with its boiler being used at the SAPFOR timber mills. The listed weight in working order of this locomotive and tender was 165 tons 1 cwt with a combined length of 73 ft 1½ in over the coupling points. For more details see Steam Locomotives and Railcars of the South Australian Railways, R.E. Fluck, R. Sampson and K.J. Bird, Mile End Museum, 1986, p. 110–11.

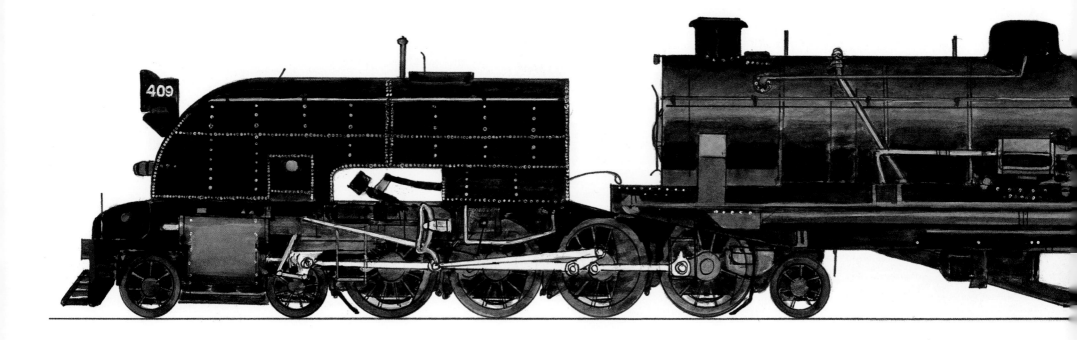

Ordered from Beyer Peacock & Co in England in 1951, the 400 class locomotives were built by Société Franco-Belge de Materiel du Chemins de Fer, of Raismes in France. Each locomotive was tested, and then stripped down and shipped from Dunkirk on the MS *Belnor*. The first to arrive were Nos 400 to 404, which left France in early April 1953 and arrived at Port Pirie on 1 June. The ship then returned and picked up Nos 405 to 409 on 6 October 1953 and arrived back at Port Pirie on 18 December. After partial assembly at Port Pirie South depot they were hauled to Peterborough for final assembly. The first into service was No. 403 on 29 June 1953, while No. 406 was last on 13 February 1954.

The problems with the 300 class were soon forgotten as the 400 class proved themselves to be

400 CLASS (SA)
WHEEL ARRANGEMENT: 4-8-2 2-8-4
ARTICULATED GARRATT
LOCOMOTIVE
10 IN CLASS
NOS: 400-409

reliable and they were able to haul the heavy goods and ore trains between Cockburn and Port Pirie. They were also used on the Broken Hill Express, and No. 402 on one occasion went as far north as Quorn.

The use of diesels in the early 1960s resulted in most of the 400 class being stored for several years, but in 1969 six were back in regular service. They hauled ore trains until 10 January 1970, when No. 404 hauled the last narrow gauge steam service out of Port Pirie. These last six locomotives were all condemned on 1 May 1970, after about seventeen years in service.

Builder: Société Franco-Belge de Materiel du Chemins de Fer 10
Preserved: No. 402, at Zig Zag Railway Co-operative Ltd, Lithgow; No. 409, at Port Dock Railway Museum (SA) Inc, Port Adelaide.

Above: *Built by Société Franco-Belge de Materiel du Chemins de Fer, Raismes, France, No. 409 entered service on 6 February 1954. It was condemned on 1 May 1970 and went to the Mile End Railway Museum on 17 November 1970.*
The listed weight in working order of this locomotive was 148 tons 19 cwt with a length of 87 ft 5 in over the couplers. For more details see Narrow Gauge Memories: The Locomotives, S. McNicol, Railmac Publications 1993, p. 173–7.

D esigned by the rolling stock engineers of the Victorian Railways, the J class was built by Vulcan Foundry in England. No. 500 was the first to enter service on 19 March 1954, with the last, No. 559, in service on 17 December 1954. They were all shipped as deck cargo from England and unloaded at Williamstown. Once in service they soon replaced the D2 and D3 class locomotives then in use on the light lines and branch lines.

With improved design and crew comfort, the Js were easier and less costly to maintain. They had been fitted with the latest designs in smoke deflectors and cow catchers, and thirty of the class were delivered as coal burners, while the rest were oil burners. As diesel locomotives entered service on more lines over the next few years, the J class hauled the last steam services on most lines in Victoria.

J CLASS (VIC)
WHEEL ARRANGEMENT: 2–8–0
GOODS LOCOMOTIVE
60 IN CLASS
FINAL NOS: 500–559

The first to be withdrawn from service was No. 523 on 17 November 1967, having travelled 134 444 miles in thirteen years in service. Nos 507 and 515 were the last two in regular use, as yard pilots at Newport until mid 1972.

Builder: Vulcan Foundry England 60

Preserved: No. 507, at Mulwala, NSW; No. 512, and No. 515, at Seymour Steam Loco Preservation Group, Seymour; No. 516, at Poulter Reserve, Poulter Avenue, Greensborough; No. 524, at park at junction of Walker and Hammil Sts, Donald; No. 526, at Steamrail Victoria Ltd, Champion Rd, Newport; No. 536, at Claude Lee Reserve, Gellibrand St, Colac; No. 539, at Apex Park, High St, Dimboola; Nos 541 and 549, at Castlemaine and Maldon Railway Preservation Society, Castlemaine; No. 550, at Rotary Park, Latrobe St, Warragul; No. 556, at ARHS Railway Museum, Champion Rd, North Williamstown.

Above: Built by Vulcan Foundry in England, J503 entered service with Victorian Railways on 1 April 1954. It was scrapped on 11 September 1968 after having travelled 181 887 miles in fourteen years of service. The listed weight in working order of this locomotive and tender was 112 tons 15 cwt with a combined length of 60 ft 5½ in from buffer to buffer. For more details see The Era of the K & J Class Locomotives in the Victorian Railways, S. Watson, 1983.

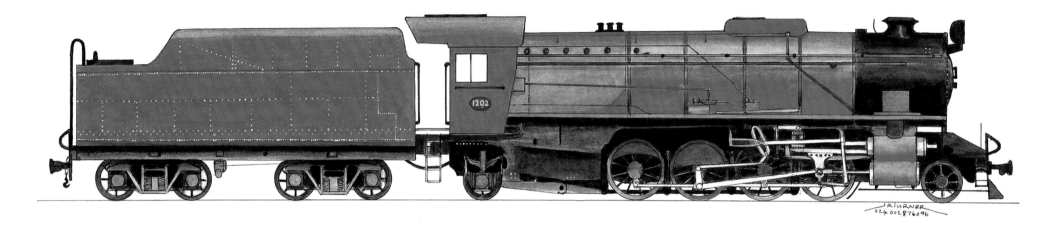

V CLASS (WA)
WHEEL ARRANGEMENT: 2–8–2
HEAVY GOODS LOCOMOTIVE
24 IN CLASS
FINAL NOS 1201–24

In early 1950, plans for several new locomotive types were submitted to the W.A.G.R. by Beyer Peacock & Co for consideration. An order was eventually placed for some 2–8–2 locomotives. When the order was amended to twenty-four locomotives on 13 November 1951, Beyer Peacock was unable to complete an order of that size by the required date. An alternative was agreed, that the locomotives should be built by Robert Stephenson & Hawthorns Ltd, with all work supervised by Beyer Peacock. By late 1951 work was ready to begin and on 17 December 1954 the first locomotives were ready for inspection at Robert Stephenson's Darlington works. The first to enter service was No. 1201 on 12 April 1955. The last, No. 1224, was built in 1956 and entered service on 16 November 1956. They arrived fully assembled, and painted green with a black smoke box.

Shortly after entering service, No. 1201 made a test run between East Perth and Brunswick Junction. It hauled a load of 1250 tons—up to that time the largest ever—and despite the weight it was able to maintain a good speed.

The V class was found to be reliable in service, and was used on heavy goods traffic on both the eastern and Great Southern main lines. On 17 June 1971 twenty of the class were withdrawn from service, with the remaining four withdrawn on 14 August 1972, after sixteen years in use.

Builder: Robert Stephenson & Hawthorns Ltd 24

Preserved: No. 1209, at Bellarine Peninsula Railway, Queenscliff; No. 1213, at Hotham Valley Tourist Railway, Pinjarra; No. 1215, at Mining Museum, Collie; No. 1220, at ARHS Railway Museum, Bassendean.

Above: Built in 1955 in England by Robert Stephenson & Hawthorns Ltd, No. 1202 entered service with Western Australian Government Railways on 10 May 1955 and was withdrawn from service on 17 June 1971 after sixteen years in service. The listed weight in working order of this locomotive and tender was 134 tons 18 cwt 2 qtr with a combined length of 69 ft 8⅙ in from buffer to buffer. For more details see A History of W.A.G.R. Steam Locomotives, *A. Gunzburg, ARHS(WA) 1984, p. 138–40.*

With the introduction of diesel-electric locomotives to the suburban passenger network, it became difficult for steam locomotives to maintain the timetable. However more locomotives were needed to meet a revised timetable in the mid 1950s, and as a result No. 664 of the U class was rebuilt as a tank locomotive and classed as Ut. It was painted green and re-entered service in July 1957. No. 664 was used on suburban passenger services, and had no trouble in keeping to the timetable. As an oil-burner it was expensive to operate and was only used when needed.

When more diesels entered service in December 1959, No. 664 went back into storage at Midland Junction with the other U class locomotives. Problems in the coalfields in early 1961 found

UT CLASS (WA)
WHEEL ARRANGEMENT: 4–6–4T
SUBURBAN PASSENGER TANK
LOCOMOTIVE
1 IN CLASS
FINAL NO: 664

September 1970.

Builder: Midland Junction Workshops 1
Preserved: No. 664, at ARHS Railway Museum, Bassendean.

No. 664 once again in service for several months, before being returned to storage.

When the Midland Railway Company was sold on 1 August 1964, along with all rolling stock and other assets, No. 664 was used to haul ballast trains while the route was upgraded. On completion of this work it was then transferred to working ballast trains on the south-west main line. It then returned to storage, and was finally withdrawn from service on 10

Above: Built in 1942 by the North British Locomotive Co and shipped to Fremantle in 1946, No. 664 entered service as a U class locomotive on 4 April 1947. It was converted to burn coal on 22 December 1954 and withdrawn from service on 6 November 1956. It was rebuilt as above and re-entered service on 8 July 1957; it was finally withdrawn from service on 10 September 1970 after twenty-three years in service, with thirteen of those as Ut class. The listed weight in working order of this locomotive was 79 tons 16 cwt and it was 42 ft 3¾ in long. For more details see A History of W.A.G.R. Steam Locomotives, A. Gunzburg, ARHS(WA) 1984, p. 129–30.

Originally built by Robert Stephenson & Hawthorns Ltd, these locomotives had entered service as the M class in 1952. In 1957 timetable changes halved the mileage travelled by the M class and it was decided that M1, M2, M6 and M8 would be altered to make them more suitable for working goods services on the north-east line. Smaller driving wheels, which had been taken from Australian Standard Garratt locomotives in storage, were fitted at the Launceston workshops. The four locomotives then became MA1 to MA4, and were back in service between October 1957 and July 1958.

While popular with their crews, the MA class showed no great improvement in performance. In the years between 1957 and 1961, however, they covered more miles than any other class of

MA CLASS (TAS)
WHEEL ARRANGEMENT: 4–6–2
GOODS LOCOMOTIVE
4 IN CLASS
NOS: MA1–MA4

Tasmanian Government Railway locomotive up to that time, working mostly on the north-east line.

In May 1964 boiler problems saw MA3 withdrawn from service, and MA1 followed in December 1969. In February 1971 MA2 and MA4 were still in service for the railway centenary celebrations, but were withdrawn from service a few months later in June 1971.

Builder: Tasmanian Government Railways 4

Preserved: MA1, at Rotary Park, near junction of Midland and Lyell Hwys, Granton; MA2 and MA4, at Van Diemen Light Railway Society, Don Village, Devonport; MA3, at The Margate Market, Channel Hwy, Margate.

Above: Built as M2 in 1951 and converted at the Launceston workshops in July 1958, MA4 was used mostly on goods services until the late 1960s when it was used on suburban passenger services. It remained in service during the 1971 railway centenary celebrations and was withdrawn in June 1971. The listed weight in working order of this locomotive and tender was 96 tons 12 cwt 3 qtr with a combined length of 59 ft 2¾ in from buffer to buffer.

For more details see Locomotives of the Tasmanian Transport Museum, Glenorchy, Tasmania, A. Dix, 1991, p. 11–13.

Based on the earlier B18¼ class, the BB18¼ included new and updated features and was arguably the most successful steam locomotive class on Queensland Government Railways. The first of the class arrived from Vulcan Foundry in England on board the vessel *Clan Macauley*, with Nos 1017 and 1018 entering service in February 1951. No. 1089, built by Walkers Ltd, was the last into service in March 1958.

The colour of the locomotives varied. Those built in England were hawthorn green with carmine buffer beams and lining, while those from Walkers Ltd were the brighter green used on the B18¼ class, with vermilion buffer beams and lining. They were used on mail and express trains to the north and west of Brisbane, and also on Brisbane suburban services to the north and south. One

BB18¼ CLASS (QLD)
WHEEL ARRANGEMENT: 4-6-2
PASSENGER LOCOMOTIVE
55 IN CLASS
FINAL NOS: 1011-1045, 1070-1089

major fault was found after they entered service when the rear bogie caused a number of derailments, but after modifications had been made, the problem was solved.

As diesels took over, the BB18¼ class were used on goods, sugar and grain trains. Nos 1014 and 1045 were the first to be withdrawn in October 1967 and the last to go, in August 1970, were Nos 1031 and 1084.

Builders: Vulcan Foundry 35; Walkers Ltd 20

Preserved: No. 1037, at Boddington St, opposite former station, Mackay; No. 1072, at Zig Zag Railway Co-operative Ltd, Lithgow; No. 1077, at Quantilan Pioneer Park, Winton; No. 1079, in QR Heritage fleet; No. 1086, Emerald; No. 1089, at QR in storage.

Above: Built by Walkers Ltd in 1958, No. 1089 was the last steam locomotive to be built new in Australia. It entered service with Queensland Government Railways in March 1958, and was withdrawn from service in June 1969. The listed weight in working order of this locomotive and tender was 101 tons 4 cwt 1 qtr with a combined length of 60 ft 2⅞ in from buffer to buffer. For more details see Locomotives in the Tropics Vol. 2, *J. Armstrong, ARHS(QLD) 1994, p. 132–43.*

PICTORIAL INDEX

Page: 6   **Class:** P   **State:** WA   **Year:** 1896

Page: 7   **Class:** H   **State:** Tas   **Year:** 1896

Page: 8   **Class:** Q   **State:** WA   **Year:** 1896

Page: 9   **Class:** Y   **State:** SA   **Year:** 1896

Page: 10   **Class:** S   **State:** WA   **Year:** 1896

Page: 11   **Class:** T   **State:** WA   **Year:** 1896

Page: 12   **Class:** R   **State:** WA   **Year:** 1897

Page: 13   **Class:** G   **State:** Tas   **Year:** 1697

Page: 14   **Class:** EE   **State:** Vic   **Year:** 1898

Page: 15   **Class:** O   **State:** WA   **Year:** 1898

Page: 16   **Class:** 4D11½   **State:** Qld   **Year:** 1898

Page: 17   **Class:** CC79   **State:** NSW   **Year:** 1899

Page: 18   **Class:** G   **State:** SA   **Year:** 1899

Page: 19   **Class:** GE   **State:** SA   **Year:** 1899

Page: 20   **Class:** GD   **State:** SA   **Year:** 1899

Page: 21   **Class:** PB15   **State:** Qld   **Year:** 1899

Page: 27   **Class:** EC   **State:** WA   **Year:** 1901

Page: 33   **Class:** CG   **State:** NSW   **Year:** 1904

Page: 22   **Class:** B15   **State:** Qld   **Year:** 1900

Page: 28   **Class:** V   **State:** Vic   **Year:** 1901

Page: 34   **Class:** 6D16   **State:** Qld   **Year:** 1905

Page: 23   **Class:** NA   **State:** Vic   **Year:** 1900

Page: 29   **Class:** J   **State:** Tas   **Year:** 1901

Page: 35   **Class:** S(636)   **State:** NSW   **Year:** 1903

Page: 24   **Class:** 6D13½ABT   **State:** Qld   **Year:** 1900

Page: 30   **Class:** C   **State:** WA   **Year:** 1902

Page: 36   **Class:** 6D13½   **State:** Qld   **Year:** 1905

Page: 25   **Class:** ME   **State:** Vic   **Year:** 1901

Page: 31   **Class:** F   **State:** WA   **Year:** 1902

Page: 37   **Class:** DD   **State:** Vic   **Year:** 1906

Page: 26   **Class:** 6D16   **State:** Qld   **Year:** 1901

Page: 32   **Class:** AA   **State:** Vic   **Year:** 1903

Page: 38   **Class:** SMC   **State:** SA   **Year:** 1906

Page: 39   **Class:** E   **State:** Tas   **Year:** 1907

Page: 45   **Class:** A   **State:** Tas   **Year:** 1909

Page: 51   **Class:** B17   **State:** Qld   **Year:** 1911

Page: 40   **Class:** A2   **State:** Vic   **Year:** 1907

Page: 46   **Class:** N(928)   **State:** NSW   **Year:** 1909

Page: 52   **Class:** B13B   **State:** Qld   **Year:** 1911

Page: 41   **Class:** T   **State:** SA   **Year:** 1907

Page: 47   **Class:** RY   **State:** Vic   **Year:** 1909

Page: 53   **Class:** E   **State:** WA   **Year:** 1912

Page: 42   **Class:** N   **State:** WA   **Year:** 1908

Page: 48   **Class:** OA   **State:** WA   **Year:** 1910

Page: 54   **Class:** M   **State:** WA   **Year:** 1912

Page: 43   **Class:** DDE   **State:** Vic   **Year:** 1908

Page: 49   **Class:** 2nd I   **State:** SA   **Year:** 1910

Page: 55   **Class:** C16   **State:** Qld   **Year:** 1912

Page: 44   **Class:** QA   **State:** WA   **Year:** 1909

Page: 50   **Class:** K   **State:** Tas   **Year:** 1910

Page: 56   **Class:** TF(939)   **State:** NSW   **Year:** 1912

Page: 57 **Class:** WX **State:** SA **Year:** 1912

Page: 63 **Class:** MS **State:** WA **Year:** 1914

Page: 69 **Class:** V(1217) **State:** NSW **Year:** 1916

Page: 58 **Class:** D & DS **State:** WA **Year:** 1912

Page: 64 **Class:** C18 **State:** Qld **Year:** 1914

Page: 70 **Class:** F(1212) **State:** NSW **Year:** 1916

Page: 59 **Class:** L **State:** Tas **Year:** 1912

Page: 65 **Class:** T(524) **State:** NSW **Year:** 1914

Page: 71 **Class:** NN(1027) **State:** NSW **Year:** 1917

Page: 60 **Class:** M **State:** Tas **Year:** 1912

Page: 66 **Class:** CC **State:** Tas **Year:** 1915

Page: 72 **Class:** G(1204) **State:** NSW **Year:** 1917

Page: 61 **Class:** 2nd O **State:** SA **Year:** 1912

Page: 67 **Class:** 2nd F **State:** SA **Year:** 1915

Page: 73 **Class:** B16½ **State:** Qld **Year:** 1918

Page: 62 **Class:** RX **State:** SA **Year:** 1913

Page: 68 **Class:** 260 **State:** SA **Year:** 1916

Page: 74 **Class:** K(1353) **State:** NSW **Year:** 1918

Page: 75　**Class:** AY/BY　**State:** Qld　**Year:** 1919

Page: 81　**Class:** C　**State:** Vic　**Year:** 1921

Page: 87　**Class:** U　**State:** WA　**Year:** 1925

Page: 76　**Class:** 2nd M　**State:** SA　**Year:** 1920

Page: 82　**Class:** R　**State:** Tas　**Year:** 1923

Page: 88　**Class:** PB15(1924)　**State:** Qld　**Year:** 1925

Page: 77　**Class:** C17　**State:** Qld　**Year:** 1920

Page: 83　**Class:** P　**State:** WA　**Year:** 1924

Page: 89　**Class:** L　**State:** WA　**Year:** 1925

Page: 78　**Class:** 6D9½　**State:** Qld　**Year:** 1920

Page: 84　**Class:** (C)36　**State:** NSW　**Year:** 1925

Page: 90　**Class:** 700　**State:** SA　**Year:** 1926

Page: 79　**Class:** T　**State:** Tas　**Year:** 1921

Page: 85　**Class:** N　**State:** Vic　**Year:** 1925

Page: 91　**Class:** G　**State:** Vic　**Year:** 1926

Page: 80　**Class:** 6D8½　**State:** Qld　**Year:** 1921

Page: 86　**Class:** 6D17　**State:** Qld　**Year:** 1925

Page: 92　**Class:** 600　**State:** SA　**Year:** 1926

Page: 94 **Class:** 500 **State:** SA **Year:** 1926

Page: 101 **Class:** 710 **State:** SA **Year:** 1929

Page: 108 **Class:** 500B **State:** SA **Year:** 1930

Page: 96 **Class:** B9½ **State:** Qld **Year:** 1927

Page: 102 **Class:** Six Wheeler **State:** Tas **Year:** 1929

Page: 110 **Class:** 2nd Q **State:** WA **Year:** 1931

Page: 97 **Class:** RA **State:** WA **Year:** 1928

Page: 103 **Class:** Big Ben **State:** Tas **Year:** 1929

Page: 111 **Class:** (C)30T **State:** NSW **Year:** 1931

Page: 98 **Class:** S **State:** Vic **Year:** 1928

Page: 104 **Class:** (D)57 **State:** NSW **Year:** 1929

Page: 112 **Class:** C19 **State:** Qld **Year:** 1935

Page: 99 **Class:** CCS **State:** Tas **Year:** 1928

Page: 106 **Class:** D3 **State:** Vic **Year:** 1929

Page: 113 **Class:** B18¼ **State:** Qld **Year:** 1935

Page: 100 **Class:** X **State:** Vic **Year:** 1929

Page: 107 **Class:** MSA **State:** WA **Year:** 1930

Page: 114 **Class:** 620 **State:** SA **Year:** 1936

Page: 115   **Class:** B13½   **State:** Qld   **Year:** 1937

Page: 124   **Class:** H   **State:** Vic   **Year:** 1941

Page: 134   **Class:** ASG   **State:** WA   **Year:** 1944

Page: 116   **Class:** S   **State:** Vic   **Year:** 1937

Page: 126   **Class:** S   **State:** WA   **Year:** 1943

Page: 136   **Class:** 520   **State:** SA   **Year:** 1944

Page: 118   **Class:** PR   **State:** WA   **Year:** 1938

Page: 127   **Class:** AC16   **State:** Qld   **Year:** 1943

Page: 138   **Class:** G   **State:** Tas   **Year:** 1944

Page: 120   **Class:** 720   **State:** SA   **Year:** 1938

Page: 128   **Class:** (C)38   **State:** NSW   **Year:** 1943

Page: 140   **Class:** DM   **State:** WA   **Year:** 1945

Page: 122   **Class:** DS   **State:** Tas   **Year:** 1939

Page: 130   **Class:** ASG   **State:** Qld   **Year:** 1943

Page: 141   **Class:** DD   **State:** WA   **Year:** 1946

Page: 123   **Class:** K   **State:** Vic   **Year:** 1940

Page: 132   **Class:** Q   **State:** Tas   **Year:** 1943

Page: 142   **Class:** U   **State:** WA   **Year:** 1947

Page: 143 **Class:** F **State:** Tas **Year:** 1949

Page: 150 **Class:** Beyer Garratt **State:** Qld **Year:** 1950

Page: 159 **Class:** M **State:** Tas **Year:** 1952

Page: 144 **Class:** (D)58 **State:** NSW **Year:** 1950

Page: 152 **Class:** 750 **State:** SA **Year:** 1951

Page: 160 **Class:** 300 **State:** SA **Year:** 1952

Page: 146 **Class:** C17 **State:** Qld **Year:** 1950

Page: 154 **Class:** W **State:** WA **Year:** 1951

Page: 162 **Class:** (D)59 **State:** NSW **Year:** 1952

Page: 147 **Class:** CS **State:** WA **Year:** 1950

Page: 155 **Class:** DD17 **State:** Qld **Year:** 1951

Page: 164 **Class:** (AD)60 **State:** NSW **Year:** 1952

Page: 148 **Class:** PM & PMR **State:** WA **Year:** 1950

Page: 156 **Class:** R **State:** Vic **Year:** 1951

Page: 166 **Class:** 740 **State:** SA **Year:** 1953

Page: 149 **Class:** New N **State:** Vic **State:** 1950

Page: 158 **Class:** H **State:** Tas **Year:** 1951

Page: 168 **Class:** 400 **State:** SA **Year:** 1954

Page: 170　**Class:** J　**State:** Vic　**Year:** 1954

Page: 172　**Class:** UT　**State:** WA　**Year:** 1957

Page: 174　**Class:** BB18¼　**State:** Qld　**Year:** 1958

Page: 171　**Class:** V　**State:** WA　**Year:** 1955

Page: 173　**Class:** MA　**State:** Tas　**Year:** 1957

ABOUT THE PAINTINGS

An outline diagram is traced onto Arches 300 g watercolour paper after which details are drawn in, using photographs as reference. This drawing is then painted using Windsor & Newton watercolours; following this, each painting is checked by an expert. Any changes that are needed are then made and the painting is checked again. The largest painting is the (AD) 60 Beyer Garratt from New South Wales, which is 76 cm long and 10 cm high.

LOCOMOTIVE BUILDERS

BUILDER	NSW	QLD	VIC	TAS	SA	WA
Addington Workshops, Christchurch, N.Z.				DS		
Armstrong Whitworth & Co, U.K.		C17			700 600 500	
Atlas Engineering, Sydney, N.S.W.	79					
Baldwin Locomotive Co, U.S.A.		B13B AC16	NA V DD	Big Ben		Ec C
Baldwin Lima Hamilton Co, U.S.A.	59					
Ballarat Foundry, Vic.			DD			
Andrew Barclay & Sons, U. K.						2nd Q
Bendigo Foundry, Vic.			DD			
Beyer Peacock & Co, U. K.	79 Cg 636 524 AD60	Beyer Garratt	ME DD G	E K L M	Y G Ge Gd 2nd I Wx	T M Ms
Cardiff Workshops, N. S.W.	38 58					
Clyde Engineering, N.S.W.	939 524 1353 36 57 30T 38	C17		Q G		740
Dubs & Co, U.K.	79 524	4D11½ 6D13½			Rx	R O F Ra

BUILDER	NSW	QLD	VIC	TAS	SA	WA
Evans Anderson Phelan & Co, Qld.		PB15 B15 C16 C17				
Eveleigh Workshops, N.S.W.	636 928 939 1027 36 30T 38 58					
John Fowler & Co, U.K.		B9½ 6D8½				
R & W Hawthorne Leslie & Co, U.K.						Q Qa
Hillside Workshops, Dunedin, N.Z.				DS		
Hudswell Clarke & Co, U K				Six Wheeler	260	
Hunslet Engine Co, U.K.	1204	6D9½				
Ipswich Workshops, Qld.		PB15 6D13½ B17 C16 C18 B16½ C17 6D17 C19 B18½ B18¼ B13½ DD17				
SAR Islington, S.A.					Y	

BUILDER	NSW	QLD	VIC	TAS	SA	WA
SAR Islington, S.A. (cont'd)					T Rx 2nd F 2nd M 710 620 720 520	
Kitson & Co, U.K.		PB15		G	SMC	S T
Lokomotivfabrik Hagans, Erfurt, Germany			J			
Lokomotivfabrik Krauss & Co, Germany			H			
Manning Wardle & Co, U.K.	1212					
James Martin & Co, Gawler, S.A.		AY/BY	F		Y	P
Midland Junction Workshops, W.A.					300	Oa P L Msa Pr S ASG Dm Dd Cs Ut
David Munro & Co, Melbourne, Vic.					2nd M	
Nasmyth Wilson & Co, U.K.		B15				N E
Neilson & Co, U.K.	524					N O
Newport Workshops, Vic.			EE NA DD A2 DDE C N S X K H		300	
North British Locomotive Co, U.K.	524	6D13½	N		Rx	F

BUILDER	NSW	QLD	VIC	TAS	SA	WA
North British Locomotive Co, U.K. (cont'd)			R New N		750	E Ds P U Pm W
Perry Engineering, Mile End, S.A.				Q	2nd F	
Phoenix Foundry, Ballarat, Vic.			EE ME V AA DD		2nd M	
A & G Price Ltd, Thames, N.Z.				DS		
Robison Bros Campbell & Sloss, Melbourne			RY			
SociÈtÈ des Chemins de Fer Franco-Belge		Beyer Garratt			400	
Robert Stephenson & Co, U.K.					2nd 0	N
Robert Stephenson & Hawthorns Ltd, U.K.			M	V		
Sharp Stewart & Co, U.K.				G		
Tasmanian Government Railway Workshops				A CC CCS MA		
Thompsons Foundry, Qld.			DD			
Toowoomba Foundry, Qld.		PB15 C16				
Vulcan Foundry, U.K.		BB18¼	J	H		E
Vulcan Iron Works, Wilkes Barre, U.S.A.	1217					
Walkers Ltd, Qld.		PB15 B15 6D16 C16 C17 6D17 C19 B18¼ BB18¼	DD	T Q	Rx T	
Yorkshire Engine Co, U.K.		B15				

ABOUT THE LOCOMOTIVE BUILDERS

ANDREW BARCLAY, SONS & CO, KILMARNOCK, SCOTLAND.

Established in 1840, this firm began building locomotives in 1859. They supplied tank engines to contractors, collieries and Scottish ironworks. In 1935 they began building diesel locomotives, and still do so today. Their last steam locomotive was an 0–6–2 tank engine which was steamed in September 1962 at the Kilmarnock factory. In 1972 the company merged with the Hunslet Group, and the Kilmarnock factory is still in production.

The total number of steam locomotives from the Riverbank and Caledonian works is estimated at 2052 during 103 years in production.

SIR W.G. ARMSTRONG-WHITWORTH & CO LTD.

The company built its first locomotive in 1847, which was probably a 2–2–2 with a vertical boiler. More locomotives were built between 1860 and 1868, followed by more locomotive building after the end of WW I. The Scotwood works built 1464 locomotives between 1919 and 1937, when the works closed. In all, about 1700 locomotives were built between 1847 and 1937.

THE BALDWIN LOCOMOTIVE WORKS, USA.

Having built its first locomotive in 1832, the Baldwin Works had built more than a thousand by 1861. By 1881 total output had reached 5921, and as mass production was introduced, the output grew dramatically, with 19 820 locomotives built by 1901. By 1923 the total output had reached 57 608 locomotives.

BEYER PEACOCK & CO, GORTON FOUNDRY, MANCHESTER.

Founded in 1854 by Charles F. Beyer and Richard Peacock, the company's first locomotive was a 2–2–2 built in July 1855. Orders from India, Scotland, Sweden and England were followed by others, with the Dutch railways buying hundreds of almost every early type of locomotive built by them. Most railways in Britain bought Beyer Peacock and some railways would use no other locomotive type on their lines.

The need for more power resulted in the evolution of the Garratt, with the first two being built for use in Tasmania in 1908. By 1907, Beyer Peacock had built 5000 steam locomotives. Local and overseas orders continued, and by 1927 the works covered 23 acres and employed 3000 people. The works was re-organised in 1961 to build diesel locomotives, but lack of orders forced its closure in 1966.

CARDIFF WORKSHOPS, NSW.

These workshops were built to replace the Honeysuckle Point Workshops, which had been gradually expanding from the 1860s until 1925. It was decided to build new workshops on a 172 acre site at Cockle Creek; the site soon became known as the Cardiff Workshops. Opened on 1 March 1928, by June 1929 it had rebuilt nineteen engines and repaired 182, while 145 boilers had been overhauled. The workshop closed in about 1993.

DUBS & CO, GLASGOW LOCOMOTIVE WORKS, POLMADIE, GLASGOW.

In 1863 Henry Dubs severed his connection with Neilson & Co and established his own locomotive factory at Little Govan, later re-named Polmadie. In 1864 construction of the works began and within twelve months the first locomotive, an 0–4–2, had been completed. Used on all Scottish and many English lines, the locomotives had a distinctive diamond-shaped builders plate, which continued to be used even after the 1903 merging of Dubs & Co with Neilson Reid & Co and Sharp Stewart & Co, to form the North British Locomotive Co Ltd. The works was then known as the Queens Park Works. Up to the time of the merger a total of 4485 steam locomotives had been built by Dubs & Co, during thirty-nine years in production.

JOHN FOWLER & CO, STEAM PLOUGH & LOCOMOTIVE WORKS, LEEDS.

Established in 1850, the company specialised in the manufacture of agricultural machinery, traction engines and steam rollers. Although John Fowler died in a hunting accident in 1864, the business continued, with the first steam locomotives, a batch of 0–6–0s, being built in 1866. The last steam locomotive was an 0–6–0WT built for a forestry railway in Pakistan in 1935. The company then built diesel locomotives for many years but in 1968 the goodwill, along with drawings and spares, were sold to Andrew Barclay, Sons & Co Ltd of Kilmarnock. Between 200 and 300 steam locomotives were built by John Fowler & Co during sixty-nine years in production.

HAWTHORN R & W LTD, FORTH BANKS WORKS, NEWCASTLE.

Founded in 1817 by Robert Hawthorn, the company became R & W Hawthorn Ltd, marine and steam engine builders and engineers, in 1820. It was 1831 before they built their first steam locomotive, a 2–2–2 which was sent to Vienna. In 1884 the name changed to Hawthorn, Leslie & Co Ltd, when the company merged with shipbuilders A. Leslie & Company.

On 1 January 1937 Robert Stephenson & Co Ltd bought Hawthorn, Leslie & Co Ltd (except for the boiler department), and the firm was then known as Robert Stephenson & Hawthorns Ltd. The last steam locomotive built by Hawthorn was an 0–4–0 saddle tank in l938, making a total of 2611 steam locomotives during 107 years in production.

HUDSWELL CLARKE & CO.

The company was founded in 1860 as an engineering firm by W.S. Hudswell and John Clarke, both of whom had worked for Kitson & Co. They built heavy engineering machinery but from 1861 concentrated on locomotive building, especially saddle tank locomotives and 0–6–0 tender engines.

From the 1920s they began building diesels and they continued this after steam orders ceased. In WW II they continued building tank engines, and the last steam locomotive built was an 0–4–0ST for the National Coal Board in 1961. The total number of steam locomotives built was 1807 during 101 years.

HUNSLET ENGINE CO, LEEDS.

Founded in 1864 by John Towlerton Leather, a railway contractor and civil engineer, and built on the site previously occupied by E.B. Wilson & Co's Railway Workshop, the Hunslet Engine Company works was surrounded by Manning Wardle & Co, Hudswell Clarke & Co, and Kitson & Co. The first locomotive built by Hunslet was an 0–6–0 saddle tank, completed on 18 July 1865. In 1902 it became The Hunslet Engine Co Ltd. In 1909 it built its one thousandth locomotive, a 2–4–2T which went to India.

In 1960 Hunslet acquired Robert Stephenson & Hawthorns Ltd's industrial locomotives, along with the goodwill and drawings of Kitson & Co and Manning Wardle & Co. They continued to supply spare parts as well as building new locomotives. In 1972 Hunslet purchased the equity of Andrew Barclay & Co. Over 107 years to 1972, a total of 2236 steam locomotives were built by Hunslet.

LOKOMOTIVFABRIK KRAUSS AND CO.

In 1866 the company opened its first plant in Munich, Germany, followed by a second plant in Linz, Austria in 1880. Krauss merged with J.A. Maffei A.G. in 1931 to form Krauss-Maffei, which built diesel locomotives. Between 1866 and 1931 Krauss built a total of 8512 engines, with 1171 built at Linz before it became independent.

MANNING WARDLE BOYNE ENGINE WORKS, LEEDS

Established in 1858 by Alexander Campbell and C.W. Wardle, the company's first locomotive was an 0–4–0ST, built in 1859. The company concentrated on building 0–4–0 and 0–6–0 saddle tank locomotives, and the excellence of their product brought many sales locally and overseas. In 1927 they went into voluntary liquidation, and the goodwill was bought by Kitson & Co, while the Hunslet Engine Co bought part of the Boyne Engine Works. In the sixty-seven years between 1859 and 1926 a total of 2004 steam locomotives were built.

NASMYTH GASKER & CO, BRIDGEWATER FOUNDRY, PATRICROFT.

Established in 1836 by James Nasmyth, the Bridgewater Foundry designed and made steam engines and special engineering products. In 1839 nine locomotives were built. By 1880, 158 locomotives had been built, and as production increased, many were sent overseas to Japan, Russia, New Zealand, India, Australia, Spain and South America. In 1882 the name was changed to Nasmyth Wilson & Co Ltd. Of the total of 1307 locomotives built by the company between 1873 and 1938, 1188 were sent overseas.

NEILSON REID & CO.

Founded by Walter Neilson and James Mitchell in 1836–7, the company built stationary and marine engines. The first locomotives were built at the Hyde Park Street works in 1843, and initially they were all sold locally, mostly to lines in the Glasgow area. In 1855, production of marine engines ceased and the company name became Neilson & Co.

Locomotive production increased, the name was again changed, to Neilson, Reid & Co in 1898. By the early 1900s the low price and quick delivery of American locomotives was creating problems for builders in England. As a result, Neilson Reid & Co, Dubs & Co and Stewart Sharp & Co joined forces in 1903 to form the North British Locomotive Co. Over sixty-six years an estimated 5864 steam locomotives were built by Neilson Reid & Co.

NEWPORT WORKSHOPS.

Established by the Victorian Government, the Newport Workshops' first locomotive, built in October 1902, was the pattern engine of the DD class. The workshop went on to build more than a hundred of this class, along with many of the best known steam locomotives to be used on Victorian Railways during the twentieth century. The company still services diesel locomotives and employs about 340 people.

PHOENIX FOUNDRY LTD, BALLARAT.

The company was founded by William H. Shaw, George Threlfell and Richard Carter in 1855, in Armstrong Street South in Ballarat. Initially they manufactured mining equipment for gold mines in Australia and New Zealand, and the business grew steadily as mining activity increased. The first locomotive built by Phoenix was an 0–6–0 named *Ballarat*, which made a successful trial run on 21 October 1871 and was then shipped to the Rockingham Jarrah Co in Western Australia. In 1904 the foundry built its last government order, which was for seven DD class. Government orders were then given to the Newport Railway Workshops, which in turn caused the Phoenix works to close in 1906.

ROBERT STEPHENSON & COMPANY, FORTH ST, NEWCASTLE-ON-TYNE.

Established in 1823 by George Stephenson and his son Robert, along with Edward Pease and Michael Longridge as partners, the company's first locomotive was *Locomotion No 1*, built in 1825.

More than a thousand locomotives of a wide variety of types and gauges had been built by 1855, many being exported overseas. On 1 January 1937 Robert Stephenson & Co Ltd combined with R.W. Hawthorn & Co to become Robert Stephenson & Hawthorns Ltd. During its 112-year span, Robert Stephenson & Co produced 4185 steam locomotives.

ROBERT STEPHENSON & HAWTHORNS LTD, DARLINGTON & NEWCASTLE-ON-TYNE.

This company was established on 1 January 1937, when Robert Stephenson & Co bought the locomotive department and goodwill of R & W Hawthorn, Leslie & Co. It was decided that the industrial locomotives should be built at the Forth Banks works which had been used by Hawthorn Leslie, while main line locomotives would be built at the Darlington Works.

The last conventional steam locomotive was an 0–6–0ST in October 1958. The Forth Banks works closed in 1960, and the building of diesel & electric locomotives then transferred to the Darlington Works on 1 January 1967. The name of the works became English Electric Co Ltd, Stephenson Works, Harrogate Hill, Darlington. Between 1937 and 1959 about a thousand steam locomotives were built.

SHARP ROBERTS & CO, ATLAS WORKS, GREAT BRIGEWATER ST, MANCHESTER.

Established in 1828 by Thomas Sharp and Richard Roberts, the company intially manufactured machinery for cotton mills and machines for shearing, planing, punching and drilling. The first locomotive, a 2–2–0, was built in 1833. Prior to 1862, the largest locomotives to be built were 0–6–0s and 2–4–0s. In 1862, the first 4–6–0ST was built, followed in 1865 by the 0–8–0 tender locomotive.

During the seventy years between 1833 and 1903, Stewart Sharp & Co built a total of 5088 steam locomotives. In 1903 the company joined with Dubs & Co and Neilson & Co to form the North British Locomotive Co.

TODD KITSON & LAIRD, AIREDALE FOUNDRY, LEEDS.

The Airedale Foundry was established in 1835 by James Kitson with Charles Todd as a partner. Capital was provided by David Laird, a farmer. The first locomotive was an 0–4–2 built in 1838. A wall of the factory had to be pulled down to enable it to be delivered. In 1851 the company became Kitson & Hewitson, until the death of William Hewitson in 1863, when it became Kitson & Co.

Fewer than a hundred locomotives were built between 1925 and 1938. An 0–8–0T for the Jamacian Government was the last locomotive to be built. During one hundred years in production, approximately 5405 steam locomotives were built.

VULCAN FOUNDRY LTD.

Established in 1830 and known as Tayleur, Charles & Co, Vulcan Foundry was established near Warrington and built its first locomotive, an 0–4–0, in 1833. Between 1907 and 1918 India and Ceylon took 977 of the 1032 locomotives built in that time. Production of steam locomotives in the Vulcan Foundry gave way to diesel and electric locomotives, and in March 1955 Vulcan Foundry along with Robert Stephenson & Hawthorn Ltd became members of the English Electric group. A total of 6210 steam locomotives was built during 122 years in production.

WALKERS LTD.

The company was founded in 1863 by John Walker, Thomas Braddock, W.T. Sandry and James F. Wood in Ballarat. In 1867 Walker visited Gympie in Queensland and bought land in Bowen St, Maryborough for a new works. With Ws Ltd. since 1982, Walkers Ltd is still at the same site in Maryborough, and employs 600 people. It builds diesel and electric locomotives as well as mining equipment.

YORKSHIRE ENGINE CO.

Established in 1865, the company built its first locomotive in 1866. Production was concentrated on tank engines for quarries and mines. The company built its last steam locomotive in 1956, by which time a total of about 800 had been built during ninety-one years.

BIBLIOGRAPHY

Abbott R.L. 'NA Class Locomotive performance Victorian Railways'. *ARHS* No 490, August 1978, pp. 182-7.

Armstrong J. *Locomotives in the Tropics* Vol. 1, ARHS (QLD).

——. *Locomotives in the Tropics* Vol. 2, ARHS (QLD), 1994.

Armstrong J. & Verhoeven G.H. *The Innisfail Tramway*, ARHS (QLD), 1973.

——. ARHS(NSW) *Along the Line in Tasmania*. Book 2 *Private Lines*, ARHS (NSW), 1983.

Bakewell G. 'Awakened Memories of the Rx-Class Locomotives'. *ARHS* No 324, October 1964, pp. 196-7.

——. 'The Victorian Railways Y Class No 108'. *ARHS* No 343, May 1966, pp. 116-17.

Belbin P & Burke D. *Changing Trains*, Methuen, Australia, 1982.

Relhin P & Burke D. *Full Steam Across the Mountains*, Methuen, Australia, 1984.

Bentley J. *Black Smoke Blue Mountains*, John Brown & Associates, 1988.

Buckland J.L. 'Early Baldwin Locomotives of the Queensland Railways'. *ARHS* No 342, April 1966, pp. 86-9.

——. 'Order of appearance of A2 class locomotives'. *ARHS* January 1951, p. 3.

——. 'Order of appearance of A2 class locomotives'. *ARHS* No 160, p. 34

——. 'DD class order of appearance'. *ARHS* May 1950, p. 19.

——. 'DD class order of appearance'. *ARHS* No 152, p. 34.

——. 'Heavy Freight Locomotives of the Victorian Railways'. *ARHS* No 344, June 1966, pp. 134-7.

——. 'Consolidation Locomotives on the Queensland Railways'. *ARHS* No 514, August 1980, pp. 186-7.

——. 'Locomotives of the Tasmanian Main Line Company'. *ARHS* No 331, May 1965, pp. 96-100.

——. 'An "All-Lines" Ticket in 1932'. *ARHS* No 333, July 1965, pp. 138-9.

Buckland J.L. & Clark M.H.W. 'Metamorphosis of an ugly duckling the D3 Class Locos of Victoria'. *ARHS* No 475, May 1977, pp. 97-111.

Burke D. *With Iron Rails*, New South Wales University Press, 1988.

Castle B.J. 'The 400-Class Beyer-Garratt Locomotives SAR'. *ARHS* No 213, July 1955, pp. 85-8.

Clark M.H.W. 'The Ee-Class 0-6-2 Shunting Tank Engines VR'. *ARHS* No 518, December 1980, pp. 258-63.

——. 'The Evolution of the DD Class Locomotives'. *ARHS* No 167, September 1951, pp. 113-15.

——. 'DD Class Locomotives of the Victorian Railways'. *ARHS* No 130, August 1948, pp. 12-13.

Clark M.H.W. & Buckland J.L. 'The Jubilee of the A2-Class Locomotive'. *ARHS* 13 No 243, January 1958, pp. 1-13.

——. 'The AA-Class 4-4-0 Express Locomotives'. *ARHS* No 406, August 1971, pp. 169-75.

——. 'The Victorian Railways V-Class Vauclain Compound Locomotives'. *ARHS* No 305, March 1963, pp. 37-41.

——. 'Intro of American Designed Locomotives of Victorian Rail 1877-1898'. *ARHS* No 473, March 1977, pp. 49-61.

Clark M.H. & Madden A. 'The Tank Locomotives of the Victorian Government Railways'. *ARHS* No 384, October 1969, p.p 221-40.

Colouhoun D, Stewien D & Thomas A. *The 700 series Locomotives of South Australian Railways*, ARHS (SA), 1979.

Cooley T.C.T. *A History of Trains and Trams in Tasmania*, Government Printer, 1987.

Cooper G. & Goss G. *Tasmanian Railways 1871-1996 A Pictorial History*, Regal Press, 1996.

Dix A. Beck D & Dix M. *Locomotives of the Tasmanian Transport Museum, Glenorchy, Tasmania*, October 1991.

Dix A. 'The High Pressure Q Class Locomotives of the TGR'. *ARHS* November 1966, pp 256-9.

Dunn I. *Years of Change. An album of NSW Railways in Transition*, NSW Rail Transport Museum, December 1983.

Eardley G. 'The Second O-Class Locomotive of South Australia'. *ARHS* No 411, January 1972, pp. 21-3.

——. 'The Second M-Class Locomotives of South Australia'. *ARHS* No 421, November 1972, pp. 223-5.

——. 'I Class Locomotive No 161 of SAR'. *ARHS* No 350, December 1966, pp. 281-4.

——. 'The Gb Class Locomotives of South Australia'. *ARHS* No 423, January 1973, pp. 16-17.

——. 'The Gc Locomotive of the South Australian Railways'. *ARHS* No 409, November 1971, pp. 241-3.

——. 'The Ga Class Locomotive of South Australian Railways'. *ARHS* No 406, August 1971, pp. 184-5.

——. 'Locomotive No 155 of South Australia'. *ARHS* No 428, June 1973, pp. 146-8.

——. 'Locomotive No 154 of the South Australian Railways'. *ARHS* No 410, December 1971, pp. 286-7.

——. 'The G-Class Locomotives of South Australia'. *ARHS* No 272, June 1960, pp. 81-4.

——. 'The Gd Class Locomotives of South Australia'. *ARHS* No 351, January 1967, pp. 14-17.

——. 'The Ge Class Locomotives of South Australia'. *ARHS* No 381, July 1969, pp. 158-9.

——. 'The Tx-Class Locomotives of South Australia'. *ARHS* No 459, January 1976, pp. 16-18.

——. 'The Rise and Fall of the Glenelg Railway Companies. The Glenelg and South Coast Tramway Company'. *ARHS* Bulletin No 153, July 1950, pp. 37-9.

Fluck R.E., Sampson R.& Bird K.J. *Steam Locomotives and Railcars of the South Australian Railways*, Mile End Railway Museum, 1986.

Grunbach A. *A Compendium of NSW Steam Locomotives*, ARHS(NSW), 1989.

Gunzburg A. *The Midland Railway Company Locomotives of WA*, Light Rail Society of Australia, 1989.

——. *A History of WAGR Steam Locomotives*, ARHS(WA), 1984.

Harrigan L.J. *Victorian Railways to '62*, Victorian Government Printer, 3/12/1962.

Higham C.J. *One Hundred Years of Railways in Western Australia 1871-1971*, ARHS(WA).

James P.C. & Stokes H.J.W. 'Locomotives of the Tasmanian Main LC'. *ARHS* No 327, January 1965, pp. 1-8.

Knowles J.W. 'Early Baldwin Locomotives of the Queensland Railways'. *ARHS* No 348, October 1966, p. 327.

Knowles J.W. *The Mount Morgan Rack Railway*, 1982.

LGCB *Preserved Locomotives of Australia and New Zealand*, 1989.

Lowe J.W. *British Steam Locomotive Builders*, TEE Publishing.

McNicol S. *Beyer Peacock in South Australia*, Railmac, 1986.

——. *WAGR Steam Locomotives in Preservation*, Railmac, 1994.

——. *Narrow Gauge Memories The Locomotives*, Railmac, 1993.

McDonald G. *Australian Trains*, Viking O'Neil, 1989.

McKillop R.F. *Rail Scene Australia*, Issue 3, ARHS(NSW), 1995.

Manny L.B. 'Railways of the Zeehan District'. *ARHS* No 313, November 1963, pp. 165-9.

Medlin P. *Steam on the Two Foot Six* Volume One-*Locomotives*, 1992.

Oberg L. *Locomotives of Australia*, AH & AW Reed, 1975.

Potts D.G. *The"N"-Class 2-8-2 "Mikado" Locomotives of the Victorian Railways* 8/10/1966.

Potts D.G. 'Centenary of the River Murray(Echuca) Railway Victorian Railways'. *ARHS* No 332, June 1965, pp. 114-9.

Public Transport Commission of N.S.W. *Steam Locomotive Data*, July 1974.

Revitt J. *The Magic of Steam*, ABC Enterprises, 1992.

Seletto J. 'The Closure and Demolition of North Melbourne VR'. *ARHS* No 339, January 1966, pp. 2-3.

——. 'The Last of the D3-Class Locomotives'. *ARHS* No 327, January 1965, pp. 10-14.

Singleton C.C. 'Modern Steam Locomotives of the Tasmanian G R'. *ARHS* No 208, February 1955, pp. 21-3.

Singleton C.C. & Burke D. *Railways of Australia*, Angus & Robertson, 1963.

Sloggett R.T. 'New R Class 4-6-4 Locomotives'. *ARHS* No 168, October 1951, pp. 125-6.

Southern J.L.N. 'Notes on the DD-Class Locomotives of the Victorian Railways'. *ARHS* No 346, August 1966, pp. 182-7.

Stokes H.J.W. 'The Decline of Steam Power on the Tasmanian GR(1945-65)'. *ARHS* No347, September 1966, pp. 193-202.

——. 'The Decline of Steam Power on the TGR (1945-1965) P2'. *ARHS* No 348, October 1966, p.p 217-29.

——. 'The F-Class 2-6-0s of the Tamanian Government Railway'. *ARHS* No 55, September 1983, pp. 194-200.

——. 'Locomotives of the Marrawah Tramway'. *Light Railways* Spring 1972, pp. 4-7.

——. 'The Tasmanian G class 2 ft gauge Locomotive'. *Light Railways* Summer 1973-4, pp. 11-15.

——. Victorian Railways Rolling Stock Branch Diagrams & Particulars of Locomotives, Cars, Vans & Trucks Spencer St, 1904.

Victorian Railways Rolling Stock Diagrams & Particulars of Locomotives, Steam, Electric,Diesel Electric,etc. 1926-1961

Watson S. *The Era of the K & J Class Locomotives of the Victorian Railways*, 1983.

——. *The Era of the N Class Locomotives in the Victorian Railways*, no date.

——. *The Era of the S Class and H220 Locomotives in the Victorian Railways*, no date.

——. *The Era of the C & X Class Locomotives in the Victorian Railways*, no date.

Watson S. & Cameron A. *The Era of the R Class Locomotives in the Victorian Railways*, 1972.

——. *The Era of the J Class Locomotive in the Victorian Railways*, no date.

Wilson J. *The Mile End Railway Museum - The First Ten Years*, Railway Museum Publication, 1974.

Woodhouse R.K.E. 'Locomotives of the Tasmanian Main Line Railway Co'. *ARHS* No 327, January 1965, pp. 225-6.

Author not known. 'New 520 Class 4-8-4 Locomotive South Australian GR'. *ARHS* No 77, March 1944, p. 31.

——. 'Modern Australian Passenger Locomotives 600 class'. *ARHS.SA* No 111, January 1947, pp. 2-3.

——. 'Rx Class Locomotives of South Australian Railways'. *ARHS* No 456, October 1975, pp. 241-3.

——. 'New Zealand Locomotives sold to Tasmania'. *ARHS* No 396, October 1970, pp. 228-31.

——. 'DS Class Locomotives of TGR'. *ARHS* No 396, October 1970, pp. 232-3.

——. 'The Victorian Railways Y class'. *ARHS* No 546, April 1983, pp. 92-3.

——. 'The "New R" Class VR' *ARHS* No 311, September 1963, pp. 139-42.

——. 'Modern Australian Locomotives N Class 2-8-2 Locomotives Victorian Railways'. *ARHS* No 161, March l951, pp. 37-9.

——. 'Modern Australian Locomotives N-CLass 2-8-2 Locomotives Victorian Railways'. pp 55 April 195

——. 'VR Locomotive Classes, Dates in service & Road Nos'. *ARHS* No 19, May 1939, pp. 43-4.

——. 'X-Class Locomotive of Victorian Railways'. *ARHS* No 343, May 1966, pp. 113-15.

——. 'The M & Me class Locomotives of Victorian Railways'. *ARHS* Bulletin No 384, October 1969, pp. 230-3.

——. 'The Dde class Locomotives of Victorian Railways'. *ARHS* Bulletin No 384, October 1969, pp. 236-9.

——. 'DD Class locomotives'. *ARHS* Bulletin No 546, April 1983, pp. 88-9.

INDEX